# WISEST LEARNERS

## PARENT EDITION

*Unlock the Secrets*
*to Your Child's*
*Academic Success*

---

☑ Practical Applications for Real Results
☑ Proven Expertise with Research Support
☑ Holistic Principles and Comprehensive Strategies

DR. WALLACE PANLILIO II | DR. ARTYOM ZINCHENKO
Ph.D. in Educational Psychology | Ph.D. in Cognitive Neuroscience

A *PQ Unleashed* Book

We would like to dedicate this book to our parents, who instilled a lifelong love for learning in us in so many wonderful ways.

# CONTENTS

## Part III - Learning Strategy Management | The Tree Branches

## LIST OF FIGURES

# INTRODUCTION

*If we did all the things we are capable of,*
*we would literally astound ourselves.*

—*Thomas Edison*

It may be hard to imagine, but Thomas Edison wasn't a good student. At least not in the opinion of his elementary school teacher, who described him as "difficult." He was imaginative and inquisitive, but he had a hard time hearing as a result of numerous ear infections and scarlet fever. Additionally, most of his traditional schooling was based on dull, uninspiring memorization and repetition tactics, and he was often bored as a result.[1] He acted out and was a classroom nuisance. Edison, renowned for his significant advancements in the practical application of electricity, his influential role in the development of the motion picture industry, and his experiments with X-rays, was often described as difficult, hyperactive, and prone to distraction.

But thanks to the attentiveness and action of Edison's mother, a former teacher herself, that categorization didn't stick. After an estimated 12 weeks of school, his mother decided it would be best to oversee his education on her own. Whereas our world has seen exponential growth in homeschooling in recent years, in Edison's time, homeschooling was even more commonplace as a nationalized system of publicly supported "common schools" was only beginning to be formed.[2] Edison's mother was willing to try different methods of schooling until she found what worked for her son. Guided by his mother, Edison developed an insatiable thirst for knowledge and reading. She cultivated in him a method for independent learning and self-education that would benefit him all his life.[3]

Born as the seventh and final child to Samuel and Nancy Edison, Thomas Edison didn't come from a family with significant wealth or resources. But his parents modeled a strong work ethic and the ability to overcome difficult circumstances, characteristics that seemed rooted in Edison's psyche and that would help him overcome his significant hearing loss that worsened throughout his life. His accomplishments are a credit to his persistence and tenacity to overcome poverty and embrace opportunities when they were presented. But when considering his educational roots, much regard must be given to his parents for their guidance and example, especially to his mother for her vigilance and involvement, which set him on a path to success.

Now let's consider the early life of a modern-day success story. Oprah Winfrey was America's first African-American billionaire. She is a prominent figure in media and philanthropy, most recognized for her famous talk show, *The Oprah Winfrey Show*, which was broadcasted for 25 seasons.[4] Born in the countryside of Mississippi in 1954, her journey of overcoming a challenging upbringing to achieve immense fame and success is widely recognized. She spent many of her formative years in poverty and high-crime neighborhoods. She moved across the country many times, living with her grandmother, mother, and father and experiencing radically different lifestyles in each home. At a young age, she was sexually abused and assaulted by family members.[5] She experienced a teen pregnancy and the loss of a son at two weeks old. Her circumstances could have easily held her back, and yet, somehow, her early trauma wasn't the end of her story. She went on to be a high school honor student and earn a full scholarship to Tennessee State University.

Winfrey had a strong spirit and plenty of spunk. The challenges she faced at a young age gave her deep empathy for others who had also experienced childhood suffering. These were all traits that would lead to her success as a young adult, enabling her to convert television viewers into dedicated fans, setting her on a course to become the first black female billionaire and to win a Presidential Medal of Freedom, the highest civilian award in the United States. But like Edison, there were also pivotal moments and standout influences that helped to guide Winfrey when so much of her life seemed lost. Her father and stepmother, who she went to live with in Nashville as a young teenager, were a much-needed steady and often strict presence, as was the church they attended every week. Winfrey has shared that "When my father took me, it changed the course of my life. He saved me." As strict as he was about appearance and tradition, her father was stricter about education, which he viewed as the key to success. "I remember coming home one time with Cs," Winfrey says, "and my father saying, 'This is not acceptable.' And I said, 'Unacceptable? C is average. This is not a bad grade.' And he said to me, 'If you were a child who could only get Cs, then that is really all I would expect of you. I wouldn't demand any more from you than Cs. But you are not. And so in this house, for you, Cs are not acceptable.'" [6]

When considering the lives of Edison and Winfrey, a few parallels can be extracted. They both experienced hardships early in life. They had to overcome grief, disappointment, and difficulties that could have held them back. They also had parents and mentors who shaped and supported their education in exceptional ways. They had models and guides who helped them envision a different path for their lives. It was due to these positive role models and their own internal drive to beat the odds that Edison and Winfrey were able to identify and take hold of the opportunities that did come their way.

Throughout most of his life, Edison could be found in one of his laboratories, pursuing theories and testing ideas. Even into his 80s and the final years of his life, Edison was pursuing an idea about electric trains and looking for a domestic source of natural rubber. He found success in numerous fields as an inventor, businessman, and entrepreneur, amassing a fortune estimated at around $200 million (in today's dollars)[7] along the way. Similarly, Winfrey has shown no signs of slowing down. Compelled by their hardships and lack of opportunity, she started a Leadership Academy for Girls in South Africa. After the wrapping of her popular talk show, she debuted a highly successful monthly magazine, launched her own TV Network, and wrote several books, just to name a few of her accomplishments. The lives of both Edison and Winfrey are defined by an insatiable appetite for learning, curiosity, and exploration.

This kind of learner, the lifelong curator of new ideas who is never satisfied to stop chasing new possibilities, is what we like to call the *wisest* learner. The wisest learner knows no limit to what they can attain. They're rarely bored. They see possibilities for growth all around them. And if Edison's and Winfrey's early years prove anything, it's that the wisest learner can grow out of the rockiest of soil. Even if you have what society deems as a difficult, hyperactive, or problematic child, with the right strategies, effective tools, and some positive modeling, you might actually have a budding success story under your roof.

Training parents to raise the wisest learners is the goal of this book. Standing on the shoulders of educators and psychologists Dr. Paul Pintrich, Dr. Barry Zimmerman, and Dr. Monique Boekaerts, we'll build upon their classical strategies and pull insights from the latest empirical findings, thorough meta-analyses, neuroscientific studies, and modern developments in the science of learning to underscore the strategies we propose. Rather than singularly focusing on one element or characteristic of learning, we'll take a holistic approach, considering all the factors that contribute to the development of a lifelong learner.

Most children will have obstacles they must overcome on the path to becoming the wisest learners. Even if their upbringings are primarily positive and nurturing, they will still have to work hard to strengthen their learning muscles and develop the discipline needed to be successful. As described in one of Boekaerts's learning models,[8] there is an emotional side to learning, and it is critical for parents to find the balance between the pursuit of learning and the well-being of their children. A child's mental capacity to learn new things (often referred to as their cognitive abilities) must be taken into account. As new ideas and opportunities are presented, children won't be mentally able to pursue these ideas if their brains are already preoccupied with other emotional distractions. Parents will need to ensure their children are emotionally sustained and guide them in how to clear away mental clutter. Only then can there be room to implement the learning strategies we'll soon discuss and the higher-learning states of automaticity and flow state that will become the goal for the wisest learner.

The encouraging news is that research overwhelmingly indicates that a love for learning and the skills needed to be the wisest learner are things that can be taught and caught through good parental modeling. It's a spirit and a mindset that you, as parents, can cultivate in your home. It's why your influence will be referenced again and again throughout this book.

The learning process is a complex system that involves multiple overlapping factors, or roles, with each contributing to the overall success of the learner. These factors can be thought of as three overlapping circles (see Figure 1), with each circle representing a different role. One role is that of the learner or child. The second role is that of the parent, demonstrating the proximal role of parents in the learning process. The third circle is the learning process itself. This book will address each of these areas—each circle represents a character in this story with a valuable role to play. While we'll speak directly to parents, it's the children who will ultimately benefit from our discussion. The learning process is the means by which wise learning will be established. Each of these concepts is interconnected, and each idea builds upon the last. One circle won't be complete without the other.

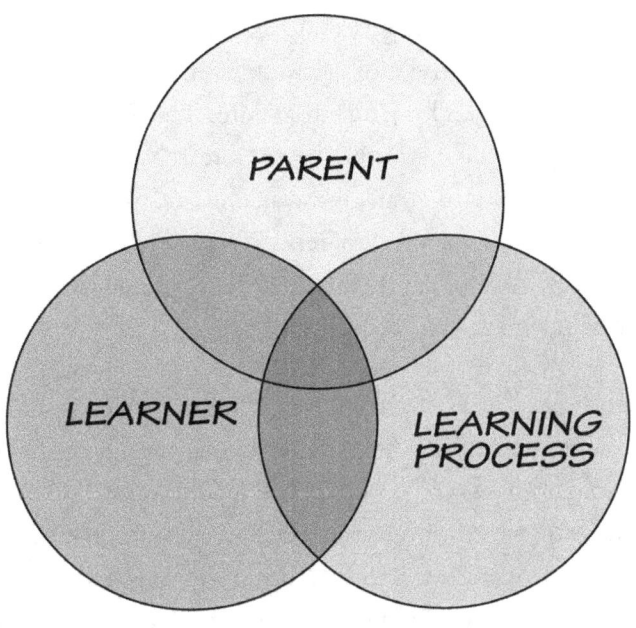

*Figure 1: The Three Overlapping Circles*

While this book was written primarily for parents raising young learners, it's important to note that it's never too late to start learning something new. Consider Leonardo da Vinci, who didn't apply himself to higher mathematics until he was 30 years old. While the formative early years of a child's life are the ideal time to initiate good learning strategies, the application of the ideas and strategies in this book can be effective whenever they are started. The wisest learners, regardless of age—even high school and college students ready to take the initiative to learn these strategies independently—will find the insights shared on these pages infinitely valuable. Additionally, while we *are* speaking directly to parents, we understand that not every child can be raised under the care of their biological parents. In some cases, the term "parent" can extend to cover a grandparent or guardian. For simplicity's sake, we will use "parent" to cover the adult or adults emotionally invested in raising, supporting, and nurturing a child. The Wisest Learners™ has gathered the gems of all the tested, researched, highly effective learning principles and strategies available and made them easier and more accessible for every parent to find and apply. Ideas that have long been available only to academics with exclusive privileges will now be open and available to all.

The important role of parents in their children's success can be seen in the story about Edison's life. People would often describe Edison as a genius, and he would counter that "genius is hard work, stick-to-it-iveness, and common sense."[9] He was also known to say that "genius is one percent inspiration and ninety-nine percent perspiration." Clearly, he understood that no one could advance themselves without a lot of hard work. According to the Edison Innovation Foundation, Edison was taught by his mother to follow four simple principles:

1. Never get discouraged if you fail. Learn from it. Keep trying.
2. Learn with both your head and hands.
3. Not everything of value in life comes from books—experience the world.
4. Never stop learning. Read the entire panorama of literature.

With these principles, Nancy Edison provided the scaffolding—the framework, mindset, and perspective—that Edison would build upon throughout his life. In this book, we'll demonstrate the art and science of what good scaffolding looks like for today's children.

We'll also highlight the notable traits of other well-known historical figures, such as Abraham Lincoln, and reflect on the patterns that lead to a lifelong love of learning. We'll identify patterns that contributed to the marked success of sports figures such as Stephen Curry and Giannis Antetokounmpo. We'll consider how, as parents, it all starts with us and the choices we make, starting today, to model the character we hope to see develop in our children. Owning our role in all of it may be the hardest lesson of all.

---

[1] Thomas Edison - New World Encyclopedia

[2] 1850-1877: Education: Overview - Encyclopedia.com

[3] Thomas Edison - Biography.com

[4] Oprah Winfrey - Biography.com

[5] Oprah opens up to Hoda Kotb about how her childhood trauma informed her life's work - Today.com

[6] The Man Who Saved Oprah Winfrey - Washingtonpost.com

[7] 37 Quotes From Thomas Edison That Will Inspire Success - Inc.com

[8] Boekaerts, Monique. "Self-regulated learning at the junction of cognition and motivation." *European Psychologist* 1, no. 2 (1996): 100.

[9] A Brief Biography of Thomas Edison - nps.gov

# The Blind Men and the Elephant[1]

Once upon a time, in a village in India, there lived six old men who were all born blind. The villagers loved and protected the old men, but since they could not see the world for themselves, they had to imagine its wonders based on the stories they heard from travelers. They were particularly curious about elephants. They had heard stories about elephants being powerful giants, graceful and gentle creatures fit for a princess to ride on, and terrifying beasts that could pierce a man's heart with their horns.

The old men argued day and night about elephants, each insisting that their version of the creature was the correct one. The villagers grew tired of their arguments and arranged for the curious men to visit the palace of the rajah to learn the truth about elephants. A young boy from their village was selected to guide the blind men on their journey.

When the blind men reached the palace, they were greeted by an old friend who worked as a gardener on the palace grounds. The gardener led them to an elephant in the courtyard. The blind men stepped forward to touch the creature that was the subject of so many arguments. Each man touched a different part of the elephant and drew their own conclusions about what an elephant was like.

The first blind man, who touched the elephant's side, said, "The elephant is like a wall."

"No, the elephant is like a spear," declared the second blind man, who touched the elephant's tusk.

The third blind man exclaimed, "You're both wrong. The elephant is like a snake," as he touched the elephant's trunk.

The fourth blind man, who touched the elephant's leg, said, "None of you know what you're talking about. The elephant is like a tree."

Touching the elephant's ear, the fifth blind man argued, "You're all mistaken. The elephant is like a fan."

And finally, the sixth blind man, who touched the elephant's tail, said, "You're all fools. The elephant is like a rope."

*Figure 2: The Six Blind Men and the Elephant*

They argued loudly about what an elephant was really like, and their shouts woke up the rajah. He asked them how they could be so certain they were right, when they only touched one part of the elephant. The rajah suggested they put all the parts together to see the truth.

The six blind men became silent and considered the words of the rajah, who was known to be a very wise man.

On their journey home, the six men discussed the rajah's advice and realized that to learn the truth, they must put all the parts together. They traveled home, with each man putting his hand on the shoulder of the man in front of him, ready to put all the parts together to finally learn the truth about elephants.

---

[1] The Blind Men and the Elephant - peacecorps.gov

# PROLOGUE

The process of becoming the wisest learner cannot be oversimplified. The strategies outlined in this book must be practiced again and again over time to be effective. Additionally, it's crucial that parents and children be flexible and willing to learn new ideas. We shared the parable of "The Blind Men and the Elephant" in its entirety because we believe it holds an important lesson for the start of this learning journey and the need for openness to new ways of thinking. In the parable, each man's perspective is correct but, at the same time, incomplete. They were each only experiencing one part of the enormous animal. Similarly, many books already in print provide singular, simplified approaches to learning. But in reality, there's no one quick or cursory shortcut to wise learning. In this book, we'll address the subject of learning with broader strokes, accounting for the elephant as a whole, not in part. We'll speak to the character of the parents and children, a learner's motivation and attitude, and how learning is modeled, as much as instructed.

We, the two authors, hope to widen the frame of reference on this topic, to give a larger-scale view of the learning process, of what the elephant looks like as a whole, and to present the complete, rich reality of what it is to embrace learning in its fullest. With a more holistic viewpoint, we believe parents can more effectively help their children to become the wisest learners.

To begin with, let's address why it is so important to become the wisest learner. Considering the volume of instruction children are expected to consume today versus 100 years ago—with grade school, college, and graduate school—it's a tremendous increase in the amount of information they must intake. Additionally, even after the traditional school years have passed, continuous education is still needed throughout our professional lives. We must keep pace with how jobs are evolving and how the world is evolving. To be successful as lifelong learners, our children need to be equipped with the techniques, strategies, and mechanisms that will supercharge their learning. Our goal is to provide you with the scaffolding for wise learning, so you can pass it on to your children. This scaffolding will be their learning foundation, making wise learning second nature for them, a set of behaviors that will automatically be triggered when new learning opportunities arise.

Knowing when and how to apply these learning strategies will come with practice and eventually become ingrained in a young learner's everyday behavior, creating mental muscle memory. The wisest learner will know how to bypass lower-level learning processing (this learning will become automatic and second nature!) so they can spend more time focused on higher-level thinking and learning. With this efficiency, they will be able to learn better and faster.

We, parents, knowing learning principles and strategies is one thing but being able to help our children learn and apply them is a challenging task on its own. Since this book is designed for parents, let me share my experience as a 12-year-old adolescent that highlights the importance and difficulty of parenting. In Filipino-Chinese culture, young adults are expected to go to work every summer. For me, those summers were spent working at my grandpa's store, selling auto parts. These summers were primarily enriching experiences for me, instilling the value of hard work and allowing me to hone my entrepreneurial instincts. Very often, my job was as a cashier. One day I realized that the sales for that day were falling short of expectations. I felt empathy for my grandpa; I didn't want him to be disappointed when the sales for the day were low. I had a "brilliant" idea. I decided to hide some of the money under the cashier's drawer. My thought was "today my grandpa will already be sad over poor sales, so why not make today *really* sad and tomorrow, he'll be so happy this money is added back in and there's a surplus."

What I didn't realize was that my dad, the store manager, was already tracking the sales for the day. He knew it was a slow day and expected the cash in the drawer to reflect as much. So, when the cash drawer added up even shorter than expected, there was confusion. As the cashier, I was held accountable. When questioned, I froze. I couldn't explain my reasoning. Even though I knew I had good intentions, I couldn't translate my thoughts into words. My dad and grandpa were left with only one logical explanation; they had to assume I was trying to steal. I was sent home and was in a great deal of trouble. I could not blame them because I was not able to explain myself properly. Even if I was able to express my "noble intentions," it would have been difficult to believe as well.

I've never forgotten this experience, and it's a lesson I've carried with me as an educator and as a parent. It highlighted the difficult task that we have as parents. How could my father have discerned my motivation from my silence? The experience has taught me to dig deep and not to accept anything at face value when it comes to children. Sometimes children can't or won't explain where they're coming from or what they're really feeling. I encourage parents to create a safe environment so that communication between parents and children will be engaging such that the children will listen and learn well when we mentor them about life and learning.

Children won't always understand the value of their education. They won't always be motivated to work hard and make wise choices at every turn. The characteristics of wise learning will only develop with time and with a lot of open and interesting conversations between parents and their children.

We carry this mindset about child development with us as we write this book—recognizing the emotional layers and elements that contribute to a child's maturity as we share our tools and strategies. Keeping these foundational needs in mind, this book will unfold in the form of the Wisest Learners™ Learning Tree (see Figure 3), a symbol of strength and longevity. We'll divide our discussion into the following sections:

1. The Roots: The Parental Engagement Cycle
2. The Trunk: Foundation
3. The Branches: Strategy Management

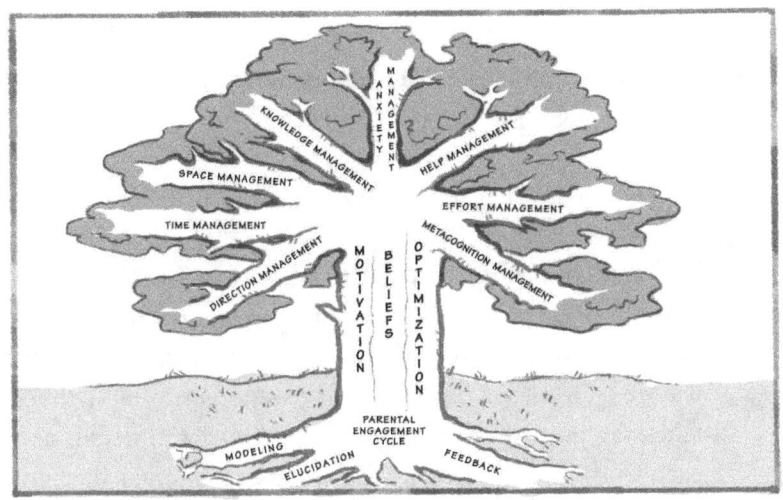

*Figure 3: The Wisest Learners Tree*

This framework will serve as a guide as we work through this book. The roots section will further address the role of parents in their child's learning development and provide a helpful parental engagement cycle for success. From there, we'll travel up the tree trunk and uncover the secrets to activating a young learner's motivation, attitude, and optimization skills. The tree branches will identify numerous applicable and practical learning strategies that are proven to significantly improve learning outcomes.

We know that each parent reading this book will have a different objective in mind, and it's important to consider those expectations before diving in. Your approach to reading and engaging with this content will depend on your goals. You can skim these pages with the objective of simply gaining a cursory understanding of the topic, knowing that your time won't be wasted. You and your child will benefit from the insights you gather. But if you're able to put in more time and you're looking for deeper impact and a more engaging experience, that's available within these pages as well. Either way, as you read this, you can benefit from the material. And how much you benefit from this book is up to you.

Here are some tips on what to look for as you read:

- We worked hard to ensure that all our points are based on research. Research study summaries are included throughout the book, followed by short Research Recaps, which will be featured in callout boxes (to make sure you caught the key takeaway points). You can read more in-depth details about each study, if you like, at the Reference section at the end of the book.
- The end of each chapter will offer an Action Plan. Take a few minutes to answer the questions posed and consider the suggestions offered in these sections. We included these Action Plans in an effort to make the book more useful. We want to help you consider ways to apply and practice what is discussed throughout the book.
- Keep a notebook with you as you read and capture ideas that stand out to you. You can review them when the book is done, and you'll have a record of the key concepts you wish to apply.
- For those interested in a deeper connection with this book and the lasting impact that can come with the application of these ideas, consider digesting only one chapter per week. Be patient in how you intake the content. Slowly digest and find ways to apply the strategies and concepts presented.

Now, as parents on a quest to support our children in this pursuit of learning, let us begin to unravel the truths hidden within the wisest learning tree and embark on the process of training, nurturing, and developing lifelong learners.

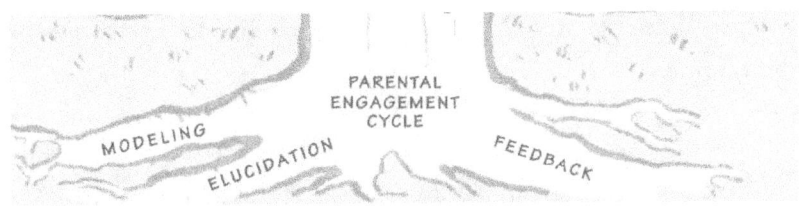

# Part I
# PARENTAL STRATEGIES
## The Roots of the Learning Tree

## Introduction to Parental Strategies

President Abraham Lincoln, that we know and love, didn't become that way on his own. Rather, a critically important figure in his childhood helped guide and shape his early development, preparing him for the important, challenging role that he would face as an adult.

"After the death of their mother, little Abraham Lincoln (Abe as he was often called as a child) and his sister Sarah began a dreary life," writes William Herndon, Lincoln's law partner and biographer. Eleven-year-old Sarah struggled to take up domestic duties in their one-room cabin with a dirt floor.[1] When his father remarried, young Abraham Lincoln—filthy, hungry, and starved for affection—immediately began calling his new stepmother, also named Sarah, "Mama." Thankfully, the good feelings were mutual. Sarah Bush Johnston washed her new stepchildren thoroughly and dressed them in clothes from her own children. She also insisted her new husband install a floor, a proper door, and windows in their home.

Lincoln once reflected on his childhood, characterizing it as "joyous and happy," which he attributed largely to his stepmother's love. Despite her illiteracy, she obtained books for him and stimulated his intellectual development, playing a crucial role in providing the sparse formal education he received. "I induced my husband to permit Abe to read and study at home as well as at school," she later said. "At first, he was not easily reconciled to it, but finally, he too seemed willing to encourage him to a certain extent. Abe was a dutiful son to me always."

Sarah Bush Johnston filled an enormous void in Lincoln's life after the loss of his biological mother. She furthered his birth mother's work, cultivating Abe's reading comprehension and intellect. "Sarah had an appreciation for the value of an education," says Jeff Oppenheimer, author of *That Nation Might Live*, a historical novel based on his extensive research into the strong bond between Lincoln and his stepmother. "She recognized early on there was something special about this boy and defended his right to pursue his intellectual development." She treated Lincoln as if he was her flesh and blood by offering love, kindness, and encouragement.

"She recognized a boy of tremendous talent and saw the diamond when virtually everyone else around this gangly, awkward boy saw the rough," Oppenheimer says. "That's what mothers do."[2] She supported him with much-needed love and attention, without which he may have succumbed to despair and devastation.

As parents, we're the glue that holds our families together and the reference point that children look to for guidance as they learn and grow. We're also their source of emotional stability. We're typically their first examples of what love and a healthy relationship should look like. It is critical for parents to understand the major role they play in the kind of learner their child will become. Parents often spend significant energy considering their children's school environment, researching factors like school graduation rates, testing scores, and student-teacher ratios. All these factors will certainly influence a child's education. But they should be weighed in equal measure with the child's home environment and the attitude of their parents toward learning. A child's home life will heavily influence their cognitive and psychological state *as well as* their academic performance.

The impact parents have on a child's academic performance was explored in a study by Priscilla Yau and colleagues.[3] This study found that supportive characteristics such as being highly responsive and setting up clear rules were some of the most effective in facilitating a child's learning. The research additionally highlighted other beneficial parenting traits such as demonstrating affection (i.e., showing love to the child), engagement (i.e., dedicating time to the child), and fostering independence (i.e., leading the child towards self-reliance), all of which were found to be associated with academic achievement. A high occurrence of each of these characteristics was positively associated with an increase in the student's GPA scores.

Not to be overlooked, the research also found that certain negative parenting characteristics can lead to academic difficulties. Inducing guilt (i.e., causing the child to feel guilty) and devaluation (i.e., dismissing the child's thoughts and expressions) can harm academic performance. An example of devaluation would be when the child feels that their mother or father always finishes their sentences whenever they talk. Guilt induction can be felt when mothers or fathers blame the child for other family members' problems. Both of these negative parenting characteristics can be categorized under the umbrella of parental psychological control, which refers to a parent's attempts to manipulate and control their children's thoughts and behavior. Some parents will use these control tactics to keep children emotionally dependent on them.

An additional study on this topic from the *Journal of Family Studies* evaluated parenting styles such as the expression of affection, communication, involvement, rule-setting, and the provision of autonomy to see how these styles of parenting can impact a child's ability to learn math, language, and the natural and social sciences.[4] The results showed that many of these parenting strategies, particularly the opportunity for a child to show autonomy with different aspects of their personality, can positively impact students' grades and academic achievement. Notably, these strategies were associated with improved academic performance in language learning and math—two of the most foundationally important subjects for children to master.

These studies are particularly interesting to us because they demonstrate the effects of parenting on learning in ways you may not automatically expect. They touch on the many elements of parenting—things such as affection and the amount of autonomy given to a child—that can translate to academically accomplished children almost as readily as a strong set of good learning strategies.

With all this research and focus on parents, you may be feeling the weight of your parental responsibility more heavily than ever. But before you cave under pressure, let's take a collective breath. The need for wise parenting is notable, but the expectation for perfect parenting is not. We, parents, should be learning, improving, trying, and retrying different strategies as we go. Our children will benefit greatly from our honesty as we work through this process; they need to see us learning and growing too. They *want* to learn from us. So, if you don't feel fully prepared to model-wise learning yet, don't worry! The work of raising the wisest learners is ongoing and something we all must work at. But if you're willing to try and you're open to experimenting and failing until you find a "good rhythm," then you'll be just fine. There's no better example you can provide.

Part I of this book is dedicated to equipping you with strategies on how to find that "good rhythm." Based on our experience in the world of education and the insights we've gathered from a great deal of research, we can give you a leg up in your learning journey. We handled the heavy lifting of reading thousands of research journal pages. We aim to maximize your efforts and give you the tools to ace your role as parents raising the wisest learners. We've got simple, important ideas you can start implementing today—things that can radically improve the impact you're having.1

To begin with, consider these two thoughts:

- The high standards of parents are important
- But those standards *must* be accompanied by warmth and love

We like to call this "The Double S" (see Figure 4). Standards *and* sweetness.

*Figure 4: The Double S*

## RESEARCH RECAP:

- Supportive parenting characteristics such as being **highly responsive** and setting up **clear rules** are some of the most effective in facilitating a child's learning. Additional beneficial parenting traits associated with academic achievement include **expressions of love**, **active participation**, and **encouragement of independence**.

- Sometimes, the best way to encourage a child's willingness to learn is by providing lots of **affection** and an **openness** to hearing their ideas and perspectives, even when they are different from your own.

- When parents try to **control** their children's thoughts and behaviors through **guilt**, **manipulation**, and **devaluation**, this can lead to a decline in academic performance.

It's okay to have high standards for what you want your child to accomplish, but your child will need those standards to be supported by your warmth and love. Be firm, yet gentle. Gentleness manifests love and warmth, while firmness manifests the standard. High warmth and high demand can be exhibited and expressed through three practices—Modeling, Elucidation, and Feedback. We've created a framework called the Parental Engagement Cycle that visualizes how these ideas work together.

## The Parental Engagement Cycle (See Figure 5)

The Parental Engagement Cycle (PEC) is a tool that parents can use to better understand their role in their child's learning process. It's a cycle that we will explain in more detail in the next few chapters, and it's something that will be referenced throughout the rest of the book.

The three spokes of the PEC are Modeling, Elucidation, and Feedback. The hub of the PEC is the family culture. The family culture influences how Modeling, Elucidation, and Feedback are manifested. Family culture can be defined as the prevalent attitude, spirit, or mindset that exists within a home. It's the recurring characteristics on display in a home and the common bond that ties together parents and children. A warm and harmonious family culture will support the development of the wisest learners.

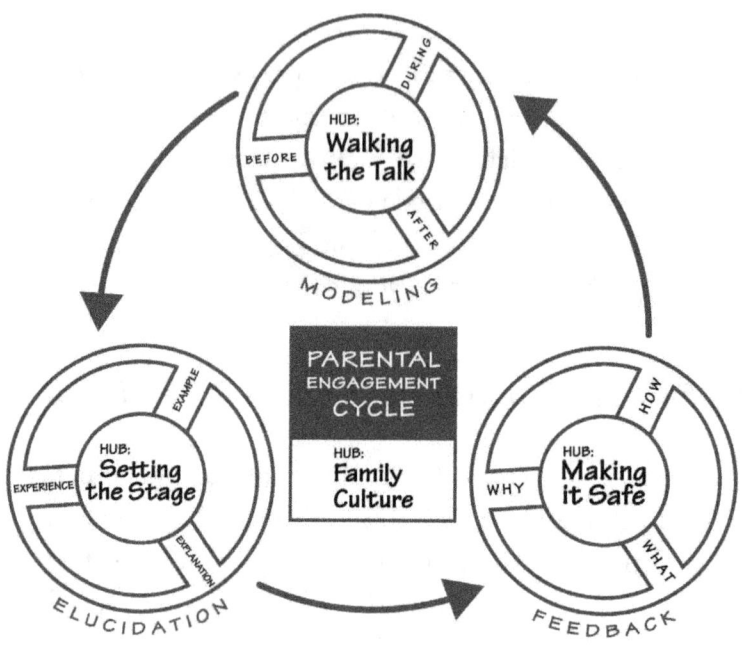

*Figure 5: The Parental Engagement Cycle*

The PEC is circular in nature on purpose, as each spoke of the wheel is tied to and supportive of the next. Also, it's a cycle that's not meant to end. Referencing back to our discussion about not needing to be perfect, just willing and open to work and try new things, the PEC is a process that you will continue to work on throughout your life as a parent.

**We created the PEC with the following goals in mind:**

- To help parents understand themselves
- To help parents understand their children

As we mentioned in the Prologue, this book is broken down into sections based on the Wise Learning Tree. The PEC and the engagement strategies of Modeling, Elucidation, and Feedback are the roots of our tree. These roots will provide a sound parental foundation from which our tree can grow and flourish. The root structure will become more established and stronger as the months and years go by and you actively put the PEC into practice. The following three chapters will focus on these forms of engagement, discussing each individually and in-depth, but also identifying how they are connected. We'll also discuss ways you can start using these strategies in your daily life.

To show the importance of the PEC for effective parenting, let me share the story of my sister Vian, whom I like to call "super mom." She's overcome many challenges in her lifetime. Rather than letting those challenges get the best of her, she's choosing to let them inform how she lives and how she chooses to parent her children. She's a great example of someone who, I believe, is exhibiting the kinds of traits that positively support good learning.

Before her current marriage, my sister had come close to marriage once before. However, three months before the ceremony, her fiancé discovered he had colon cancer. He passed away not long after his diagnosis. In the face of this immense tragedy, she found the strength to quell her grief and pursue new dreams, carrying with her a deeper respect for how suddenly life can change. She met someone new, and soon after, they were married. Pregnancy didn't come easy for her at first, but with persistence and patience, they eventually started a family. They now have three beautiful children and a greater sense of gratitude for life. "Our struggles with pregnancy were so difficult," shares Vian, "but the way people encouraged and supported me helped to center and strengthen my faith. Once I was pregnant with my son, I knew his life had value and purpose. I wanted to make sure he was aware of it as well."

All of their children are high achievers, both in their academic and personal pursuits. The eldest was a great swimmer and archer but was forced to walk away from those endeavors when he was diagnosed with lymphoma. After my sister's earlier encounter with her fiancé's colon cancer, she recognized the gravity of this turn of events. She was able to share with her son the wisdom she'd gained from her past experience, and I believe he took her guidance to heart. Rather than letting his diagnosis get the best of him, he decided to purposely make the most of the rest of his life—however long it may be. Vian's son decided to enroll in an international baccalaureate program, choosing the hardest classes in order to push himself and glean all that he could from the program. This was a high-stakes risk as higher grades in this program led to better schools—but he went for it anyway, not wanting to take the easy route. He performed above average but was one grade point shy of graduating. Still, he learned everything he could from the experience. He persevered, applied, and earned a scholarship to a great technology college. He's currently in Sydney, Australia, pursuing an engineering degree in mechatronics, and he's excelling! He's consistently making the dean's list for outstanding academic achievement.

I believe the success of my sister's oldest son (and, in fact, of all her children) is in part due to the losses and heartache she faced earlier in her life—how she was able to grow from those experiences and pass on her hard-earned wisdom to her children. She has provided a positive example as someone who has already overcome hard, unplanned life circumstances and still found a way to thrive. She has gained a better appreciation for what's most important in life (strong character and faith), and that's guiding how she encourages, disciplines, and motivates her children.

This story highlights the role of the PEC in good parenting. By being transparent with our children about our past struggles and failures, we can model resilience and perseverance, which are key elements of the PEC. This can help our children learn how to overcome challenges and lean on us for support and guidance, reinforcing the Elucidation and Feedback aspects of the PEC. By welcoming their questions and encouraging open dialogue, we can create a positive family culture that fosters communication and trust, which are fundamental components of the PEC. Positive parenting is possible even for those of us who are learning as we go (which is most of us, if we're honest!). The PEC serves as a framework for nurturing a healthy parent-child relationship and promoting optimal learning and growth in our children. Let's embrace the PEC and strive to be the best parents we can be, using it as our foundation to navigate the challenges of parenting with confidence and raise resilient and successful learners.

In this next chapter, we're going to take a closer look at Modeling specifically and the role it can play in raising the wisest learners.

## ACTION PLAN

- Do you feel you have an open mindset when it comes to learning new things? Your children will learn as much from your open and willing attitude as they will from your instruction. As you consider the action plan at the end of each chapter, look for ways you can model an openness to learning for your children.

- Take a moment to reflect on your home environment. Keep in mind that no home environment is ever perfect! Jot down some ideas for how to make more room for warmth and quality time.

- Do you let your children see you struggle and then witness your growth over time? Reflect on a time recently when you've faced something challenging and consider how it could be helpful to let your child learn from your experience.

- How do you feel when your children ask questions that challenge you? Is there room for open dialogue and hard conversations? Consider ways you can encourage open discussions in your home.

[1] Abraham Lincoln's 'angel mother' and the second 'mama' who outlived him - Washingtonpost.com

[2] The Two Mothers Who Molded Lincoln - History.com

[3] Yau, Priscilla S., Yongwon Cho, Jacob Shane, Joseph Kay, and Jutta Heckhausen. "Parenting and adolescents' academic achievement: the mediating role of goal engagement and disengagement." *Journal of Child and Family Studies* 31, no. 4 (2022): 897-909.

[4] Aguirre-Dávila, Eduardo, Miguel Morales-Castillo, and Manuel Moreno-Vásquez. "Parenting, autonomy and academic achievement in the adolescence." *Journal of Family Studies* (2021): 1-14.

CHAPTER 1

# MODELING

One of the world's best-known humanitarians, Mother Teresa, was born into a devout Catholic family. Her parents were actively involved in their local church, exposing the young Mother Teresa—then known as Agnes—to a life of faith at a very early age. At just eight years old, her father tragically fell ill and died. After his death, Agnes became especially close to her mother, a woman known for her compassion and generosity. In many ways, her mother shaped her perspective on what it meant to be charitable toward others.

Residing in Skopje, now the capital of the Republic of Macedonia, Agnes and her mother, Drana Bojaxhiu, were not wealthy by any means. Yet, they frequently welcomed the city's impoverished to share meals with their modest family. "My child, never eat a single mouthful unless you are sharing it with others," Drana is said to have counseled her daughter. When Agnes asked who the people eating with them were, her mother would explain that "Some of them are our relations, but all of them are our people."[1] She was planting seeds of kindness and altruism in Agnes, the fruit of which would be visible later in her life.

When raising the wisest learners, good parental modeling is about showing our children how to be dedicated students in every area of life. Be it in academic endeavors or social interactions, we model for our children how to act, talk, and relate to those around us. Good modeling will happen naturally as we exhibit a consistent, honest interest to be lifelong learners ourselves—displaying a willingness to try new things, have new experiences, and face new challenges.

It's important to remember that your posture, attitude, and outlook will be more influential than your words alone. This may bring to mind a commonly known saying that "more is caught than taught."

This idea takes root in a study by Siu-Cheung Kong and Yi-Qing Wang,[2] which revealed that parents' perceived usefulness of tasks, along with nurturing parental support, can effectively foster students' learning efficiency and motivation. This research showed that a parent's perception of how useful and relevant a subject, task, or educational program is (i.e., our perceived usefulness) can be passed on to our children through simple conversations and modeling. Let's consider, for example, how you, as a parent, communicate your feelings about math, reading, or science. When faced with a difficult math problem, do you put yourself down and announce that you are "no good at math"? Or do you model a positive learning mindset and a willingness to keep trying until you figure it out? If you model a willingness to learn a hard subject, your child is highly likely to pick up on your attitude and adopt it as their own.

How about your attitude toward formal education? If you didn't have a good experience with school, consider how you may be passing that on to your children in the way you recall stories from the past or express your thoughts about how school let you down. You can alter your child's views on school by first changing your outlook and then setting your sights on helping them to have a better experience. Wounded people tend to wound people, as the saying goes. As parents, we must first adopt a positive attitude toward learning, potentially resolving and addressing past issues, before we can model a good attitude for our children.

A story about my parents offers a good example of positive modeling. When my Ph.D. adviser asked me if there were educators in my family who inspired me to take graduate studies, I said that there were none. She was quite surprised when I shared with her that my father had only finished grade one, and my mother had finished second-year high school. But the one impactful thing that both of them modeled to me was the love of learning. My father would share stories of how and what he learned from different people, especially from elders like his parents, and how much he appreciated them. My mother would spend the time learning different skills that would then be converted into various businesses. They would support my inclination to spend the whole day at the bookstore reading. Every summer, my parents would enroll my siblings and me in various summer skills activities such as painting and playing the piano, among others. Those are quite common nowadays, but they were not as common in our community then. I still marvel at our summer learning experiences because my parents did not have large financial resources. They had to sacrifice a lot to allow their children to have various learning experiences outside of the traditional school system. My parents modeled a learning environment that impacted my perspective toward learning.

This idea that, as parents, we will undoubtedly pass on our convictions about learning through our attitude and actions is so fundamental to raising the wisest learners that we've integrated it into our Parental Engagement Cycle. "**Walking the Talk**," or when parents *show* how to act, not just talk about how to act, is the central hub of the Modeling wheel. As parents, we're showing our children what we believe about learning, whether we intend to or not. It's critical that we own our influence and recognize our impact. Our children internalize our perceptions into their own value systems. If we demonstrate openness to learning, speak positively about acquiring new skills, and model a lifestyle that is welcoming to the discovery of new ideas, then, in turn, our children will be more motivated to do the same.

## RESEARCH RECAP:

- Children *internalize* and *mimic* the actions of their parents. If we model a positive and open attitude toward learning, our children will too.

- Our perception of how valuable a subject or task is can be passed on through *simple conversations*, the *positivity or negativity* of our words, and our *attitude or posture* toward a subject or task.

The three spokes of the Modeling wheel are the three stages of when modeling should occur—Before, During, and After learning.

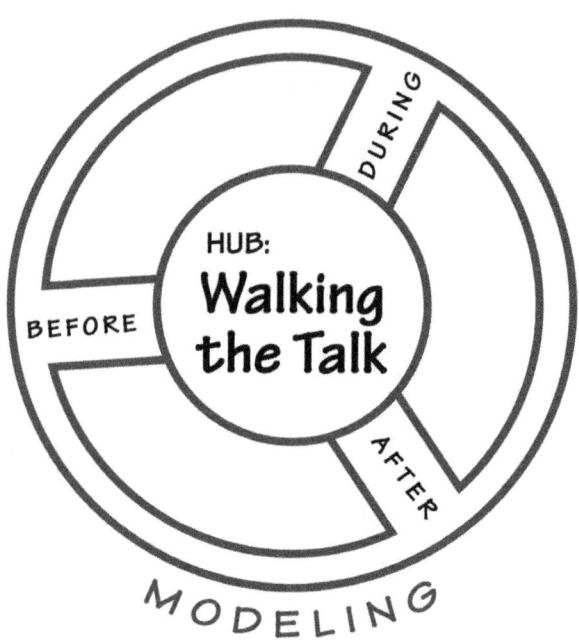

*Figure 6: The Modeling Wheel*

- **Before learning:** This refers to the work parents can do to create positive conditions for learning to take place. Chapter 9 will be dedicated to a discussion about space management and the importance of structuring a physical environment in a way that will optimize learning. This can include things such as providing an organized, quiet, naturally lit learning space where productive work can be done. "Before learning," as it relates to Modeling, takes into consideration space management, but it's more than that, as well. It also refers to the ways that parents can set their children up for success by modeling good learning behavior—a willingness to tackle hard things and an openness to explore new ideas. Before children tackle learning on their own, we can show them how to do it well.

- **During learning:** This part of Modeling addresses what's taking place during the time dedicated to studying and learning new skills. When you, as parents, are focused and working to understand something new, what kinds of actions will your child witness? Will they see you using a whiteboard to visually map out your thoughts? Will you be quiet and thoughtful, or do you express your ideas out loud as you work them out? How much time do you dedicate to learning, and what do you do to avoid distractions? The way you go about learning yourself can be a positive modeling experience for your children to see. This step also takes into consideration the specific learning strategies that can be applied during a study session for optimal learning and a flow state to be triggered. Part III will discuss the various learning strategies that we recommend. Parents will need to play an integral role in helping their children determine how to apply the various learning strategies and, when possible, modeling for them what it looks like to practice the strategies they find to be most helpful.

- **After learning:** This modeling will occur after learning has taken place and involves identifying what went well, what didn't, and where improvements can be made. Consider how, when learning a new sport or when working with a trainer, it's common for there to be check-ins with the coach after a workout to discuss how you performed. Good post-learning modeling will accept the advice of the coach. Time will be spent thinking about how to apply their suggestions in the next workout session. Negative post-learning can take the form of a bad attitude, giving up because advancements aren't happening as quickly as hoped, or blaming the coach for lack of progress. Parents can model for their learners how to process their progress, take the advice of instructors, and apply the recommended steps toward improvement.

Good modeling can be illustrated by a real-life event that occurred on the Hudson River in 2009. Captain Chesley "Sully" Sullenberger III, a seasoned pilot with decades of experience, was tasked with a seemingly impossible mission—safely landing a commercial plane with 155 passengers on board after both engines were disabled by a bird strike.[3] As the leader in a critical situation, Captain Sullenberger recognized that his team, including the co-pilot and flight attendants, was in crisis. With the plane rapidly losing altitude, time was of the essence.

Captain Sullenberger took decisive action and skillfully landed the plane on the Hudson River, executing a textbook-perfect water landing. He remained calm, composed, and focused throughout the entire ordeal, reassuring and guiding his team and passengers. His actions demonstrated the highest level of professionalism and competence under extreme pressure. The media later dubbed him a hero for his remarkable feat, calling the incredible water landing a miracle.

Captain Sullenberger's actions were not only heroic, but they also served as a powerful example of modeling for his team and the world. His self-awareness, decision-making, and response to the learning experience of an unprecedented emergency landing were a testament to his expertise and leadership. His courageous and skilled modeling inspired confidence and trust in his team, leading to a successful outcome. Captain Sullenberger's story continues to be studied and celebrated as a remarkable example of the power of modeling in a high-stakes situation.

Our real lives may hopefully not involve dramatic and dangerous events like what Captain Sullenberger had to go through, which would make us the hero of all our children's stories. However, we can still be role models by displaying good character, a strong work ethic, and an openness to learn. If we choose to model kindness, graciousness, and hospitality in our daily lives, our children will take notice and are likely to follow our example. Our children will reflect on what we teach them through our actions.

Let us return to the story and influence of Mother Teresa (or Agnes). Agnes's mother was a role model for her, but Agnes herself became a globally known role model for an entire generation. Even after her passing, she continues to be an icon of charity movements across the globe.

BBC reporter David Willey noted the following about Mother Teresa when he interviewed her in 2016: "By the time I met her in the late 1980s, Mother Teresa's sisters and affiliated brothers and fathers had already grown to become an international family of 1,800 nuns and many thousands of lay workers. Today they number nearly 6,000 and are active in 139 countries. Her order knows practically no territorial boundaries, and she was already setting up homes and hospices and recruiting in Eastern Europe long before the fall of the Berlin Wall and the end of the Soviet Union."[4]

The modeling done by Agnes's mother contributed to the development of a modern-day saint. Their mother-daughter story is a reminder to us of the powerful influence we have as parents. We can show them, through our actions, how to be overcomers who value effort over results. We can determine, as their parents, which characteristics and values are of utmost importance to our family and then be living examples of what it means to strive for those standards. It's our responsibility but also our beautiful opportunity to shape the next generation of the wisest learners.

## ACTION PLAN

- What concerns do you have about your child's attitude toward learning? Take note of specific positive and negative tendencies that you've seen in their attitude that you would like to either reinforce or work to improve.

- Do you feel your child's learning attitude reflects how you feel about learning? Jot down some ways you want to adjust your attitude toward learning. What actions, opinions, or behaviors would you like to change in order to model a more open posture toward learning new or hard things?

- Is there a new opportunity or challenging task you would like to take on? Consider how you can include your child in the process and let them witness your growth as a learner.

[1] Mother Teresa - Biography.com

[2] Kong, Siu-Cheung, and Yi-Qing Wang. "The influence of parental support and perceived usefulness on students' learning motivation and flow experience in visual programming: Investigation from a parent perspective." *British Journal of Educational Technology* 52, no. 4 (2021): 1749-1770.

[3] Captain 'Sully' and Passengers Reunite for 'Miracle on the Hudson' Anniversary: 'We're Like Extended Family'

[4] Mother Teresa: The humble sophisticate

PARENTAL
ENGAGEMENT
CYCLE

MODELING

ELUCIDATION

FEEDBACK

# CHAPTER 2

# ELUCIDATION

My wife and I have been blessed with the opportunity to travel extensively. With our daughter now in her 20s and jobs that can often be done remotely, we've taken advantage of the chance to see many different countries. These travels provide us with the opportunity to experience a wide variety of cultures and lifestyles. It's also a wonderful way to meet and spend quality time with friends who are spread around the world.

During one such trip to Nashville, Tennessee, my wife and I had dinner with some friends with two young boys. Not surprisingly, their boys were busy, energetic, and very inquisitive. As we swapped stories over supper, we came to the subject of scary animal encounters. My wife and I had been in the Smoky Mountains the previous weekend, and she'd had a nerve-wracking but exciting experience with a few black bears. The father of this family went on to share some of his own chance meetings with dangerous wildlife, which naturally stoked the fires of imagination in the minds of the young boys, who were eager to learn more about their father's adventures. The father's patience struck me as he thoughtfully answered each of their questions. He didn't just provide rote, simple answers to appease them, a tactic that would have enabled him to focus on the adult conversation. Rather, he paused each time their curiosity was sparked and provided detailed explanations, painting colorful pictures with his words and filling his sons' minds with wonder. They longed to know more, and their interest in bears, wildlife, and outdoor adventures grew with each detail of their father's tales.

For the few short years that our children are under our roof, we, as their parents, are the lens through which they will view much of the world. Our experiences will become their experiences—enlivening their imaginations and opening their minds to the possibility around them. We get the chance to impart our hard-earned wisdom, framing tough concepts in ways that are real, digestible, and comprehensible to them as young learners. This process is known as Elucidation.

Elucidation means to explain or clarify. The goal of Elucidation is to make a topic more clear and easier to grasp. As children grow, learn, and experience new things, their curiosity will take them on many adventures. There are an endless number of possibilities to be explored. Some things will come naturally to them, but much will need some measure of explanation. They will often need a guide to help them make sense of what they encounter throughout life. As their parents, we are uniquely positioned to provide these insights.

Elucidation is the second wheel in our Parental Engagement Cycle. Parents will often have to work to master the patience and openness needed to skillfully respond to their children's many questions to help them better see and understand the world around them. Regular, thoughtful elucidation will set children up to be lifelong learners. When children's questions are met with willing answers, they will come to see all of life as a stage for learning. Every opportunity will be a new chance for them to expand their understanding.

That is why the central hub of this wheel is "**Setting the Stage**" (as seen in Figure 7). It's an idea that is manifested as parents identify and live out the family values, principles, and practices they want their children to embrace. Parents clear the path for the kind of learning environment that will exist in their homes. It's up to parents to provide an accommodating, open environment where children feel the freedom to ask questions. It's parents who can foster their children's trust that curiosity will be met with a listening ear and a willingness to learn together.

Parents can "set the stage" by proposing standards for the kind of learners their children should strive to become. These can be standards such as always doing your best, working hard, and committing to do something well if you're going to do it at all. Parents can explain the value of learning and help their children dream about what they can accomplish through learning. They can also reinforce verbally their belief that their children can meet these standards, providing the faith that they *can* be successful. All these things can be communicated directly and indirectly to children through conversations and explanations.

Three separate research analyses focused on examining parental involvement from three distinct angles—home-based involvement, school-based involvement, and academic socialization.

1. **Home-based involvement** included parents' involvement in activities at home, such as supervising or checking homework and talking about school life. This could also include doing

extra homework exercises to reinforce what the child is learning at school.

2. **School-based involvement** covered activities carried out within the school, such as interactions with teachers, attendance at class meetings, and active participation in school-related events. This might also include fundraising or involvement in school campaigns—any number of ways that parents can be more present and active at their child's school that aren't directly related to the learning that is taking place.

3. **Academic socialization** is related to the ways parents talk to their kids about school and learning to communicate their expectations and views on education. Academic socialization can include when parents ask their children questions such as "Why is it necessary to go to school or have good grades?" "How is what you're learning related to your future life?" and "How will what you're learning help you in your future career?"

All three of these studies sought to determine which of these forms of parental involvement was most helpful in predicting a child's GPA and academic attainment (the highest level of schooling they would achieve). While you might be inclined to think that the first of these three types of involvement—home-based involvement, where parents are helping with homework and actively trying to find new ways to reinforce school material at home—would be the most effective, in reality, all three studies identified *academic socialization* as the most valuable.

The initial research carried out by Day and Dotterer demonstrated that a blend of increased academic socialization and school-based participation positively impacted the grade point averages of all adolescents involved. Interestingly, the reports from parents in this study highlighted their feeling that academic socialization had a minimal impact. In other words, the parents didn't think that how they talked to their kids about school made that big of a difference. However, their children's reports painted a different picture. According to the adolescents, academic socialization *was* perceived to have a stronger, more significant effect on their academic achievement.

School-based involvement was the second most impactful form of involvement. It seems that when you're involved in your child's school, this action backs up the conversations you're having about the importance of school. Your participation shows that you value school activities—your kids see you taking school seriously. Additionally, teachers seem to value parental involvement, taking a child more seriously because of their personal connection with the parents. Parental involvement in school activities creates a form of psychological bias toward the children whose parents are more involved.

Finally, home-based involvement was shown to have no reliable correlation with long-term academic outcomes. This was based on reports from both the parents and students involved in the study. There was even a slight negative impact reported by the students with regard to home-based involvement. It seems that when parents push too much at home, it can backfire and have a slightly negative impact on a learner's GPA.

The second study by Benner, Boyle, and Sadler[2] demonstrated that school-based engagement was especially helpful for less privileged children. At the same time, parents' academic socialization appeared to foster the academic achievement of more privileged children effectively. There were considerable associations between school-based engagement and parental expectations and a student's overall grades and level of education. However, home-based involvement was unrelated to either GPA or educational accomplishment.

The third study, carried out by Duan, Yuan, and He,[3] aligned with the previous two studies, finding no meaningful influence of home-based involvement on academic performance. However, the other two types of engagement played a significant role in predicting achievement, with academic socialization emerging as the strongest. In other words, speaking, explaining, and showing the importance of education through direct conversations with children was the strongest predictor of a high GPA.

While home-based involvement is seemingly getting a bad rap, this third study did highlight an interesting detail. Home-based involvement *was* a strong predictor of school behavior, which includes attendance, attitude toward studying in school, and staying out of trouble. It is reassuring to know that our efforts to support homework and talk about school life are not all in vain.

All in all, these three different studies, each with large sample sizes, uncovered similar findings. They highlight how conversations about education at home can positively and significantly impact a child's GPA. They further illustrate how school-based engagement and academic socialization can positively influence educational achievement, or the extent of schooling a child is likely to pursue. When parents explain and discuss the value of their child's education, they help their child to grasp the importance of learning. Children are then more motivated to succeed and are more likely to not only finish school but go on to earn postgraduate degrees.

Verbally setting a standard, expressing how you value learning, and then communicating your faith in your child—your belief that they *can* learn what's before them—all of this will set your child up for academic success.

## *RESEARCH RECAP:*

- The way parents *talk* to their children about *school and learning* can have a direct impact on their academic success.

- *Being involved* in your child's school, participating in events, volunteering, and attending on-site meetings, will *reinforce your conversations* about how you value their school and learning experience.

- *Extra assignments*, *homework*, or *at-home exercises* are *not as important as direct conversations* with your children about the value of their education. Parents need to explicitly express why learning is important, how schooling will benefit their child in the long run, and how they have faith in their child to be successful.

With these powerful research results in mind, let's revisit the Parental Engagement Cycle and the Elucidation wheel. We've already established that **"Setting the Stage"** is the central hub of

Elucidation. The three spokes are the three ways parents can effectively elucidate for their children—through Experience, Example, and Explanation.

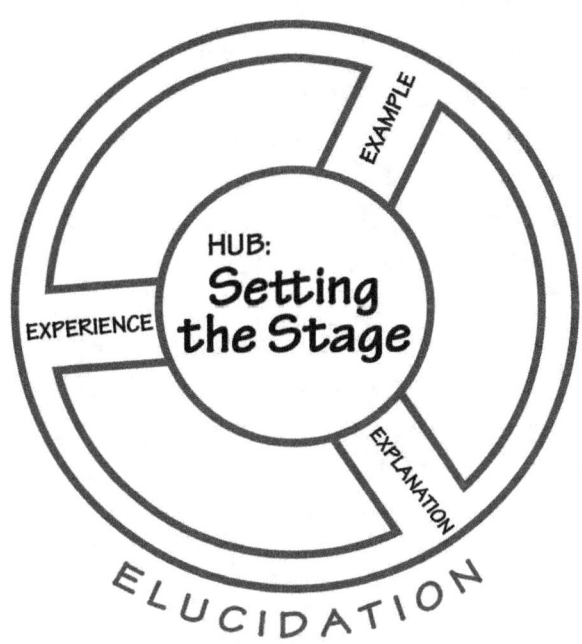

*Figure 7: The Elucidation Wheel*

- Experience: This type of learning involves hands-on engagement with the subject matter. For instance, if a child is learning about gardening, experience-based learning would involve actually planting and tending to a garden. Through this kind of learning, the child can interact with the plants, soil, and tools involved in gardening, allowing them to develop a deeper understanding and appreciation of the subject matter. Experience-based learning can be a powerful way to engage multiple senses and create lasting memories of the subject matter.

- Example: This type of learning involves using visual or auditory aids to help illustrate and explain the subject matter. For example, if a child is learning about the solar system, this type of learning could involve looking at images and illustrations of the planets and their orbits or watching videos about space exploration. While not as immersive as experiential learning, this type of learning can still provide a substantive understanding of the subject matter, especially when combined with other types of learning.

- Explanation: This type of learning involves discussing or explaining a subject through lectures, discussions, or conversations. For instance, if a child is learning about the scientific method, this type of learning could involve a teacher or mentor explaining the principles of the scientific method and how it is used in scientific research. While not as immersive as experiential or example-based learning, this type of learning can still be valuable for developing an understanding of a subject, even if fewer senses are engaged. Nevertheless, it may not be as effective for creating lasting memories or strong retention of the topic as experiential or example-based learning.

Learning will happen most effectively when all three spokes of the Elucidation wheel are engaged. The more directly a subject can be experienced, the more examples that can be seen, and the more explanation that can be given, the more clearly a topic will be understood by a young learner.

Let's consider some specific instances that bring to life these spokes of the Elucidation wheel. We'll begin with Singapore math, a mathematics teaching approach that provides a great example of what it's like to **Experience** a subject. In case you are unfamiliar with Singapore math, it was originally developed by Singapore's Ministry of Education in the 1980s for Singapore public schools.[4] It has been widely adopted in various forms around the world over the past 20 years. Earlier in my career as an educator, I spent six years in Singapore, where I had the opportunity to meet with and learn from many of their icons of education. One such educator was Dr. Yeap Ban Har, the author of many Singapore math textbooks. We were so fortunate to have him later become a consultant for our school.

With Singapore math and the CPA (Concrete, Pictorial, Abstract) progression[1] that is used, mathematical concepts are first taught with the use of simple, physical representations and concrete objects, usually in early grades. This can include the use of tiles or blocks. This allows children to learn by tangibly *experiencing* math problems. It's been shown that learning mathematics this way builds stronger mathematical abilities in the long run, and children are more adept at handling challenging and abstract forms of math later on.

When thinking about the **Example** spoke of our Elucidation wheel, one of the most impactful movies I've ever seen, *Schindler's*

---

[1] The CPA (Concrete, Pictorial, Abstract) is a way of teaching math in Singapore that helps kids learn step by step. First, they use real objects and hands-on materials to understand math concepts. Then, they see pictures or drawings that represent the math ideas. And finally, they move on to working with numbers and symbols. This gradual approach makes it easier for kids to grasp and remember math concepts."

*List*, comes to mind. This movie enabled me to confront the pain of the Holocaust in a unique way. Through the compelling nature of how the story was visually depicted, I felt more connected to the suffering of the victims. I've since been driven to seek more opportunities to learn about this difficult time in history, visiting Holocaust-themed museums whenever possible. I recently toured the Dachau Concentration Camp Memorial Site in Germany, where I came as close as possible to *examples* of life in that camp. I was able to see, hear, and feel a sense of what the victims endured. I now feel a deeper sense of empathy with regard to their experience.

Finally, when considering the **Explanation**, I think we can circle back to the story we started this chapter. The key to a good *explanation* is to deliver the information with the most descriptive and direct language possible. My friend in Tennessee did a superb job of this, using vivid storytelling about his adventures in the wild. His compelling description helped his sons to visualize what it must have been like to be in his shoes, coming in contact with these animals.

As we said earlier in this chapter, the goal of Elucidation is to make a topic more clear and easier to grasp. Whenever we can do this for our children by providing engaging experiences, captivating examples, and compelling explanations, they will be more likely to fully grasp and retain whatever subject is set before them.

## ACTION PLAN

- Do you feel you have directly stated the value of learning to your children? Do they understand the need for school and what they will attain by getting a good education? If you feel there's room for growth here, jot down some specific learning goals you can share with your children.

- When considering foundational learning subjects such as math and reading, sketch out some ideas for incorporating the spokes of the Elucidation wheel—Experience, Example, Explanation—into their learning process.

- As you consider how to "Set the Stage" for your child, it can help to create a written document that outlines your family's values, principles, and practices, particularly as they relate to education and schooling. Once completed, share this with your child.

[1] Day, Elizabeth, and Aryn M. Dotterer. "Parental involvement and adolescent academic outcomes: Exploring differences in beneficial strategies across racial/ethnic groups." *Journal of Youth and Adolescence* 47, no. 6 (2018): 1332-1349.

[2] Benner, Aprile D., Alaina E. Boyle, and Sydney Sadler. "Parental involvement and adolescents' educational success: The roles of prior achievement and socioeconomic status." *Journal of Youth and Adolescence* 45, no. 6 (2016): 1053-1064.

[3] Duan, Wenjie, Yuan Guan, and He Bu. "The effect of parental involvement and socioeconomic status on junior school students' academic achievement and school behavior in China." *Frontiers in Psychology* 9 (2018): 952.

[4] Singapore Math - https://www.singaporemath.com/

CHAPTER 3

# FEEDBACK

If you're not familiar with Toastmasters, it's an educational organization that exists to promote communication and public speaking. Toastmasters students regularly deliver speeches—some are prepared beforehand, and some are given off the cuff. After any speech is given, there's an evaluation that follows. Typically, positive or constructive criticism is given first, followed by negative feedback. All feedback is delivered publicly in front of the group. At the end of the process, someone will even assess the work of the evaluator.

I have quite a bit of experience with Toastmasters. I joined many years ago with the hope of improving my public speaking. After one of my speeches, the evaluation I received was harsh. Constructive or not, the critique was hard to take, and I took it personally. I felt defeated and, quite frankly, my feelings were hurt. It was several months before I attended another session.

Rather than taking the feedback for what it was—an opportunity to improve my skills and become a better speaker—instead, I lost out on the chance to learn. I let the feedback get the best of me; I didn't leverage it as motivation to improve.

I learned many things from my time with Toastmasters, and one was the value of good feedback. Another was that the maturity to accept feedback must be taught and practiced. Welcoming the critique of others is hard for adults, even when it's well-intentioned. So naturally, we can expect that children will struggle with it too. But the feedback our children receive from other teachers and us is vital to their growth and development. So as parents, we must learn how to deliver our feedback effectively, and we will need to train our children on how to accept it with openness and wisdom.

I applied this understanding when I launched a program called Projects and Presentations at my school. Similar to Toastmasters, both teachers and peers give each other feedback on the quality of their project and the delivery of their presentation. As part of the program, the students are trained on how to give good feedback and how to accept and handle feedback, whether it's negative or positive. Both sides of the process are critically important to learn. It has proven to be a very helpful and productive program for our school.

While feedback can be defined in several ways, for our purposes, we will discuss the validation and/or critique that parents give to children in response to their work or performance. The way parents deliver their feedback is as important as the specific words used. It's possible to have good intentions, but when feedback is poorly given, it can be harmful and not helpful. It must be provided in a way that is affirming as well as clear. That's why the central hub of the Feedback wheel is "**Making It Safe**" (see Figure 8). Parents must learn to effectively deliver their feedback in ways that will build their children up while still getting across the right message.

It's important to foster a welcoming, safe environment in the home for intaking and processing feedback. Especially between a child and parent, the feedback loop needs to be healthy, constructive, and regular. To do this, we must guard against giving feedback in anger. We need to be levelheaded and in control of our emotions so we can frame the discussion for our child and so our child knows the feedback is meant to be constructive and not hurtful. Keep in mind that we all have an innate fear of being evaluated by others. We all want to be fully accepted as we are! This inborn desire can inhibit our children's ability to accept feedback. But when critique is delivered in love, it's a lot easier to swallow.

You'll want to put on your modeling hat and *show* your young learner not only how to give good feedback but how to receive it as well. You can do this by opening yourself to hearing whether or not you're delivering your feedback in a way that is helpful to your child. Ask them for ways to improve how you give feedback. A child's personality and unique disposition will determine the style of feedback that will be most effective for them. You'll want to be flexible, teachable, and willing to alter your style if your initial attempts fall flat.

In a *New York Times* article,[1] Dr. Adam Grant, a Harvard graduate and an organizational psychologist at the Wharton School, introduced the idea of praising with nouns instead of verbs. To help explain this idea, let's start with a quick refresher on basic grammar.

A noun is an identifier for a person, place, object, or concept identifier. A verb, on the other hand, is a word that communicates an action or a condition. As it relates to how we give feedback to our children, good examples of noun phrases are "you are kindhearted" or "you are a big helper." Conversely, the alternate verb phrases are "you have been kind today" and "you have been helpful this afternoon." While seemingly a subtle distinction, Dr. Grant describes why it's so impactful. In his article, Dr. Grant shares that it is "22 to 29 percent more effective" to encourage children with nouns than verbs. He adds that "When our actions become a reflection of our character, we lean more heavily toward the moral and generous choices. Over time it can become part of us."

While using nouns to praise positive behavior can be effective, when it comes to giving negative feedback, it's generally better to use verbs. Using verbs to describe the specific behavior that needs improvement, rather than labeling the child with a negative trait, can be more helpful in addressing the behavior without damaging the child's self-esteem. Consider the difference between these negative noun and verb phrases. If your child is told, "You're a poor math learner," this thinking can become part of their identity. These negative sentiments are strong and can have the wrong kind of staying power. But instead, if your child hears, "You didn't do well on this one test," the impact will probably be temporary. Your child will be much less likely to internalize and latch onto the second critique. More so, using a verb phrase can be more effective in communicating what needs to change without making the child feel like their behavior is a reflection of their character.

Let's take this line of thinking one step further. Let's assume you want your child to be a hard worker, but if you're continuously belittling them for falling short, not working hard enough, or failing to meet your standard of what defines a hard worker, they will likely only become discouraged. Rather, consider speaking to your child as if they are already a hard worker (the way you *want* them to be), even if they aren't yet there. Use language such as "you are a 100% effort person," essentially willing their hardworking-ness into life. Even if your child has not yet achieved this point, you can vocalize the positive version of what's to come, providing your child with a visual of who they want to become and a path to follow. When this is done, your child will be clear on the goal of who they should be striving to be.

In her book *Mindset*, Dr. Carol Dweck,[2] a professor at Stanford University and one of the globally recognized leading researchers in personality, social psychology, and developmental psychology, discusses another crucial element of providing effective feedback. Dr. Dweck discusses how praising a student for getting good grades by attributing this success to their natural abilities is actually detrimental feedback. Similarly, telling a child they did a great job, even if they really didn't, can set them back, giving them a false sense of confidence. The more effective alternative is to focus on their effort during the project and not the results. If they get a good grade but didn't work hard for the grade, then the feedback should focus on their effort. The goal is not just good grades. The goal is to instill good habits in learning. So, it's important that the feedback you provide reflects this goal.

A 2020 analysis[3] explored the role of feedback in education and found that valuable feedback is critical to a child's overall success and development. Specifically, feedback was shown to have a higher impact on academic achievement and the development of motor skills.

## RESEARCH RECAP:

- The **right type of feedback can significantly influence academic performance**, encompassing student accomplishments, knowledge retention, and cognitive test results.

- Praising children with **nouns can promote positive character traits**, and using **verbs for negative feedback prevents children from internalizing failure**s. This approach encourages children to strive towards embodying positive identities (like being a "hard worker") without linking their self-worth to occasional shortcomings.

- Feedback has also been shown to **impact physical performance** and the **development of motor skills**.

With all these considerations about feedback in mind, we can see why the three spokes of the Feedback wheel include the Why, How, and What of delivering effective feedback.

*Figure 8: The Feedback Wheel*

- **Why:** Start by internalizing and processing your motivation for delivering feedback. Consider pausing and appraising your emotional state the next time you're set to give feedback. Are you speaking out of anger or frustration? Are you upset or venting? If so, consider ways to cool down and center your emotions first, so you can provide helpful and effective feedback to your learner.

- **How:** Consider the way your feedback is being delivered. Is it passive (talking about how another child has been successful), is it in anger (condescending or belittling), is it flippant (there's no standard or the child can do no wrong), or is it positive and affirming?

- **What:** As we've discussed, not all words and phrases are equal when it comes to giving our children feedback. As often as possible, use noun phrases, focus on their effort, and speak to your child with feedback that points them toward how you want them to act, even if they're not quite there yet.

While the Why, How, and What of the feedback we give is important for the many reasons we've already stated, it can also greatly impact your child's self-talk. Self-talk is the way we talk to ourselves, our inner voice.[4] This inner voice combines conscious thoughts with inbuilt beliefs and biases to create an internal monologue throughout the day. Parents indirectly inform and teach their children how to self-talk. A parent's feedback provides the scaffolding for how a child will manage their inner monologue. Consider, as an example, a discussion you may have with your child about their goals. Your feedback can encourage them not just to focus on where they are now but to reflect on how far they've come. Help them to look back and see where they started and consider how much they've progressed. This kind of feedback can spur them on to reach the finish line. You're essentially equipping them with language that can translate to positive and affirming self-talk.

Similarly, if your child is working toward a financially related goal, there's a fine line between giving them a lot of money and hoping they'll figure out how to manage it versus helping them, with the right age-appropriate tools, learn how to manage their money. Our feedback is akin to one of the "right tools" that can inform how your child will process the many life experiences that will come their way. This isn't a perfect science, and mistakes may be made, but with trial and error, parents can establish good scaffolding through their feedback.

As we've described throughout this chapter, feedback is critically important for children to learn to receive so they can grow and develop. It's also a discipline that will be necessary for them to apply throughout life. The earlier they can learn it, the better off they'll be. My co-author, Dr. Artyom Zinchenko, has shared with me his experience in supervising a graduate student who was working on his master's thesis. It's common practice for students at this stage to develop an experiment on their own. Artyom codes the experiment, the student runs it, and they analyze the results together. The student will then write the results in a scientific publication-style format. There are often other writers and contributors involved at this point and there is usually heavy editing and the back-and-forth exchange of accepting and rejecting changes that can go on for several rounds. Feedback is a critical part of the process.

For this one student though, the feedback process was too hard to accept. He was strongly insulted and felt he was being too harshly criticized through the many rounds of changes. The project came to a grinding halt as the student could not accept the feedback from Artyom and his peers. It took a great deal of effort and a lot of discussion about the process before he was willing to come back on board and move on with the class. And remember, this was a graduate student! He'd already completed many years of school, and yet, he'd never mastered the skill of accepting feedback. It almost halted his education altogether.

I've experienced a similar challenge in one of my businesses. I oversee a team that prepares exams and training manuals for commercial truck drivers. There are many writers and editors involved and early on, I had to set expectations for how feedback would be given and received. It was important for me to be able to communicate needed improvements to the team, and they had to be willing to handle the changes with a spirit of humility. It was a situation where they could have easily become defensive, but if they had, the project would have suffered.

Consider other professions as well, such as the work of a software developer. Often, robust and intricate websites are collaboratively built by a team. It's common in this profession for each stage of development to undergo a code review, where every section of code is reviewed by the team before the project can move forward. For the process to be successful, every developer on the team will need to know how to give and respond to feedback without becoming overly defensive. If pride gets in the way, the team will not be effective.

In all these scenarios, it's vitally important that feedback is both given and received effectively. We all must develop this set of skills in order to grow into successful, thriving adults. With the strategies described in this chapter, your family will be equipped to establish a healthy feedback loop in your home, and your child will be on the path to developing a wise mindset toward the value of feedback in their life.

## ACTION PLAN

- With a fresh understanding of the importance of feedback, take a moment to reflect on some specific ways you can start *making it safe* for feedback to be given and received in your home.

- When giving your child negative or positive feedback, is your tendency to use noun or verb phrases? Jot down some feedback you've given your child recently. How can you tweak your feedback to use noun phrases more often?

- Remember that it can be helpful to give feedback that points them toward how you want them to act, even if they're not quite there yet. Consider actions that you see your child do regularly. List ways to give feedback that will encourage them to act in a more positive or productive way.

- We are all juggling an inner monologue. Do instances come to mind of how you can be more intentional in the ways you inform and teach your child to manage theirs? When you see them struggling, potentially with a situation where they feel they are failing, help to frame their self-talk by pointing out how far they've come and how much they've already accomplished.

[1] Raising a Moral Child, https://www.nytimes.com/2014/04/12/opinion/sunday/raising-a-moral-child.html

[2] *Mindset: The New Psychology of Success* by Carol S. Dweck, https://www.amazon.com/Mindset-Psychology-Carol-S-Dweck/dp/1400062756/ref=tmm_hrd_swatch_0

[3] Wisniewski, Benedikt, Klaus Zierer, and John Hattie. "The power of feedback revisited: A meta-analysis of educational feedback research." *Frontiers in Psychology* 10 (2020): 3087.

[4] What is self-talk? https://www.healthdirect.gov.au/self-talk

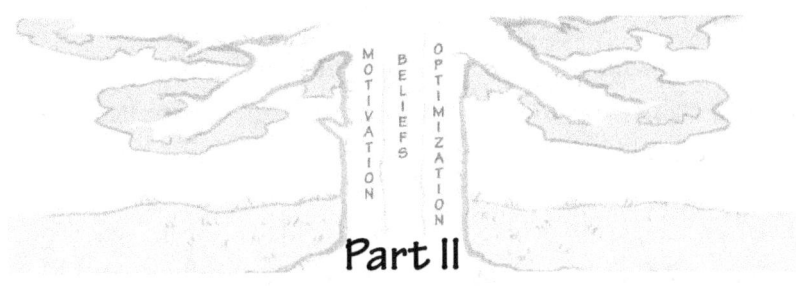

# Part II
# LEARNING FOUNDATIONS
## The Tree Trunk

## Introduction to Learning Foundations

Jessica Cox was born in the Philippines. Having a son already, her parents had been thrilled to add a little girl to their family. But in the delivery room, when the doctor announced that their new baby had no arms, her mother had been inconsolable. After all, Jessica's mother had grown up in a time and culture in which disability was considered a tragedy—she was afraid that Jessica was facing a homebound life sentence.[1]

But in the months and years following her birth, Jessica's mother and family found ways to adapt to her disability. Things were far from easy, but her parents especially drew strength and encouragement from the opportunities available for people with disabilities in their new home in Tucson, Arizona, where they moved when Jessica was 14. Her mother overcame her own fears and emerged as Jessica's strongest supporter. Her instinct was to integrate her into a regular environment as much as possible, including traditional public school.[2] Her parents wanted her to believe she could overcome any challenge and do anything an "able-bodied" person could do,[3] including swimming and dancing. She eventually developed a connection with tae kwon do, a sport she excelled at and one that would later lead her to her future husband.

Even as her parents worked to keep her life "normal," Jessica was keenly aware of her disability. At recess, teachers and other children were often overprotective, preventing her from climbing too high or trying new things. She often experienced what she calls the "unspoken societal misconception that people with disabilities struggle, and therefore, should achieve less,"[4] an unfortunate reality that can often hold people with disabilities back. She experienced anger and frustration with the daily challenges she faced and the limitations others put upon her.

Jessica tried for years to adapt to prosthetic arms, enduring hours of therapy every day after school. But even as she found ways to acclimate to the awkward limbs, she never connected with them. Her inner spirit as an overcomer longed for more. She yearned to set aside the boundaries placed upon her and the conventional means for overcoming her disability. She longed to pursue a way of life only she could define. One way she did this was by embracing the use of her feet to accomplish tasks that most people reserved for their hands. Most notably, piloting an airplane.

Though she had a fear of flying from a young age, it was something her family did often, as her mother wanted her and her siblings to regularly visit their home country and to know their Filipino heritage. Even while taking regular international flights though, the idea of losing contact with the ground never came naturally to her. But the summer after earning her bachelor's degree in psychology, she was invited to speak before a Rotary Club in Tucson, Arizona. At the end of the speech, a retired U.S. Air Force fighter pilot offered to take her on a flight through Wright Flight, his nonprofit that uses aviation to inspire students to set and achieve higher goals for themselves. She was terrified of the opportunity but also didn't want to turn down this invitation.

Before she could embark on that flight, Jessica was asked to deliver a speech at the Flying Samaritans International Annual Conference. They wanted one of their pilots to fly her to the event, which would take place in Guaymas, Mexico, two hours from home. Here she'd been psyching herself up for the short flight through Wright Flight, and now she faced an additional trip as well—an international flight in a small airplane, at that. But this speaking opportunity was a significant one. It was her first international invitation, and she was compelled to spread her story to new audiences. She had begun to see how her words of encouragement, based on her experience of overcoming many challenges, were a source of hope to those she reached, especially for people who were facing their own disabilities. She decided to say yes to both flights—facing her fear of flying head-on. Jessica shares the following story on the website flyingmag.com:

"The day came, and I climbed into the back seat. The whole time leading up to takeoff I was holding my breath. I was holding back my anxiety with prayers. My nerves made me feel like I was going to jump out of my skin.

"Then, as we took off, I realized we were at the point of no return, which in a way, was a relief. As we finished our climb, I remember feeling like this was not as big a deal as I made it out to be. I was finally breathing, and we finished the uneventful flight to Mexico.

"On the way back, the pilot let me sit in the right front seat. He asked me if I wanted to try putting my foot on the controls. As I put my foot on the yoke and he let go, I had this moment of flying an airplane. I was the only one touching the controls.

"That was the moment that changed everything.

"It was empowering—probably the second-most empowering moment of my life."

The first-most empowering moment of her life? That would be her first solo flight. Once Jessica realized she could not only be a passenger in an airplane without fear but a *pilot* too, there was no stopping her will to succeed. Jessica now holds the esteemed title of the first and only licensed armless pilot in aviation history. She worked through 30 hours of training and a three-hour oral exam before earning that solo flight. As had been the case throughout her life, nothing about learning to fly with her feet came easy. But flying had opened her eyes to a whole new world of possibility. Once she knew it was within reach, there was no turning back.

*Figure 9: Jessica Cox, the First Armless Pilot*

Jessica shares on her website, jessicacox.com, that "after an arduous three years, [she] became a certified pilot, earning the title of the first woman to fly an airplane with her feet." Today, Jessica travels the globe motivating people to overcome their perceived limitations with her inspirational speeches. Acknowledging how instrumental her parents' support is in her success, she started her nonprofit that allows her to mentor children and adults with limb differences, especially those who may not be getting enough support from others.

Jessica's story is a great example of the learning foundations this part of the book will discuss. Furthering our understanding of the

Wise Learning Tree, the next three chapters will focus on the tree's trunk and the three pillars that comprise this part of the tree—motivation, beliefs, and optimization. They are each unique and important but also connected. Together, they provide a base from which learners can build upon and activate the learning strategies discussed later in the book.

These three traits—motivation, beliefs, and optimization—are critical traits that we, as parents, will need to cultivate in our learners. They are also traits that are clearly at work in Jessica's story.

- **Motivation is what drives someone to act.** Jessica was *motivated* to work hard. She felt the limitations of her disability through the boundaries placed upon her by others, but her spirit couldn't be quenched. She knew she could do more than others could envision for her.

- **Beliefs, as we'll consider them, are a learner's view of knowledge, and whether they consider knowledge to be simple and fixed or nuanced and obtainable through reasoning.** Jessica's *beliefs about learning* were the latter. She refused to let her limitations, fear of flying, or her disability hold her back from realizing her dream to be a pilot; she willingly took on the many hours of instruction required to become certified.

- **Optimization speaks to a learner's ability to bypass lower-level thinking to become more efficient, so that they can learn more and faster.** Jessica found ways to *optimize* through the use of her feet. Traditional wisdom for someone without arms had her trying for years to use prosthetic arms. But only Jessica could envision a better way. By learning to use her feet in place of her arms, she enabled herself to do so much more than anyone could have imagined.

Up to this point, this book has heavily focused on the role of parents. That will not end here, as we must learn how to encourage our learner's natural motivation, support beliefs about acquiring knowledge that fosters a wise learning posture, and activate their ability to optimize through it all. But moving forward, we'll begin to discuss the role of our children—both parents and children have important parts to play. Your child must take ownership of their learning, while as parents, we must allow them space to do so. If we are too often in the way, running the show, our children will not have the opportunity to do their part.

As parents, we will need to guide our children to the wise learning door. Then, we must move aside and allow them to step up, find their inner initiative, and walk through. In the process, it's also important for us to foster a safe environment where mistakes can be made. Inevitably, as our children own more responsibility, they will sometimes fail. But if we're quick to pick them back up and encourage them to try again and again, we let them see that it's okay not to be perfect. It's acceptable for them to take shots and sometimes miss. If they live in fear of disappointing us, they won't have the assurance they need to try something new. It's important for them to have the security to go through this process at home, among the boundaries of a loving family, so they are better equipped to experiment and take calculated risks when they're on their own.

## ACTION PLAN

- As we pivot to discuss the role of our children in learning, do you find yourself hesitating? Do you often do things for your children, rather than giving them space to own responsibility? Consider some small ways you can encourage your child's independence and make it safe for them to try and (sometimes) fail.

- Jessica's inspirational story of overcoming offers helpful parallels to wise learning. Take a moment to reflect on the connections between Jessica's story and how it can relate to your child's growth as a learner.

---

[1] Flying Over Adversity: Aspiring to Be a Pilot, flyingmag.com

[2] Jessica's History, jessicacox.com

[3] Remembering the incredible Inez Cox, rightfootedmovie.com

[4] Being Overlooked, flyingmag.com

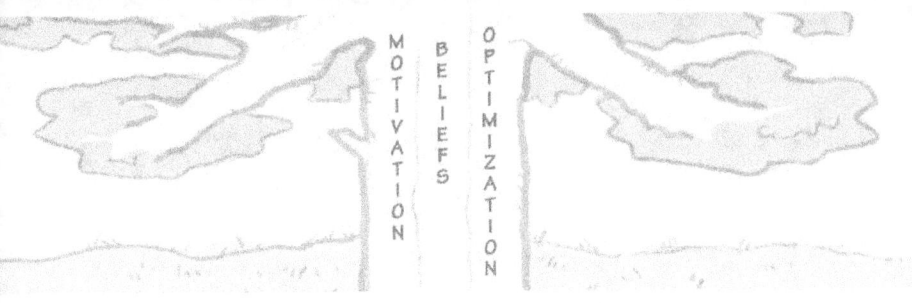

## CHAPTER 4

# MOTIVATION

To kick off our discussion on motivation, I want to highlight the story of one of my favorite athletes. I'm referring to Giannis Antetokounmpo, a professional athlete who plays basketball for the Milwaukee Bucks,[1] who has made a significant impact in the sports world.

Giannis was born to Nigerian immigrants but raised in Athens, Greece. As foreigners without official Greek citizenship, Giannis and his family faced a plight familiar to many immigrants—they were marked as outsiders and often ostracized from Greek society. Giannis and his brothers supplemented their family's modest income by peddling bags and sunglasses on the bustling city streets. They suffered housing evictions and often missed meals.

While Giannis had a tough childhood, it was also marked by love, joy, and a tight family bond. He saw his parents model selflessness, kindness, and hard work. He grew up with a deep respect for them and a desire to be just like them. Additionally, "Giannis's brothers were his best friends, his comrades," shares Mirin Fader, author of the book *Giannis: The Improbable Rise of an NBA MVP.*[2] She goes on to add that "when you share everything, there's not much to bicker about."

Giannis's parents saw sports as a positive outlet for their sons. They involved them early in the popular national sport of football. But Giannis's size and physicality caught the eye of a basketball coach in the area, who encouraged his transition to basketball as a young teenager. Compared to many of his fellow players, Giannis was getting a late start. At 13 years old, he showed up on the basketball court, not even knowing how to dribble or make a layup. But there was something about him that struck his teammates even then. Christoforos Kelaidis, his then-team captain, shares that "He was very competitive. He didn't like to lose. He couldn't do that much, but he had spirit."[3]

Antetokounmpo often remained in the gym, committing to his practice until nearly midnight. He chose to sleep on an exercise mat in the weight room rather than going home in the dark.[3] He was motivated and driven to be the best and to find a way to overcome his circumstances. He wanted to win. As far-fetched as it seemed, he had dreams of one day playing in the NBA.

Over time, his work ethic and his drive to make something of himself (combined with the good fortune of his size and natural athleticism) were paying off. By the age of 16, he had established himself as one of Greece's premier players, despite still playing in the country's secondary amateur leagues. Soon his performances were attracting attention from scouts across Europe and even America. Three years later, at just 19 years old, he was selected in the first round of the 2013 NBA draft. With such little experience, the Milwaukee Bucks took a gamble on him, banking on his size, speed, and obvious physical potential. Once in Milwaukee and under the tutelage of professional trainers, Giannis's willingness to put in long hours, push himself, and work hard were again evident. He learned to lift weights and transformed his body into that of a professional athlete. He practiced nonstop, undistracted by his new status as a millionaire. He remained humble and dedicated to his sport.

Milwaukee's gamble on Giannis paid off. Not only had they recruited a player with potential, but they'd also gained someone who was motivated to win. In his third season, Giannis was averaging an impressive 16.9 points per game. Moreover, during his initial five seasons with the Bucks, they made it to the playoffs thrice. His accolades continued to snowball when in December 2020, he signed the most lucrative deal in NBA history—$228.2 million for five years.

Giannis's difficult childhood (his family was so poor that he often had to share one pair of shoes with his brothers), his vulnerability as a child to attacks by racist militants, and the regular threats of deportation to Nigeria his family often received—it's all part of his story as an overcomer. He gives hope and inspiration to other young immigrants facing their own harrowing childhoods. His dreams of becoming an NBA star, to be the best in the world, drove Giannis to work harder and push himself further. His motivation was the spark that set him apart. It was there as a teenager, and it still drives him today.

Giannis is recognized for expecting top-notch performances from both himself and his teammates on the court. However, he's also noted for his lack of interest in being viewed as the face of the league. Whereas many players become enamored with the fame, pomp, and glamour of life as a professional athlete, Giannis has maintained the grounded inspiration of his youth.

"Growing up and how tough life was for my family and me, I'm always going to stay humble. I've just got to keep working hard, trying to get my team better," Giannis shares. "I don't like all these flashy cities like L.A. or Miami. I don't know if I could be the same player if I played in those cities."

As we began to define earlier, motivation is what propels someone to act in a certain way. It's their "why." Healthy eating habits can be due to an interest in living longer or maintaining a certain weight. Regular attendance at church will happen when there's an interest in growing spiritually. For Giannis, his motivation has always been to be the best player he can be and to do what he can to improve his family's circumstances. Three of his four brothers now play in the NBA too. He is often involved in programs to elevate basketball opportunities in his home country of Greece, and yes, he wants to win games for his longtime team, the Bucks. But the allure of fame doesn't seem to draw him in the same way it does other players. His motivation has remained firmly grounded by the principles that have always driven him.

A student's motivation to learn will come initially from their parents and teachers. Children will internalize why they should act in certain ways through what they see modeled. Parents will elucidate why certain learning pursuits are more important than others and then provide feedback that will keep a child going when their motivation is flagging. Eventually, motivation will need to be transferred to and internalized by the child if it is to take hold. Jessica Cox built upon the strength of her parents, who were the first to see she was capable of doing anything an "able-bodied" person could do and proceeded to put her in traditional school, dance classes, and tae kwon do. Giannis saw his parents' dedication to their family and their sacrifice and hard work. These were traits he came to admire and emulate. Parents can help learners to find their passion, to uncover what energizes them. They can model the right behavior for their students to copy. Eventually, if they are to become successful learners in their own right, these motivations will become their own.

There are two important types of motivation: internal (or intrinsic) and external (or extrinsic). In the next section, we will discuss the differences between these types of motivation and explore whether they both can lead to a positive learning outcome.

**Intrinsic Motivation and Extrinsic Motivation**

Intrinsic motivation comes into play when a student learns out of personal desire, without being pushed. They approach a new subject out of sheer interest and personal inspiration. There are no external rewards, but rather, internal satisfaction. They want to learn and discover new things based on their own initiative.

A student with high intrinsic motivation may respond to learning in the following ways:

- "I enjoy coursework that truly challenges me so I can learn new things."

- "I love taking classes that pique my curiosity because then I discover a lot of things."

- "When I get the chance in this class, I will pick tasks that help me learn even if they do not guarantee a decent score."

All the above statements emphasize the "Why?" component of being a part of a class. The learner is more involved in their academic activities because of an internal drive and interest in acquiring knowledge. A study conducted by researchers Zaccone and Pedrini found that intrinsic motivation levels correspond with a student's improved learning and course grades. As students gain a better understanding of a subject, they also gain more intrinsic motivation.[4] In other words, as their knowledge increases, so does their internal motivation to learn more. The motivation behind a student's participation can play a crucial role in their academic performance.

When learners can identify areas of study that naturally interest them and are given space to pursue those curiosities, they will be more motivated to learn all they can about the subject. The key is for parents to be attuned to what drives their learners. Keep encouraging them to learn more about the things they are drawn to and, when needed, look for ways to connect areas of learning that lack a natural attractiveness to the topics or subjects they are motivated to pursue.

Consider household chores, for example. These are commonly encouraged through external rewards—money, treats, or a special outing. These motivators can help to jump-start a child's interest, but the ultimate goal is for these chores to become common enough that they're almost second nature, things your child may even do without prompting (or at least without grumbling). Sounds like a dream? Maybe not, with the right tactics.

Identify chores they seem to enjoy or that they're proud to complete. Do they feel grown up when they're given the responsibility of managing the Windex bottle and wiping the windows? Do they think it's fun to get a little wet while washing the dishes? It's bath time for the plates and forks! They may like performing tasks alongside Mom and Dad, getting special one-on-one time while you work together. While you could offer rewards at first, if you do, then set the expectation that there will not always be a reward. Communication here is key. Remind them that they're helping things at home run more smoothly. Eventually, the knowledge that they're positively contributing becomes the reward, along with the enjoyment they may find from doing tasks they find (at least relatively) fun.

With intrinsic motivation, there are four key considerations:

1. A child's **Desire to Learn** new things

2. Their **Natural Interest** in a particular subject

3. Their **Autonomy** over learning

4. An identifiable **Task Value**

Children are born curious. Their motivation to discover the world around them is how they learn to crawl, walk, and talk. They learn in those early days by touching seemingly everything and putting much of it in their mouth. They're pulling up on tables, opening every drawer, and, once they're able to, chattering nonstop. Most often, they're asking questions about why things are the way they are. This inborn interest in the world around them lives on as they reach school age. It's our job as parents and educators to feed their natural **desire to learn** and to help them connect the dots between the interests they already have and the new subjects they have yet to discover.

Maybe they love to be the center of attention and to dress up and act out stories. A future in the theater may indeed be developing. What if they seem drawn to every kind of ball they find? They throw, kick, and scramble to catch everything that crosses their path. A lifetime spent at the ballfield may be to come. Parents can tune in to these **natural interests** and then find ways to connect them to other areas where a child may not be as inclined. When it's time to read, look for books that will speak to their love of make-believe and fantasy or find stories about successful ballplayers. When tackling math concepts, creatively introduce ways of adding or subtracting using some of the objects they are already interacting with.

When I was young, my mom enrolled me in an art program and sketching course as well as piano lessons. In both cases, I didn't do well. Even though I'd been supplied with great teachers and received regular prompts to practice, my parents never saw much progress. Why? I was not intrinsically motivated to develop my skills in these two areas. Nothing about either opportunity had captured my natural interest.

Connecting a natural interest to a new endeavor can provide the scaffolding a child needs to build an intrinsic connection to a new activity. When I was learning both art and piano, I was also an avid watcher of *Voltes V*, a Japanese cartoon series about robots and how the heroes fought the villains. It may have been a more interesting learning experience if I had the opportunity to sketch robotic figures or play the piano using the theme song of the cartoon series. In hindsight, and based on the experience I now have as an educator, I believe that such efforts could have paid off. I may or may not have gone on to pursue a lifelong career in the arts, but such attempts likely would have extended and deepened my intrinsic interest to practice and develop my skills in the area of art and music.

This kind of thinking can carry over to almost any area of learning. Associating natural interests with new learning challenges is a way to open the door to learning, and often, your child's natural motivation will take over with time. As we come to better understand our child's skills and strengths, as well as interests and desires, we'll be better equipped to use the right motivation to encourage them to learn. If your young boys are drawn to comic books and war stories, you can seek out age-appropriate, history-themed graphic novels for their reading practice. If your daughter loves animals and art, you can encourage her natural interests with regular trail walks with a sketchbook in tow so she can draw or paint the wildlife she encounters and develop her art skills and understanding of nature along the way.

A third key aspect of intrinsic motivation is *autonomy*. When children feel they have a say in how they are learning, they'll have more ownership over the choices they make. Autonomy will push a child to consider the consequences and trade-offs of their choices, which can empower them to learn how to make good choices. When they've made a choice to do something, they will be more intrinsically motivated to stick to that decision.

It can be tricky for parents to know when to step in and when to step back and let their child work things out on their own, to make their own choices and mistakes. The move toward autonomy can start in small ways though. Allow them to choose what clothes they want to wear for the day. Give them options when possible. "Do you want milk or water?" There are small, harmless ways they can feel they have a say in what's happening. This will help them build the mental muscles needed to make wise decisions in the future.

As parents, we'll want to be available to help our learners wrestle with uncertainty, weigh their opportunities, and deal with the challenges they face when their decisions go awry. It's a balancing act of providing just enough guidance to provoke their interest and then the right amount of support when they need it. Ultimately, intrinsic motivation can't bloom with too much parental interference. Children need space for it to take root and grow.

Lastly, parents can increase motivation by highlighting *task value*. Task value, in the context of learning, refers to a child's perceived usefulness of the subject they are learning. It's their understanding of how the work they are doing will benefit them or the advantage they will gain by performing an activity. It's their mental measurement of a task's worth.[5] Task value will also include an accounting of the cost—an assessment of the time, energy, or mental stamina that will be required for a child to learn a subject or complete an assignment.

It's so important for learners to value what they're doing. Adding task value makes the work less abstract. It enables a learner to understand the significance of what they are studying and appreciate the reason why they are learning the new subject. Task value is an important pillar that will support the development of an intrinsically motivated learner.

Substantial research supports the idea that task value can lead to higher academic achievement.[6] When children understand and, even better, *appreciate* the value of their learning tasks, they will be more intrinsically motivated. This triggers a positive self-reinforcement loop. Higher intrinsic motivation will likely lead to better academic results, which, in turn, will improve one's confidence. The more that students find difficulty in certain subjects or lessons, the more compelling the need for an understanding and appreciation of the task value.[7]

Another interesting consideration of task value is how it differs with varying learning settings—online learning versus in-person learning, for example. Online learning requires a great deal of self-discipline, time management, and commitment relative to in-person learning, since a teacher is not present for online learning to manage their students' behavior. Therefore, it is understandable that self-discipline is an important part of positive online learning outcomes.[8] As discussed earlier, when learners have a deeper task value understanding and appreciation, their intrinsic motivation is likely to become stronger, which can only help in developing their self-discipline.

The importance of task value was brought to life for me by one of my students who had attended my school's "life lessons skills boot camp." This boot camp teaches our students practical skills, such as how to change the tires of a car. This student found these lessons to be especially helpful later in life when a friend got a flat tire. The student remembered what he'd been taught and was able to save the day by changing the tire. He later told me that in the moment of learning that skill, he'd not recognized the value, but he certainly saw the value when the skill was later put to use. His story is one that is now shared with students in that boot camp—so they have a better understanding of the value of what they're learning and are motivated to pay attention!

Finally, task value is something that is needed throughout life, even after the formal years of education are over. When my daughter graduated from college, she thought her days of intense study and test-taking were behind her. In a sense, her task value for learning was at a low point. She didn't see the value of continuing to pursue another course of study—she had earned her degree! That soon changed when, not long after graduation, she was drawn to apply for a business analytics position. It was a field different from her degree and an area where she had no experience. After the initial rounds of interviews where she wasn't offered the job, her perspective on learning began to shift. She was coming to see that while her official school days may have wrapped, learning is a lifelong sport. If she wanted to get a job in this field, she was going to have to better understand the work performed in this role. She had to regain her task value for learning.

Driven by her own intrinsic motivation and with a full appreciation of the task value, she took additional business analytics courses to better prepare her for the role. The idea of lifelong learning may not come naturally. But, with the right motivation and an appreciation for the value of the activity to be learned, lifelong learning can become a reality for any child, adolescent, or even adult student!

## RESEARCH RECAP:

- **_Higher task value_** is positively correlated with more component learners and **_better academic achievement_**.

- There's a positive relationship between **_task value and self-efficacy_**, or a learner's confidence in their ability to do what's needed to reach a specific goal.

- Task value is beneficial **_for both in-person and online learning_**.

Let's take a quick moment to consider the life of Dr. Jose Rizal, as his story is a great testament to the value of intrinsic motivation. In my home country of the Philippines, Dr. Rizal is a national hero. An avid and talented writer, Dr. Rizal is well known as the leading spokesman of the Philippine reform movement.[9] During his lifetime, Filipinos were oppressed by Spanish rule. Rizal was a prolific writer, gifted artist, political campaigner, and multilingual individual with proficiency in 22 languages and dialects.

In the midst of so many worthy pursuits, Dr. Rizal also earned a degree in ophthalmology, driven by a love for his mother, who was going blind due to cataracts. She had been his first teacher and she had recognized early on his sharp mind. "His suffering Motherland [the Philippines] was under an abusive and oppressive foreign power and through his written work he hoped to open the eyes of his countrymen and the Spanish authorities. He longed to give his mother sight just as he longed to bring vision to his 'blind' countrymen. He wanted to heal them both," shares Ma. Dominga B. Padilla, MD, FPAO.[10]

In addition to his university studies, Dr. Rizal received personalized training in Paris under the famous oculoplastic surgeon Dr. Louis de Wecker and in Heidelberg where he trained under Dr. Otto Becker. When he returned home from studying abroad, he established an ophthalmology practice and successfully operated on his mother's left eye, restoring her sight.

By all accounts, Dr. Rizal was unjustly arrested and found guilty of sedition by the military. He was publicly executed by a firing squad in 1896. His martyrdom motivated many Filipinos to push for independence from Spain. Growing up and hearing the history of Dr. Rizal has always inspired me. He accomplished so much in an effort to spur the independence of my country, but it's the story about his medical pursuits that has resonated with me the most. With so many diverting areas of interest, he had to maintain a great measure of intention, diligence, and determination to become a doctor. His motivation sprung from a deep and enduring love for his mother. He had a clear and decisive understanding of the value of the work he was pursuing. Powered by such strong convictions, he was able to accomplish tremendous things.

You can take heart in knowing that, when empowered by the right motivation, your learner will be able to reach big goals as well. Your efforts to encourage and motivate them the right way will not be in vain. When captivated by an intrinsic drive to pursue a dream, they will be able to accomplish great things.

In contrast to all we've discussed about intrinsic motivation, let's now consider extrinsic motivation, which is driven by external rewards that are leveraged to encourage a behavior or action. These rewards could include the desire to make good grades or to earn a promised reward. It could come as a result of a fear of failure or of disappointing parents. When a student's extrinsic motivation is high, engaging in a learning activity is seen as a means to an end.

A student with high extrinsic motivation may respond to learning in the following ways:

- "The most fulfilling thing for me right now is getting a perfect score in this class."

- "The most essential thing for me right now is improving my total grades, therefore obtaining a perfect score in this subject is my top concern."

- "I wish to do well in this class because I want to prove my abilities to my family, friends, and relatives."

This form of motivation—external sources of encouragement such as good grades, awards, and a sense of competitiveness—is what parents and educators often gravitate to first, as it feels like the easiest to implement. However, inappropriate or excessive use of extrinsic motivation can be detrimental to learning in the long run. Because of this, extrinsic motivation should only be used sparingly, and intrinsic motivation should instead be reinforced.

Numerous research studies have been dedicated to the study of motivation and learning, to uncover which method of motivation is most productive. Time and again, it has been found that extrinsic motivation will either have no effect on learning or, on occasion, even a negative impact. By comparison, intrinsic motivation is consistently tied to high learning achievement.[11] The overwhelming majority of our research and experience points to the value of intrinsic motivation as the stronger of the two options. A 2021 study by Howard and colleagues[12] even demonstrated that intrinsic motivation led to students' overall feeling of well-being, while external motivation was associated with decreased well-being. These authors concluded that intrinsic motivation is one of the key factors for successful learning and general academic performance in school.

*Figure 10: A Child Receiving Extrinsic Reward*

Nonetheless, some studies on extrinsic motivation showed that it could be helpful in encouraging school attendance,[13] eating vegetables,[14] athletic performance,[15,16] and some aspects of online learning.[17] In other words, when used properly and in the right situations, extrinsic motivation can be helpful in driving learners to reach their goals, improve their performance, or learn specific tasks.[18]

## RESEARCH RECAP:

- When your child pursues a learning-based activity or task for the pleasure of doing it and for the intrinsic joy of understanding something new, they will be more motivated to complete it, even when faced with challenges, and they will be more likely to understand the task or to successfully complete the activity.

- Intrinsic motivation is a key factor for long-term and stable successful learning and general academic performance in school.

- In contrast, extrinsic motivation can have a negative impact on a child's academic performance. It is best when this form of motivation is used sparingly or as a short-term solution until the more sustainable intrinsic motivation can take hold.

Based on my education administration experience, one should only use extrinsic motivation in the context of instilling intrinsic motivation or when the task at hand does not require long-term retention of knowledge or skills. When used in select situations and possibly in some of the ways referenced earlier such as to encourage school attendance or athletic performance, this form of motivation can have a positive impact, even if it's a short-lived one. It's intrinsic motivation, though, that will help students to have more dynamic and longer learning experiences, particularly when they also take the time to practice as part of their skills development whether in sports, arts, or academics. I've also noticed that when students (on their own and not because of their teachers or parents) consciously and regularly take the initiative to motivate themselves externally using token rewards, such as having their favorite dinner or taking some free time, to reach specific goals, these students tend to develop natural intrinsic motivation toward reaching the goal. The key is that it is their own initiative that drives them. This is further the case when such students consciously recognize that these external motivators are stepping stones toward not only achieving their goals but also instilling intrinsic motivation. This is probably also due to their exercise of an important learning pillar that we will discuss in subsequent chapters—metacognition.

I'm reminded of an experience I had as an intern in Japan, fresh out of college and with minimal funds. In an attempt to save money, I purchased meals daily from vending machines that can be commonly found around the city. I didn't initially see the harm in regularly eating the filling but nutritionally lacking instant noodles. But after a week or two of this, I got sick. There weren't enough good nutrients in the noodles! They were a quick fix but not something that should be eaten daily. Similarly, extrinsic motivation can often seem like a quick fix to behavioral issues, and for a time, this form of motivation may drive some good results. But it's less likely to provide the long-term, positive impact that intrinsic motivation will.

As parents, we should be mindful and selective in how often we utilize extrinsic motivation—recognize its limitations and use it sparingly. It's not only an unsustainable form of motivation, but it can also be detrimental to fostering more effective intrinsic motivation. Always remember that it's best to use extrinsic motivation as a way to *feed* intrinsic motivation.

## ACTION PLAN

- Has extrinsic motivation been your go-to form of incentive in the past? Based on the feedback in this chapter, list ways you can pivot and begin to use "intrinsic prompts" instead.

- Do you have a clear understanding of your child's natural interests? Take a moment to write down a few that come to mind. How can you connect their desire to learn and their natural interests with other learning objectives such as math and reading?

- What are some things that you've been intrinsically motivated to learn in your lifetime? Consider a story of encouragement you can pass on to your children, based on your experience with intrinsic motivation.

[1] Giannis Antetokounmpo: From poverty in Greece to NBA's most lucrative player - Olympics.com

[2] The Humble Superstar: New Giannis Antetokounmpo Biography Explores Champion's Family Life, Legacy - Wisconsinlife.org

[3] Giannis Antetokounmpo Is the Pride of a Greece That Shunned Him - NYTimes.com

[4] Zaccone, Maria Cristina, and Matteo Pedrini. "The effects of intrinsic and extrinsic motivation on students learning effectiveness. Exploring the moderating role of gender." *International Journal of Educational Management* (2019).

[5] Neuville, Sandrine, Mariane Frenay, and Etienne Bourgeois. "Task value, self-efficacy and goal orientations: Impact on self-regulated learning, choice and performance among university students." *Psychologica Belgica* 47, no. 1 (2007).

[6] Al-Harthy, Ibrahim S., and Said S. Aldhafri. "The relationship among task-value, self-efficacy and academic achievement in Omani students at Sultan Qaboos University." *International Review of Social Sciences and Humanities* 7, no. 2 (2014): 15-22.

[7] Metallidou, Panayiota, and Anastasia Vlachou. "Children's self-regulated learning profile in language and mathematics: The role of task value beliefs." *Psychology in the Schools* 47, no. 8 (2010): 776-788.

[8] Lee, Daeyeoul, Sunnie Lee Watson, and William R. Watson. "The relationships between self-efficacy, task value, and self-regulated learning strategies in massive open online courses." *International Review of Research in Open and Distributed Learning* 21, no. 1 (2020): 23-39.

[9] José Rizal, New World Encyclopedia

[10] "Yes, Dr. Jose Rizal was a real ophthalmologist" by Ma. Dominga B. Padilla, MD, FPAO, paojournal.com

[11] Taylor, G., Jungert, T., Mageau, G. A., Schattke, K., Dedic, H., Rosenfield, S., and Koestner, R. (2014). "A self-determination theory approach to predicting school achievement over time: The unique role of intrinsic motivation." *Contemporary Educational Psychology* 39(4), 342-358.

[12] Howard, Joshua L., Julien Bureau, Frédéric Guay, Jane XY Chong, and Richard M. Ryan. "Student motivation and associated outcomes: A meta-analysis from self-determination theory." *Perspectives on Psychological Science* 16, no. 6 (2021): 1300-1323.

[13] Wilken, Eric Conrad. "The effects of extrinsic motivation on high school attendance." PhD diss., Lindenwood University, 2016.

[14] Shim, Jae Eun, Juhee Kim, Yoonna Lee, Kristen Harrison, Kelly Bost, Brent McBride, Sharon Donovan, et al. "Fruit and vegetable intakes of preschool children are associated with feeding practices facilitating internalization of

extrinsic motivation." *Journal of Nutrition Education and Behavior* 48, no. 5 (2016): 311-317.

[15]Amorose, Anthony J., Dawn Anderson-Butcher, Tarkington J. Newman, Mickey Fraina, and Aidyn Iachini. "High school athletes' self-determined motivation: The independent and interactive effects of coach, father, and mother autonomy support." *Psychology of Sport and Exercise* 26 (2016): 1-8.

[16] Vallerand, Robert J., and Gaétan F. Losier. "An integrative analysis of intrinsic and extrinsic motivation in sport." *Journal of Applied Sport Psychology* 11, no. 1 (1999): 142-169.

[17]Azzahro, Rana, Ana Maghfiroh, and Niken Reti Indriastuti. "Maintaining Students' Extrinsic Motivation in Online Learning: Teachers' Problem." In International Conference of Education, Social, and Humanities (1ST INCESH). Web of Science, 2021.

[18] Barajas, Nancy H. "The Influence of Extrinsic Motivational Factors on Upper Elementary Students in Reading." PhD diss., 2020.

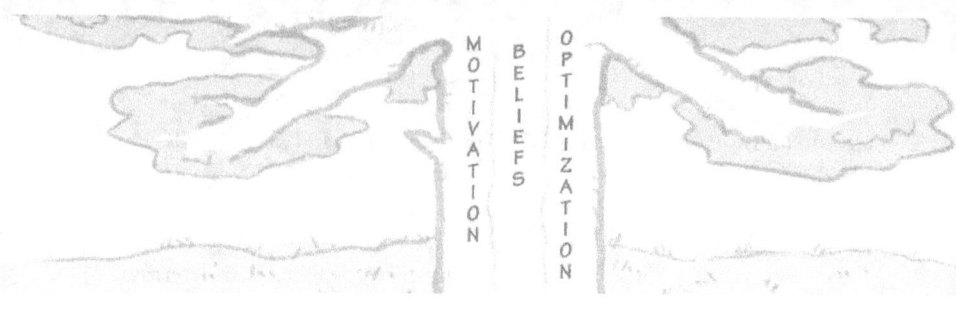

## CHAPTER 5

# BELIEFS

A group of researchers studied the intellectual and ethical development of college students and found that as students progressed through their college years, their beliefs about learning and knowledge changed.[1] They discovered that learning outcomes improved as the students' beliefs changed. It was found that the longer a student retained particular beliefs about learning and knowledge, the lower their academic achievement.

Children's beliefs about learning and knowledge are likely to influence how they learn and the outcomes of that learning.[2] The wisest learners need to be self-aware of their beliefs to jump-start the process of optimizing their learning journey. There are five essential beliefs that we will discuss in detail in the next section: Diversity, Standards, Fluidity, Connectedness, and Control.

**Five Essential Beliefs of Learning and Knowledge**

1. **Diversity** - *Diversity* recognizes that knowledge can come from different sources.

Some learners will listen to what a teacher has to say or read what is in their textbook, and they will immediately perceive all the knowledge as the truth. On the other hand, there are students who will recognize that the knowledge can be enhanced, better understood, or contradicted by doing research and considering other reliable sources (or viewpoints) before deciding if the knowledge taught is acceptable or should be modified. This second attitude toward learning is the more sophisticated and desirable of the two. It is a wiser way to learn. As a result of the student's pursuit of a deeper understanding of a subject and their desire to seek out more than one authority's opinion, they will walk away with a stronger conviction and a more thorough understanding of the subject than the student who accepts at face value the first version that is handed down to them from a single teacher or textbook.

This can be a challenging quality for parents to cultivate and foster in their children as it requires a delicate balancing act. On the one hand, when children are still toddlers, parents understandably require children to accept their teaching and authority at face value. These teachings can include not playing with fire or electrical outlets or being respectful to others. Most parents want their children to accept such instructions as the absolute authority for that season. However, as children become older and their thinking and reasoning competencies develop, it is natural that they will start asking questions or even outright refusing to follow instructions. Many parents struggle during this transition period with being able to dictate to their children in absolute terms and encountering varying levels of resistance, whether overtly or subtly.

Parents must establish a safe space for their children to ask questions even under challenging circumstances. Making room for discussion will empower a child to think critically and independently. As our children grow, they need to be able to reason the hows, whats, and whys of what they are being taught. As subjects become more complex, they will also become more nuanced, and there will often be more than one perspective that needs to be considered.

When openness to discussion and critical thinking are not embraced at home, this can carry over to a child's classroom experience. Instruction passed on from teachers may be immediately accepted; by extension, textbooks will be too. In addition, when a child tends to depend on absolute authorities for their knowledge base, the adopted learning strategies, e.g., rote memorization, will tend to be more superficial as well.[2]

Consider the idea of how perceptions of history can change based on the author of a text, or whether a book is published in the U.S., Japan, or Russia. The context in which an author is writing will undoubtedly color the language chosen and the viewpoint presented. If misinformation has been infused in a textbook and that book is viewed as an authoritative text, then what is stated in the text will be all the next generation of learners will know as truth. Conversely, if an environment has been cultivated in which children are encouraged to ask questions, then children will feel safe to engage in discussion beyond what they are being told. This sets the stage for a more positive and open setting in which learning can happen, where critical thinking is not only allowed but encouraged. When children believe they are part of the learning process, that they have choices, and that their voice matters, they will in turn feel autonomy over their decisions and will be more motivated to engage in learning opportunities.

Many parents (and educators) are concerned that allowing such open discussion might lead their children toward adopting the wrong ideas. Such fears are understandable, but in an age where people can get information through the internet easily, it becomes even more important for children to be trained on how to use appropriate tools to research, discuss, and weigh the various viewpoints available.

My first significant encounter with educators who taught me to question and think critically about what I learned was at my university. Even though it was a secular university, it was there that I learned to have a deeper understanding and appreciation for my faith and other truths and values that I'd been taught earlier in life. It was a season in which I processed and asked questions about my beliefs, but this didn't lead me to abandon my faith. Instead, it allowed me to strengthen my faith and, more importantly, make it my own.

The wisest learners will be better equipped to learn only when they start to think and process independently. Parents, it's worth remembering that we don't always have to have the final say. Granted there are many cases where it is critical for young learners to implicitly trust the instruction that is handed down to them by parents and teachers, but as they become older and subjects become more complicated, it's also vital for learners to be capable of handling more sophisticated thinking and of grasping the reasoning behind what they are being taught. Eventually, they should be able to discern between falsehoods and trustworthy information, based on supporting evidence and reliable sources. Instilling this open-mindedness toward critical thinking is something parents must model and teach at home, throughout the life of their children.

2.  **Standards** - *Standards* recognize that the curation of knowledge is better served when there are standards in use, such as reasoning and experimentation. Students who have this belief are more likely to be more intrinsically, rather than extrinsically, motivated to learn as well as use more meaningful learning strategies.[2] Their focus is not on proving they can memorize and recall teachings passed on from an instructor or textbook. Rather, students who value the process of digging deeper into a subject so that they can fully understand the justification for a way of thinking are more likely to excel academically. Eventually, these students will be more skilled in separating facts from opinions, sifting through a wide range of information to find the truth of a subject. They can classify whether something they've been taught is trustworthy or if it requires further investigation.

It will be worth noting that they may not necessarily have higher grades compared to other students who do not go through the process of thinking through the evidence that supports justification. However, understanding and applying the value of *standards* provide a deeper foundation for conceptual and subject-matter mastery.

My co-author Artyom recalls how he struggled with this concept during one of his graduate school courses. In this class, his instructors would provide a research study, something often written by a world-famous, respected expert. Their assignment was to analyze, critique, and identify areas of weakness in the report. At the time, Artyom found this to be incredibly challenging. His tendency was to believe everything written by these sources—they were published, trusted experts, after all! But over time and with the guidance of his instructors, he found ways to read more critically, identify claims that were not well backed, and spot evidence that was lacking or had weak reasoning. It was an eye-opening experience that helped him learn how to think critically about other published articles, even those published in respected journals.

This practice of training critical thought regularly happens in graduate programs in the form of peer reviews, where work is evaluated and critiqued by others in the same field. As parents, we can foster this form of thinking by making fewer statements and asking better, open-ended questions that stimulate reasoning rather than simple acceptance. Remembering our discussions on modeling, this particular attitude toward learning is one that can be most successfully taught through example.

As parents, we won't be with our children every day for the rest of their lives. In this day and age of the internet, they will be faced with an overwhelming amount of information and knowledge. Helping them build knowledge *standards* based on reasoning and experimentation will equip them to curate knowledge—that is, knowledge for them to accept, revise, and/or reject. As parents, we should be able to guide our children to be able to scrutinize these various sources of information and weed out the fallacies from the facts. The wisest learners can then develop a wide array of *standards* to help them sift through the increasingly abundant body of knowledge available to them. In doing so, they will be better prepared to handle the complex questions they will face later in life.

*Figure 11: Sources of Information*

3. **Fluidity** - *Fluidity* is based on the belief that one's knowledge is constantly evolving. If students believe that knowledge is evolving, then they acknowledge there is a vast amount to be learned throughout life, and it is ever-changing. With the appropriate beliefs about knowledge, learners will view a new course or area of study as a chance to expand their awareness of the world—their understanding of how a scientific study was accomplished, a math problem was completed, or an art project was created. They'll view their surroundings with interest and intrigue, aware of the learning potential all around.

If students think that knowledge is fixed and unchanging, then they have closed their minds to its expansive nature. On the other hand, students who believe that knowledge is *not* fixed have been observed to have more confidence in their ability to learn a particular subject.[2] They were also observed to use deeper, instead of surface-level, learning approaches that make use of higher-order thinking skills.

Fluidity will play a crucial role in the job market of the 21st century. Consider these realities for the current workforce:

- Technology continuously evolves, demanding that users keep pace with every update or risk being left behind.

- Information, media, and news are reported at light speed and one week off can have you feeling disoriented and out of touch.

- Work can now be accomplished from any location at any time thanks to various online collaboration technologies such as Zoom and Asana.

Fluidity is a critical belief for today's workers, whether by necessity or by choice. To illustrate, 75% of Gen Z (employees ages 18 to 25) believe they would benefit from a job change.[3] "Gen Z joined the workforce just as the pandemic shook up the job market in 2020. Not surprisingly, that's changed the way this young cohort views work, with Gen Z showing a greater willingness to job hop than older generations."[4]

According to a ZipRecruiter survey,[5] 95% of Gen Z prioritizes career advancement opportunities, 93% want a manager they can learn from, and 91% are in search of professional development and training opportunities.[6] If Gen Z doesn't find these opportunities with their current employer, they're willing to leave and connect with an employer who does. We can also infer that Gen Z, compared to older generations, is more open to learning new skills and knowledge that their new jobs will entail. Without an openness toward learning, these workers will likely miss out on opportunities for career development and growth.

Artyom often experienced this fixed belief about learning when teaching undergraduate students studying statistics. Statistics is considered a precise field of study—there are formulas that are followed, often in very specific ways. As a result, when there is a paradigm shift, such as a change in the standards of how data should be distributed and modeled, this would be particularly difficult for these students to accept. Many would be challenged to change their belief, even when presented with evidence that the newer models are superior to the older ones. Their belief had been fixed that there was only one way to solve these problems.

Artyom's experience provides insight into how *fluidity* affects learning approaches and outcomes. The more fixed a student believed knowledge to be, the more they would struggle with complex, higher learning. Research studies have observed that when students believe that knowledge is fixed, they are likely to earn lower grades.[7]

To further illustrate this idea, consider the many times throughout history when prominent, well-respected thinkers have been wrong.

- In 1943, Thomas Watson, president of IBM, was famously quoted as saying, "I think there is a world market for maybe five computers." And yet today, the world sees over two billion personal computers in use, and more than three billion individuals access the internet on a daily basis.[8]

- Daryl Zanuck, executive producer at 20th Century Fox, said in a 1946 interview, "Television won't be able to hold on to any market it captures after the first six months. People will soon get tired of staring at a plywood box every night."[9] Currently, at least one TV set is found in more than 1.4 billion households worldwide.

- In 1903, Henry Ford asked his lawyer, Horace Rackham, to invest in his automobile company. The president of the Michigan Savings Bank cautioned Rackham against investing in Ford's automobile business. "The horse is here to stay, but the automobile is only a novelty," he reportedly said.[10]

Not recognizing that knowledge is fluid has resulted in close-minded thinking and led to the downfall of many respected companies. Some more recent examples are Blockbuster Video, which missed out on the streaming video revolution, and Kodak, which missed out on the opportunity presented by digital cameras. Fluidity can help avoid these failures, as the wisest learner can easily adapt to knowledge that is continuously evolving and make changes as necessary.

4. **Connectedness** - *Connectedness* recognizes that one area of knowledge is usually related to another. Knowledge rarely operates alone. If knowledge were fragmented, then ideas would

stand alone, untethered to other concepts. But this is seldom the case.

A *connected* view of knowledge recognizes that ideas can be complex and layered. In contrast, a simple view of knowledge believes that ideas can be easily categorized, black or white, and strictly based on facts. While there are times when knowledge *seems* to be simple, the reality is, as a learner matures, concepts will become increasingly complex, less black and white, and more likely to require deep consideration. The more students learn, the more they will accept that knowledge doesn't always fit neatly into one box.

It's worth noting that students who have a simple or disconnected view of knowledge will more likely be associated with lower academic performance.[11] On the other hand, students who believe in the connectedness and inherent complexity of knowledge are more likely to use more meaningful (or less superficial) learning strategies, be more intrinsically motivated, and have positive learning outcomes.

As learning progresses, concepts become more complex and, ironically, it becomes increasingly difficult to make these complex ideas digestible and simple. Consider the challenge faced by a UX designer working to make a vast amount of information easy to navigate on a website. The more complicated the service being offered, the more challenging it is to make the experience user-friendly for the customer. When a UX designer is able to master the inherent complexity of connecting different website features, he'll more effectively present the information in a way that is appealing to customers.

When I graduated from university, I had many classmates who decided to work as specialists for various multinational corporations. Some of them decided to specialize in finance, while others chose marketing. After initially wavering, I eventually opted to become an entrepreneur. As an entrepreneur, I had to learn the different aspects of running a business, such as finance, marketing, production, distribution, human resources, purchasing, etc. At first, I regretted my decision because it was quite difficult to learn many disciplines simultaneously, but eventually, I learned how valuable such learning could be. Being competent in various disciplines allowed me to see how different components relate to each other. Finance does not work separately from marketing or human resources. In the same way, distribution does not operate in isolation from production and purchasing. They are all integrated, and such relationships make such knowledge rather complex.

It's because of the integrated nature of knowledge that as a school administrator for 14 years, I've supported the adoption of spiral learning in my school. For example, consider the four areas of scientific study—biology, chemistry, physics, and earth science. In many high schools, each area is studied per year; there is a higher tendency to teach each area of science as a stand-alone area of study. By contrast, with a spiral learning approach, all the sciences are studied every year and students have more opportunities to comprehend their integration.

For parents looking to apply these principles at home, consider ways you can expose your children to a variety of disciplines, fields of expertise, and experiences. Ask questions to stimulate their imagination and spark discussion around connecting what might seem distinct or separate, if not fragmented, concepts or areas and look for commonalities that tie them together. Additional strategies will be discussed in detail in part three.

5. **Control** - *Control* recognizes that positive learning outcomes are internal and primarily dependent on a learner's choices, particularly the effort they put forth and the learning approaches they decide to use. Every learner holds a certain perception or belief of their ability to accomplish a task or achieve a goal. Most often, they aren't fully conscious of this underlying attitude, but this subtle awareness guides how they approach a new subject, project, or idea. A learner either believes they can achieve something through hard work or they feel, for whatever reason, that it's out of their reach.

Learners with a *healthy control belief* feel they can do something about their learning situation; it is within their power to reach their desired outcome. This learner is driven internally. Their belief is that *they* are the primary deciders of their learning outcomes. They believe their behavior directly dictates their performance. On the other hand, learners with an *unhealthy control belief* feel their learning outcome can be attributed to external factors beyond their control. They don't believe they have what it takes to reach their desired goals or feel they are being held back by something or someone around them. Their attitude toward ownership is such that the effort they put into learning something won't pay off. Learners will fall into one of these two categories; they will either take ownership of their learning or attribute their failure to others.

The positive role of control beliefs on a child's academic success has also been repeatedly confirmed through research. In 2019, Muwonge and colleagues published an article in the *South African Journal of Psychology* citing that higher levels of control were indirectly linked to academic success as measured via GPA.[12] They discovered that children who exhibited higher levels of control were also more likely to be critical thinkers and would show advanced organizational skills. In other words, the feeling of being in control of one's learning progress can facilitate a number of positive learning-related qualities, which in turn further facilitates academic performance.

Bill Gates has been a controversial figure since the early days of Microsoft, but whether we like or agree with him or not, it is undeniable that he has been quite impactful in many areas such as technology, philanthropy, and health. Microsoft, the company he co-founded with Paul Allen, continues to dominate many markets including desktop operating systems and office software suites. Gates's foundation has also raised the bar when it comes to philanthropic endeavors in donating over $65 billion.[13] The foundation has taken the initiative in fighting poverty and life-threatening diseases such as malaria, resulting in saving and uplifting millions of lives.[14]

How did Gates achieve such levels of success? Gates's parents shied away from taking credit for their son's accomplishments, but when questioned for parenting tips and advice, they offered some interesting insights. In a joint *Forbes* interview with Gates and his father,[15] Gates reflects on how his parents pushed him to pursue activities that didn't come easy for him, like swimming, soccer, and football. They also encouraged him to take music lessons—according to Gates Sr., his son tried the trombone but with little success.

"I didn't know why [they encouraged these activities] at the time," Gates shared. "I thought it was kind of pointless, but it ended up exposing me to leadership opportunities and showing me that I wasn't good at a lot of things instead of sticking to things that I was comfortable with." Gates Sr. added that by encouraging their son to try new things, they felt they were nurturing an *attitude of openness*; they wanted him to *see how he could learn* from every experience, even his failures. Gates's parents had sown the seeds of the control belief. Gates was learning how he is ultimately responsible for his own learning outcomes.

I went through a time of unhealthy control beliefs when I was younger. I'd intentionally create situations that would enable me to attribute my failure to something external, rather than blame my inability to do well. For example, I'd find myself watching movies instead of studying the night before my exams. By doing this, if I failed my exam, I could attribute it to watching movies instead of my "lack of intelligence."

It was only when I developed a healthier control belief that I started to achieve better learning outcomes. Recognizing that I needed to own up to my learning and not blame external factors or other people helped me in my subsequent endeavors, such as when I jump-started my graduate studies and athletic aspirations. I've learned by watching my parents and taking the advice of my teachers. I've come to realize that with hard work and dedication, I can complete difficult tasks and reach big goals. Better yet, the more I've seen my efforts pay off, the more willing I am to tackle a new challenge.

When a child feels they have control of their destiny and sees the rewards of having the right attitude toward accountability, they come to see that, with enough effort, they can do hard things.

They become more naturally motivated to dream big and put in the hard work to achieve those dreams.

A key learning point here for parents is that a botched attempt at trying something new doesn't have to spell defeat. More often than not, failure in itself is a teaching moment—an opening to discuss what new understanding or insight can be drawn from an experience. This approach to learning can encourage a child to see every experience through a different lens and may very well lead them to consider how every attempt at something new is ripe with opportunity. The key is for students to keep the right attitude and to always be on the lookout for the bigger-picture lesson that's available.

## RESEARCH RECAP:

- Children who believe implicitly in a *diversity of knowledge sources* will have more *positive learning outcomes*.

- Children who support the idea that *knowledge comes from reasoning, thinking, and experimenting*, will be more *skilled in separating facts from opinions* and sifting through a wide range of information to find the truth of a subject.

- The more a child believes *knowledge to be fixed*, the more they will *struggle with complex, higher learning*.

- When children understand how *knowledge relates to other knowledge*, it provides a deeper *foundation of conceptual and subject-matter knowledge*.

A study conducted by a team of researchers at the University College London[16] analyzed two groups of London transportation professionals. This study provides interesting evidence about how our brains are malleable and how we can be taught to embrace new habits with time and practice. In this study, one group was training to become taxicab drivers and the other training to be bus drivers. In taxi school, the drivers had to pass a difficult exam without the use of GPS, proving they had learned all the streets in London. This is no small feat in such a large city! The bus driver trainees, by contrast, had a much easier task. They had to learn only one specific set of roads, as they would be driving the same routes again and again over the course of their careers.

After several years of work, the brains of both groups were scanned, and lo and behold, the taxi drivers had increased the size of the part of their brains responsible for spatial navigation. While both groups had started their careers as drivers at the same time, and they were doing essentially the same work of transporting passengers through London, the taxi drivers' brains had increased in their capacity to learn. On the other hand, the bus drivers' brains had not changed. The taxi drivers' brains were more active because their work always kept them thinking of new routes, of how to handle a new traffic jam at a moment's notice, or considering how to juggle the needs of a variety of passengers often in a hurry. They were continuously learning new things, keeping their brain sharp and responsive. Our children's brains are malleable in a similar fashion.

The reality of knowledge and truth is that we all have a great deal to learn. There is so much that we don't know. It's important that we all—learners and parents alike—approach learning with humility. As parents, we can be the first to model the right attitude and create a safe space of openness and conversation, where disagreement and healthy conflict can exist, so that these right attitudes toward learning can grow. We should encourage open discourse so our children can express when they are struggling and we can sense when it's time to keep pushing or pull the plug and allow them to pursue another path. Growth is the goal for all of us, so give yourself and your children grace as you work through these tricky conversations together.

When parents create a family culture such that their children know that they can make an impact on their own learning, then children are more likely to achieve their learning goals. Helping our learners to develop a healthy attitude toward ownership requires healthy parental modeling and open dialogue, just like every other aspect of wise learning! It also calls for patience with ourselves, as we learn how to be good models, and with our children, as they work through the process. Together, with continued effort, it can be accomplished and the results you hope for can be achieved.

As you look to apply the principles of this section, consider ways you can give your children autonomy and room to make their own decisions and choices. Ask stimulating questions that will help your children develop their analytical and strategic skill sets. Allow your children to gradually make more autonomous decisions, starting from the most simple and graduating to the more complex, enabling them to build a foundation for independent critical thinking.

# ACTION PLAN

- Remember, we can be taught to embrace new knowledge with time and practice; in other words, **healthier beliefs can be learned**. Consider how the five essential beliefs of learning can be taught, encouraged, and modeled at home. Look for chances to incite your learner's curiosity and encourage their instinct to investigate and ask questions.

- When your learner gives you a simple response to a complex matter, gently push back and help them to see differing viewpoints on the subject.

- Ask your children open-ended questions about what they are learning and allow them time to process their thoughts and thoughtfully respond.

- Encourage your learner's input in discussions about subjects that do not have a clear-cut right or wrong answer. Tell them how you came to your personal conclusions about the subject, while reminding them that it's okay for them to form their own ideas.

---

[1] Perry Jr., William G. *Forms of Intellectual and Ethical Development in the College Years: A Scheme.* Jossey-Bass Higher and Adult Education Series. Jossey-Bass Publishers, 350 Sansome St., San Francisco, CA 94104, 1999.

[2] Kizilgunes, Berna, Ceren Tekkaya, and Semra Sungur. "Modeling the relations among students' epistemological beliefs, motivation, learning approach, and achievement." *Journal of Educational Research* 102, no. 4 (2009): 243-256.

[3] Does Job Hopping Help Or Hurt Your Career? - Robert Half Talent Solutions

[4] Job hopping is the Gen Z way - By Cate Chapman, Editor at LinkedIn News

[5] Workers Are Changing Jobs, Raking In Big Raises—and Keeping Inflation High - *The Wall Street Journal*

[6] Gen Z Characteristics Employers Need to Understand - Robert Half Talent Solutions

[7] Trautwein, Ulrich, and Oliver Lüdtke. "Epistemological beliefs, school achievement, and college major: A large-scale longitudinal study on the impact of certainty beliefs." *Contemporary Educational Psychology* 32, no. 3 (2007): 348-366.

[8] Listverse - https://listverse.com/2019/05/14/10-quotes-from-experts-who-were-proved-wrong/

[9] Darryl F. Zanuck Quotes. BrainyQuote.com, BrainyMedia Inc, 2022. https://www.brainyquote.com/quotes/darryl_f_zanuck_401896, accessed October 18, 2022.

[10] 1922, *The Truth About Henry Ford* by Sarah T. Bushnell, Chapter 4: "The First Car and the First Race," Quote Page 55 to 57, The Reilly & Lee Company, Chicago, Illinois. (Google Books Full View) https://books.google.com/books?id=YXuMzVQLOAAC&q=fad#v=snippet&q=fad&f=false

[11] Cano, Francisco. "Epistemological beliefs and approaches to learning: Their change through secondary school and their influence on academic performance." *British Journal of Educational Psychology* 75, no. 2 (2005): 203-221.

[12] Muwonge, C. M., Schiefele, U., Ssenyonga, J., and Kibedi, H. (2019). "Modeling the relationship between motivational beliefs, cognitive learning strategies, and academic performance of teacher education students." *South African Journal of Psychology* 49(1), 122-135.

[13] Bill & Melinda Gates Foundation - Foundation Fact Sheet - https://www.gatesfoundation.org/about/foundation-fact-sheet

[14] Bill & Melinda Gates Foundation - Our Story - https://www.gatesfoundation.org/about/our-story

[15] Best advice: Gates on Gates - *Fortune*

[16] Maguire, Eleanor A., David G. Gadian, Ingrid S. Johnsrude, Catriona D. Good, John Ashburner, Richard SJ Frackowiak, and Christopher D. Frith. "Navigation-related structural change in the hippocampi of taxi drivers." *Proceedings of the National Academy of Sciences* 97, no. 8 (2000): 4398-4403.

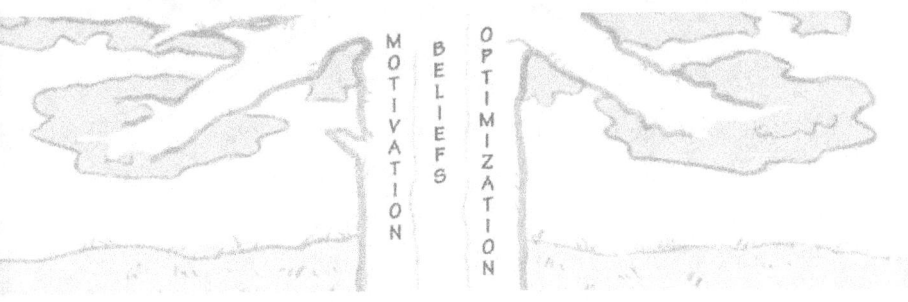

# CHAPTER 6

# OPTIMIZATION

The interest in process optimization, particularly in the workplace, has surged in recent years. Project management methodologies such as Scrum, Lean, and Agile have risen in popularity as businesses have looked for ways to optimize team collaboration and productivity. And these management strategies have worked according to *Harvard Business Review*: "Studies show that companies embracing such techniques may enjoy significant improvements in efficiency and costs."[1] This is especially true when there is support from the leadership team to implant these management philosophies into the company culture.

Optimization refers to the act or process of making something as good as it can be. It's when you find a way to make the most of a situation, procedure, or activity. Shelly Madden blogged that when you optimize a project, you increase the likelihood of streamlined operations, better resource management, reduced error, and customer satisfaction.[2] All these outcomes are desirable for businesses looking to thrive, making process optimization a priority.

Much like the benefits gained by optimizing business processes, the same can be said for learning. We all must contend with the limited time, energy, and mental space we have available and the seemingly endless learning expectations. We have to optimize our resources in order to juggle our unlimited access to information, thanks to the internet and the availability of cell phones and computers. Add to that the underlying supposition for us to maintain an attitude of openness to learning throughout life so we can pivot and expand our careers as new opportunities arise.

Our children are growing up in this reality—learning resources are unlimited, and the expectations for lifelong learning are high. That's why it's essential for them to learn to optimize their resources for the most productive learning possible. Our focus in this chapter will be on learning optimization and the three aspects of learning that we all need to optimize—our time, energy, and cognitive load, which is our mental capacity to learn new things. Think of this chapter as the icing on top of an already great cake. These practices will enhance all the ideas we've already discussed and fully round out our conversation on learning foundations.

In the pages to come, we'll introduce and discuss two new concepts that are related to the idea of optimization —the illusions of learning and non-learning. We'll also consider how to promote automaticity in learning and how to help your learner reach an "ideal state of learning" or flow. All these practices will facilitate better learning and help your student develop into a wiser, savvier learner, ready to take on any academic challenge head-on.

# The Illusion of Learning

As a school administrator, I've noticed one of the frequent causes of teachers' frustrations is when students struggle with lessons that have been discussed in previous classes. Some students who scored well on short quizzes after such lessons would also struggle. This situation makes it challenging for the teachers because they will now have to allocate precious instruction time to review the previously discussed lessons. When you replicate this situation over the course of a school year, it is not hard to imagine how students' learning can be negatively affected. In addition, teachers will likely struggle to cover all of the assigned curriculum for the school year. How can educators address this problem which we define as the *illusion of learning*?

The **illusion of learning** focuses on the period of time immediately after you hear something. Hermann Ebbinghaus, a German psychologist and pioneer in the experimental study of memory, provides a better understanding of this illusion through his research. Ebbinghaus was interested in the mechanics of how people acquired and forgot information. This led him to run a study on himself from 1880 to 1885 where he tried to commit nonsense words to memory (as it is much more difficult to remember combinations of phonemes that do not make sense—i.e., are nonsense words—relative to real words that can be linked through associations, personal experiences with these words), examining his memory at various intervals and documenting the outcomes. The graph below is a close representation of the results, which is more known today as the Ebbinghaus Forgetting Curve.[3]

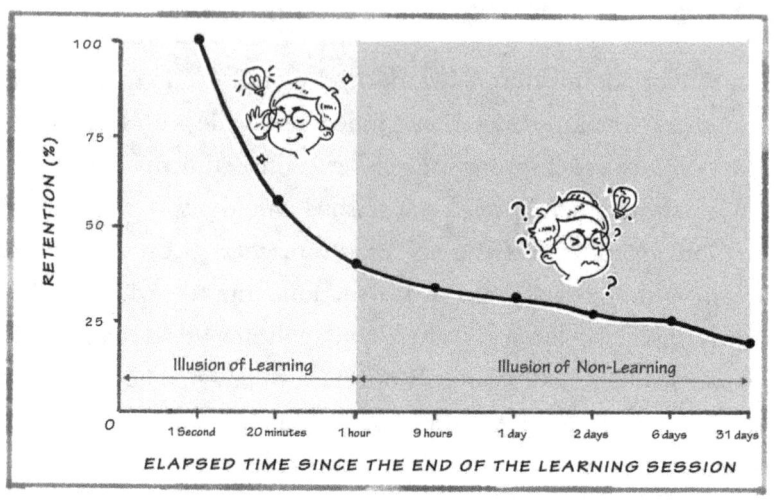

*Figure 12: The Ebbinghaus Forgetting Curve*

The Ebbinghaus Forgetting Curve illustrates how memories fade quickly over time when they're not actively engaged. As you can see, there is almost a linear trend to how fast newly formed memories are forgotten, with some 42% of memories lost in the first 20 minutes after the end of the learning session.

Ebbinghaus discovered that the metabolic processes in our brains may hinder the conversion of information from short-term memory into long-term memory. In other words, our brain protects our long-term memory from what it deems as less interesting or unimportant information in an effort to not overfill our long-term memory with unnecessary recollections. His findings remind us that memory formation is a process that requires time and effort. As we're working with our children to develop good learning practices, it's important to remember that not all the information that enters our short-term memory is guaranteed to be stored and remembered in the long-term memory. In fact, our learners will have to apply the repetition of good strategies for new information to make its way into their long-term memory.

Directly after learning new information, we can experience a feeling of knowing, a momentary belief that a new idea has been planted in our brains. This feeling is actually an illusion of learning called the recency effect. This effect is tied to how we tend to recollect the most immediate information we've learned more accurately, and we'll remember more clearly the last idea we heard over the first. What we don't realize is how quickly that information can slip from our minds.

Going back to our discussion on students struggling with lessons that have been previously taught, parents (and educators) must acknowledge and accept that the illusion of learning is a reality that children will need to contend with. Teaching a lesson to someone once does not mean the lesson has been learned. Due to the recency effect, there can be an illusion of learning after that initial teaching. Children will eventually forget much of what they have learned unless essential interventions occur. There is much work to be done before true learning can happen.

When a student crams for a test right before they take it, the recency effect will play to their advantage. They may do fairly well on the test. The knowledge will be fresh in their mind, so they will likely be able to recall the information and answer the questions with decent accuracy. Passing their test will give the *illusion* that they've learned the information. But in reality, over time, this information won't stick. If they are tested on this material several days later, they likely will remember little of it. Without continued interaction with the knowledge, most of what they crammed to retain for their test will be lost.

Similarly, rereading material several times, especially before being asked to recite or retell it, can give the *illusion* that you've learned the material. But if rereading is your child's only strategy for remembering information, it won't be enough. It's too passive of a strategy when up against our brain's tendency to forget. Rereading can have your student thinking they've captured a memory, but it's likely that the recency effect is on display more than any long-term learning.

Another common factor tied to the illusion of learning is the issue of multitasking. Multitasking is when we attempt to do tasks simultaneously. While many people feel that multitasking makes them more productive—you're accomplishing multiple things simultaneously, after all—research has proven time and again that multitasking can be deceptive and creates an illusion of learning.[4]

It simply isn't possible for someone to focus fully and adeptly accomplish more than one task at a time. And while this applies to any kind of multitasking, it is especially true in the case of learning. When a student is trying to text, scroll through social media, or watch TV while studying, their learning will suffer. This is because our attention span is a limited resource. When we try to juggle multiple activities at once, our brain will jump from activity to activity, and nothing will get our full attention. This is far from an optimal state for learning or studying.

I've often seen this illusion of learning play out with my students. Many students will cite how multitasking makes them faster or more efficient. And, while they may pick up bits and pieces of the subject they are learning, overall, it's a superficial kind of learning. Multitasking prohibits the kind of learning that sticks with a student over time.

Additionally, once a student begins to multitask, it can be a very difficult habit to break.[5] When several sources of information are competing for a student's attention, they will have less ability to focus and a greater chance of getting distracted by something else that can seem more interesting. So, especially when studying something they find difficult, it's critical to avoid multitasking altogether, as it can draw a student's attention away from what they need to learn.

While we've witnessed the challenges associated with multitasking firsthand, our experience is supported by compelling research, as well. A student's attentional control, or their ability to focus on a task without distraction, will directly impact their GPA.[6,7] Multitasking is a factor that has been proven to lower a student's attentional control. The *more* tasks a learner tries to juggle at once, the weaker their attentional control. By direct correlation, scientists can deduce that multitasking while studying can actually lead to a lower GPA. Students are much less adept at staying focused on their studies while simultaneously checking their phones or tending to other distractions.

Before we move on from our discussion on the illusion of learning, there's one more consideration tied to the forgetting curve that we want to touch on. We call it the summer gap. This common, extended break from learning that students look forward to every year provides a reason for concern, especially in light of what we've shared about our tendency to forget information. The research we have to share on this subject may have you reconsidering how your students spend this annual time off from study.

A study conducted in 1996 by researchers from the University of Missouri and Tennessee State University[8] found that students who took a full break from their education over the summer experienced a significant loss of knowledge. The study revealed that students who did not engage in activities such as reading, practicing what they learned during the school year, or taking summer classes fell behind those who did.

A second study out of Johns Hopkins University[9] took this summer gap consideration a step further, looking into what, if any, lasting consequences could result from taking the summer off. Their findings uncovered how children from higher-income families had significantly better academic scores by the ninth grade and they attributed this to two factors. The first was that these children started first grade with a learning advantage, specifically they were better readers, having entered school with a couple of years of quality preschool learning already under their belts. The second advantage was how these students spent their summers, often being schooled by tutors or under the care of parents who invested in their learning in various ways throughout the summer break.

The researchers also found that the loss of knowledge was more acute for economically disadvantaged students who didn't have access to these same opportunities over their summer break. The forgetting curve played a role here too, as the students who took the summers off would essentially have to catch back up at the start of each year. So, while during the school year, both groups of students were offered the same classes and taught the same curriculum, over time, the more economically affluent students were academically more advanced, thanks in part to their continued education over the summer breaks. Over time, the poorer students fell further and further behind.

An additional study published in 2019 by Kuhfeld[10] analyzed reading and math scores from more than 3.4 million students, looking to uncover a sum of how many months of education were lost over the summer. Across all grades, almost four months of learning were lost over the summer break. Especially as learning became more complicated in older grades, the loss was more significant.

The expectation that absolute learning has occurred during the school year and information cannot or will not be forgotten over the summer has led to the regular disappointment of many teachers when students return for the fall semester. Instead of fully taking the summer off from learning, consider alternative strategies that benefit learners and teachers alike.

Parents can consider implementing a "summer gap" review program at home where you periodically check in to review key lessons from the previous year with your child. Additionally, consider how summer can be used as a time to prep for the year to come. Ask your school what subjects will be covered during the first quarter of the following school year and look for opportunities to prepare your student before they enter the classroom. Both options can have a positive impact on your learner's self-efficacy, control beliefs, and intrinsic motivation.

## RESEARCH RECAP:

- The Ebbinghaus Forgetting Curve illustrates how *memories can quickly fade over time when they're not actively engaged*.

- On average, we forget about 42% of what we hear within 20 minutes, and more than half of memory loss occurs within just one hour!

- *Multitasking is a hard habit to break*, but if we don't address it, *it can directly impact our student's academic performance*.

- *It is possible to combat the illusions of learning and the effects of the forgetting curve.* If students regularly review and recall what they've learned and find ways to engage with new information aside from just rereading, they'll be more likely to retain their knowledge over the long haul.

## The Illusions of Non-learning

Tim Grover, the longtime trainer for Michael Jordan and Kobe Bryant, has shared how strength training was always a touchy subject for shooting guards. "They're always afraid the new routine will throw off their touch," Grover said. "And it does. There's just no way around it." Grover also shares the same qualifier he would tell Bryant and Jordan: For a short period of time, while their body was adjusting, their touch might betray them. But it would return—maybe in a week, perhaps two.

Even in the face of these known challenges, Grover preaches the benefits of pushing through and trying new training. He says that "strength training helps ligaments and tendons remain healthy and aids in recovery from injury." There was a balance of building strength while adding enough weight. Sometimes, players have to find their sweet spot.[11]

Much like what athletes experience when they attempt new training routines, there's also an adjustment period when learning that's needed to build mental strength. For Bryant and Jordan, this adjustment period left them feeling as if their new routines didn't work at all, as if their playing was getting worse instead of better. There can be a similar feeling of adjustment for learners as they acquire new knowledge. For a time, they can feel as if they aren't learning at all or even regressing. It can be quite discouraging.

We call this adjustment period an **illusion of non-learning**. As a learner continues to interact with new information well after the first time they hear it, they may struggle to retain or apply it. They can have the *illusion* of not being able to truly learn the information. The reality isn't that these children aren't learning, but rather, learning new things requires time and patience, especially if the goal is for that new information to take root in our long-term memory. Deeper learning that sticks over time requires the thoughtful use of resources and learning strategies that trigger memory activation.

Just as Jordan and Bryant would have to work through the kinks of how new strength training was affecting their shooting accuracy, sometimes students have to work extra hard through the hurdles of learning. This illusion of non-learning can also be thought of as a **dip** in learning, or essentially the opposite of what's experienced with the recency effect. Consider, for example, how some children can struggle when learning to read. They will make good progress in one week, but as new words or harder phrases are introduced, they can seemingly regress for a period as they wholly intake the new reading material. Eventually, as they practice, they will begin to understand and retain the new reading skills and regain any ground that seemed lost along the way.

The key is for these children (and their parents and teachers) not to get frustrated during the dips. The dips don't signify a period of non-learning. Rather, they are a stretch of time where the child needs further practice to fully gain mastery of the new knowledge. The progression of learning may be small and incremental, but it's there. Parents and students alike should not be disappointed during this period as learning still occurs, but time and effort are required for knowledge to sink in. It is important to be patient with your learner during this time.

Similarly, the summer gap that we referenced earlier can also present an illusion of non-learning. When learners struggle to remember information after taking the summer off, there can be an illusion that no learning had occurred during the previous school year or that the information learned was lost over the summer. And yet, the foundation was still laid during the previous year. The information may not have been fully lost over the summer. Rather, what was learned needs to be revisited and reviewed, allowing the child time to restore that learning into their long-term memory.

It's helpful to remember that our brains don't operate in a computerlike manner—we can't store information on our internal hard drives and retrieve it at any time in the future. Instead, our brains are biological systems that are constantly cycling through information. Because of that, we must work to overcome this reality by keeping our brains active, stimulated, and engaged so that the information we're trying to retain has a better chance of sticking with us for a longer period of time.

We're not suggesting that every student needs to participate in year-round schooling or attend school throughout the summer just to keep up. More practically, consider how learning can happen in a variety of settings, and summertime provides an opportunity for you and your child to engage with what they are learning in a different or novel way. This can happen through educational vacations, regular time spent reading, or in camps that encourage critical thinking. Even taking a summer job has been shown to pay off for students, both financially and mentally, as they are more prone to keep their brains active and engaged throughout the summer when they are employed.

The important takeaway from this conversation is that learning is an active, ongoing pursuit. If we allow our brains, or our student's brains, to idle for too long, knowledge can be lost. As our learners are engaged in their most involved years of education, as well as later in life past graduation, it's critical for their brains to be constantly working, learning, and engaging with the world around them. As they do so, they will benefit from the long-lasting results of a sharp mind and a greater capacity to retain new knowledge.

With a better understanding of these illusions of learning and non-learning, let's now consider several tried-and-true strategies that can be applied to address these issues.

1. **Overcoming the forgetting curve and recency effect.** Research has shown that if students review and study material directly after having learned it, either right after class or at the end of the day, they will not only understand the material more clearly, but it will also take them longer to forget the information.[12] Top students have been known to rewrite some of their notes from class, especially ones written in shorthand, helping them to digest what they've heard. They'll then take time to review the material again after several days and consider how this material fits in with other topics they are learning. Efforts such as these will help to reinforce what they've just learned and lessen the impact of both the forgetting curve and the recency effect.

2. **Recalling is more powerful than rereading.** Rather than rereading, encourage your student to recall the material they've just learned. Recalling knowledge happens when a student processes, evaluates, assesses, and regurgitates it. Simply rereading it is not effective enough for long-term retention. But by recalling, restating, or even reteaching what they've learned to a parent or friend, a student will more thoroughly understand the information. Finding ways to interact with new information beyond reading is exponentially more powerful.

3. **Canceling out multitasking.** The key to addressing the issue of multitasking head-on is to fully remove it from the equation. Parents can help their learners by setting up parameters around study time. Designate a space or quiet room for studying to take place. If you're not in a situation where you can fully dedicate a room to studying, look for ways to structure your child's environment so that it is conducive to learning. Shut off the

TV and encourage them to put their phone in another room while they are studying.

You can also set cues that signal when it's time for your children to focus. Apps that utilize the Pomodoro Technique[13] can signal when focused work should begin and when to take a break. The Pomodoro Technique encourages working in 25-minute segments, which is a manageable expectation for learners of most ages.

These strategies will give your learner guidelines for how to be productive by establishing a routine around where study time takes place and how to be productive in reasonable, short spurts. Learners will be more inclined to stay on task if there is a known stopping point ahead.

4. **Combating the illusion of non-learning.** To overcome a student's feelings of non-learning, parents can provide a listening ear for them to express their frustration. Then, help them to see where they have made progress, even if it's incremental. Insightful research from 2020 supports this idea, highlighting how higher perceived parental support is associated with better academic performance.[14]

Parents can also help by encouraging their learners to focus on *their* progress only and not to get sidetracked by the progress made by others. Additionally, helping children to maintain their motivation and stamina is key. This can be done by guiding learners to establish smaller goals that are reasonably attained so they don't get discouraged. Praise their hard work instead of their natural talents and abilities, as their continued work is what will help them ultimately reach their goal.

## ACTION PLAN

- To reduce the illusions of learning, encourage your child to review their class notes at the end of the day, rewriting shorthand and the main points learned. Encourage them to review the material again after several days and to look for ways the information ties to other areas of their schoolwork. Additionally, it can be helpful for them to recall, restate, or reteach what they are learning to you, another adult, or a friend.

- Address multitasking concerns by agreeing to rules for study time. Designate where learning will take place and ensure it is conducive to productive work. Include in your rules how electronics or other media should be handled when study time is happening.

- Consider ways you can combat the summer gap through educational camps or ongoing but engaging learning experiences over the summer break.

## Automaticity

When visiting different countries, learning to adapt to the varying driving rules has been an unexpected but recurring challenge for me. In my home city of Manila, where I learned to drive, I'm accustomed to the dense car congestion. Cars tend to drive close to one another, albeit slowly, because of the heavy traffic. I've heard from others, particularly visitors to our country, that these driving conditions can feel very stressful. The narrow spaces between cars, even at low speeds, can be anxiety-inducing. But not for me! Driving this way feels natural; I can do it without a great deal of effort. However, as I've discovered, driving practices that may feel second nature to local residents in other cities and countries can be highly distressing to me.

When driving in the U.S., for instance, I find the high speeds at which everyone travels immensely nerve-racking. From my point of view, make one wrong move and the results could be disastrous! Even knowing that, statistically, the chances of a major accident are low, there's still an adjustment period before I can drive comfortably, especially on the interstates. When visiting Australia, there was a new reality to contend with—driving at high speeds *and* a right-side drive system. Switching driving sides proved to be my biggest challenge yet. It required weeks of practice before I felt comfortable. When I needed to make a turn, I had to be very conscious of my actions, moving carefully to ensure I didn't crash into another car in the process.

When driving in Manila, I'm so comfortable that I can drive while listening to books or conversing with other passengers. But when driving in Australia, I need complete silence to think about my driving. I'm unable to do any kind of multitasking so I can focus on the road. In Australia, the practice of driving has not yet become automatic for me. I can get easily confused, miss turns, or nearly avoid an accident as I'm still learning how to drive in this new (to me) way.

Automaticity occurs when a behavior or mental process can be carried out rapidly without effort or explicit intention. For me, driving in Manila has come to feel automatic, while driving in Australia has not. For learners, automaticity comes when a child can complete a learning function effortlessly; the activity has become second nature for them. When a task is automatic, less time and energy are required to complete it.

To fully understand the importance of automaticity, let's break down two fundamental types of thinking related to automaticity and discuss why they are both valuable and needed parts of your child's learning development.

**Lower-order thinking** involves basic and primary learning and can include learning the alphabet, the mastery of basic addition and subtraction, the memorization of simple multiplication facts, or the development of typing skills. The learning process involved with lower-order thinking is often very procedural and mastered through repetition. With time and practice, your child can reach a point where they're able to complete lower-order activities automatically. As efficiency with lower-order thinking increases, children are able to learn more, faster, and can progress to more in-depth learning. Mastery of basic multiplication facts, for example, will set your learners up to tackle complex math problems later on.

**Higher-order thinking** happens when a child has formed good learning habits and they've strengthened their mental muscle memory to a point where more involved learning is possible. It occurs as a child is able to complete lower-order activities faster and with less effort, enabling them to apply those basic skills to solve more complex problems, set bigger goals, and manage their knowledge intake with greater efficiency. This goes beyond routine memorization and would require analysis, evaluation, and critical thinking. Consider, for example, a child learning English grammar. They need to first memorize basic grammar rules before writing and speaking fluently and effortlessly, concentrating on the topic of the reading assignment and not on the subject-verb agreement. Knowing how to execute basic learning functions quickly and with a high degree of automaticity, while making the most of the learning tools at their disposal, will enable them to optimize their study experience and expend minimal time and energy in the process.

Our child's brain cortex, responsible for functions like memory, cognition, learning, rationalization, problem-solving, consciousness, and sensory-related tasks[2], experiences less strain when they engage in activities that don't necessitate substantial thought or contemplation: things they can carry out habitually or automatically. Our goal is for your learner to develop the kind of automaticity that will allow them to essentially skip the thought process needed to execute lower-order thinking, reducing stress on their brain's cortex, requiring less cognitive load (or mental capacity), and making room for deeper thought processes to occur.

While automaticity is critical for our children to achieve higher-order thinking, it's also been shown through research to result in better grades and improved learning. Let us take a look at three studies that show the importance of automaticity when it comes to learning. The first study highlighted how greater automaticity in completing basic arithmetic without the aid of a calculator could be linked to higher grades for first-semester chemistry students.[15] Since chemistry requires the completion of numerous math problems, and they're often multistep computations, students who were more proficient in basic math were able to more quickly and accurately work through the formulas. The more efficient students could be with each step, the higher their likelihood to keep up as the computations become more complex.

---

[2]Sensory-related tasks involve the processing of information received through the senses, such as sight, hearing, touch, taste, and smell.

While this study doesn't *guarantee* that strong basic math skills will lead to higher grades in chemistry, or conversely, that a student who lacks strong basic math skills is doomed to struggle—other factors will be at play in determining academic performance, such as a student's intrinsic and extrinsic motivation to learn chemistry—the tie between high math automaticity and high chemistry grades is compelling. The majority of students with proficiency in basic math were able to handle the demands of chemistry *because of* their good math foundation—they didn't have to think as hard to solve each math problem, giving them the mental capacity they needed to tackle the entirety of the chemistry question. This study demonstrates how high automaticity with lower-order thinking can lower cognitive load and make space for more involved calculations.

The second study[16] considered the effect of cognitive load and automaticity on the problem-solving ability of college engineering students. It found that when students were able to complete tasks based on a high level of automaticity, they had faster response times and better performance. Conversely, when students were operating with lower automaticity, their performance was slower and their accuracy was lower. In fact, when students were able to solve problems using highly automatic thinking, they were able to work three times faster. Even as their mental capacity was taxed and students experienced a slowdown in performance, the tasks that were highly automatic could be completed faster. As these students were given more intricate, complex problems, a high degree of automaticity allowed them to keep up and continue to work with a degree of speed and accuracy.

The third study found a correlation between faster reading and the ability to quickly and easily recognize and understand words.[17] This fluency was shown to improve with the ease of processing words. Additionally, the study revealed that this ability, known as automaticity with reading, has an impact on performance in mathematical processes, computing, and reading not only in middle school but also in college.

With a mastery of literacy and numeracy skills so strongly linked to success in higher-level learning, it's essential to help our children build strong foundations in these areas in their early years of learning. One theory, presented by Gordon Logan,[18] suggests that as lower-order thinking is mastered, learners are able to bypass the steps they've had to take in the past to solve a problem. Instead, they're able to retrieve answers directly from long-term memory. When solving the multiplication problem of 5x5, for example, they would bypass the need for any small calculations and automatically know the answer to be 25. A second theory, presented by Schneider and Shiffrin,[19] suggests that learners aren't bypassing steps, but rather, they're able to compute answers at a faster rate. Automaticity helps them to process each step of a problem faster and with greater accuracy. When cooking a recipe you've made hundreds of times, for example, you don't have to reference the directions, rather, you can work through each step with extreme efficiency and speed, especially compared to how long it would've taken you to complete the recipe the first time.

Regardless of which of these theories is the most accurate, both point to the value of rehearsal[20] and repetition in achieving automaticity, especially with respect to lower-order thinking. The more a child practices saying their alphabet, answers basic addition or multiplication problems, or types on a keyboard, the higher their automaticity. Rehearsal and repetition are appropriate when the learner needs to retrieve information as presented without any further elaboration or processing. This is helpful to note as we consider how to help our children build a strong foundation in reading and math.

But keep in mind, just as a child will need to develop the skill of critical thinking as they tackle more complex ideas later in life, so here too, basic learning strategies will need to evolve as our learners move through their schooling years. As subjects progressively become more weighted, our children will need to adopt the most effective learning strategies that will enable our learners to effectively move ideas from short-term memory to long-term memory and help certain processes to become automatic. These strategies will be discussed in detail in the subsequent chapters.

The key takeaway is that automaticity is important for both lower- *and* higher-order thinking; the difference is in how it is adapted. Lower-order thinking is very content-oriented and is based on the automaticity that comes from multiplication drills and alphabet recitation. Higher-order thinking requires the recognition of patterns and the ability to determine which learning strategies align with one's strengths and weaknesses. Automaticity is a powerful way to optimize learning because by automating certain learning processes, the learner is then able to manage cognitive resources in helping achieve better learning outcomes.

# RESEARCH RECAP:

- *Automaticity*, which is critical for achieving high-order thinking, can also help our children to attain **better grades** and achieve **overall improved learning**.

- When learners are able to complete tasks based on a high level of automaticity, they can produce **faster response times with less effort**, reducing their cognitive load.

- **Learning strategies will need to evolve** as students progress from lower- to higher-order thinking. Memorization or repetition is key for lower-order thinking; higher-order thinking will require adopting intentional and optimal learning strategies.

In my years of competitive swimming, I experienced two types of swimming coaches. One was highly focused on executing drills, drills, and more drills with the goal of improving my cardio capacity. The other coach focused on technical skills and improving my strokes. The emphasis of each coach was equally important and led to my overall improvement. For our learners, rehearsal and repetition of lower-level skills are the cardio that builds endurance. Elaboration and other control strategies like what happens under the training of a technical skills swimming coach help develop higher-level skills. Our learners will need both the core, basic practice to build up endurance for learning *and* the technical understanding of how to become better learners.

As with the development of any skill, the desired level of auto-maticity that is needed for both lower- and higher-order thinking will require hard work and discipline. Knowing *what* to do isn't enough. Our learners will need to apply and adopt these practices with your help, encouragement, and good modeling. Just as tun-ing into YouTube to see how to shoot a basketball correctly won't instantly turn your child into the next Steph Curry (in fact, you and your child could watch those videos a hundred times and still not reach the skill level of an NBA shooter!), it takes hours of prac-tice for knowledge to become automatic. After Curry made his famous half-court shot, many kids tried to imitate him, thinking they could automatically do what Steph did because they'd watched him do it. But Curry will explain that he practices that skill "all the time."[21] It became automatic for him after years of practice.

With consistent application of the Parental Engagement Cycle and the nurturing of your child's interest in acquiring knowledge, it's possible for the learning practices outlined in this book to become deeply ingrained in your learner's mind, even automatic. Your chil-dren will begin to shift from learning because they're told to do so to seeing the value of learning because they're internally inspired by the desire to uncover new understandings about the world around them. A lifelong love of learning will blossom with the adoption of skill sets tied to intrinsic motivation. As learning becomes self-driven, there's the added bonus that it will also be stickier, or in other words, it will linger longer in their memory. A cycle ensues as the strengthening of automatic learning skills will inevitably increase intrinsic motivation. It will also enable your child to more easily achieve flow or the "ideal state of learning," an idea that we'll discuss in further detail in the next section.

## ACTION PLAN

- With a new understanding of the value of automating lower-order thinking, what practices will you initiate to help your child establish a strong learning foundation? Jot down some ideas on how you can help your child in mastering basic skills.

- Sometimes, the practice that's required to gain automaticity over lower-order thinking can feel repetitive. Keep your child motivated by helping them see the bigger picture. Remind them that they're mastering multiplication problems in order to one day successfully conduct exciting chemistry experiments, for example.

## *Flow*

Steven Kotler, the author of *The Habit of Ferocity*, has studied extensively what makes it possible for "maverick innovators to turn science fiction ideas into science fact technology."[22] With a desire to uncover how some people are able to accomplish things that others would consider to be impossible and essentially dream the future into life, he's examined what has enabled upstart entrepreneurs such as Larry Page, Jeff Bezos, and Elon Musk to build world-changing businesses in near record time. He's considered the work of small teams and individuals who are going after grand global challenges—issues like poverty, healthcare, energy scarcity, or water scarcity—things that in the past only large corporations could tackle. What he's discovered in all these areas is a common signature thread: the state of flow. Flow is the point at which these individuals feel their best and can perform their best. Kotler defines flow further as "moments of rapt attention and total absorption." It's when you're so focused on the task at hand, everything else disappears.

Mihaly Csikszentmihalyi popularized the flow state in his book *Flow: The Psychology of Optimal Experience.*[23] Csikszentmihalyi coined the term "flow" to describe a mental state characterized by optimal performance. His interest in this concept began during his graduate studies at the University of Chicago. He remembered being intrigued by artists he would observe in their studios, so absorbed in their work that they seemed to lose touch with everything else. He was surprised by what happened when they were done: "They'd finish a work of art, and instead of enjoying it…they would put it against the wall and start a new painting. They weren't really interested in the finished painting."[24] Csikszentmihalyi observed that these artists were driven not by the final product of their work but by the complete immersion and engrossment they experienced during the creation process.

When a child is in a learning flow, they become completely absorbed in the discovery of a new skill or concept, experiencing a heightened sense of focus and engagement. During this process, there's no stress or anxiety, and they remain undistracted, simply enjoying the rhythm of learning. Flow is a state of being where a learner is simultaneously intellectually efficient, motivated, driven, and happy (happiness that is likely due to the academic progress they're making). Sounds like a good place for our children to be, doesn't it?

Artyom shares that a state of flow is absolutely necessary for him when performing difficult tasks that require his full attention. If not in a state of flow while working, he can get distracted, stop halfway through, or never finish the task. Coding a new experiment, for instance, wouldn't work without flow. Experiments require multiple steps, each of which is coded in different subsections. A change in one parameter of one subsection may or may not work with the other sections. He must constantly keep in mind all the possibilities of what could go wrong, while also thinking about how to code each new feature. The same is true with data analysis. If he's analyzing a new dataset with some distortions, missing values, or incorrectly coded variables, he'll need to clean and transform the dataset, keeping in mind the kind of format it needs to retain based on the style of test being run.

Research has found that learners who can reach flow while working or studying will achieve higher grades in school. One research study investigated the association between academic performance and a student's learning flow while completing a research paper.[25] It uncovered that students who achieved flow as they worked received higher grades on their papers. In fact, there was a significant improvement in grades for the students who reached a flow state.

Interestingly, the feeling of flow can be reinforced by success or hindered by failure, and high anxiety can actually reduce a person's ability to reach a flow state.[26] There is also a strong relationship between positivity—how positive a person feels about themselves and their ability to reach their goal—and their ability to reach a flow state. When the state of flow is leading to productivity, this can be motivating for work to continue. It increases the likelihood that the project will reach completion. On the other hand, if work isn't progressing due to challenges and difficulties experienced while trying to find a solution, it can become more difficult to maintain a state of flow.

## RESEARCH RECAP:

- Reaching *learning flow* while studying has been shown to lead to *higher grades*.
- A child's level of confidence in their ability to succeed is strongly linked to their likelihood of achieving their goal.

As learning flow predicts higher grades, it can be inferred that learners who reach this state will have higher self-awareness and self-efficacy or a stronger belief in their ability to be successful. As a result, an amazing positive cycle can ensue. The more flow experiences a learner has, the stronger their self-efficacy will become and the more positive their learning outcomes will be. As their GPA continues to go up, the learner will be encouraged to study more. Once this cycle is in place, and the more it continues, the more it will build. But keep in mind that the opposite can be true as well. With fewer flow experiences, grades may drop and a child's motivation to work hard and study will be reduced as well. It's our job as parents to do what we can to help our children to attain this optimal experience while learning. The more flow states our children can achieve, the more profound their overall learning will be. Here are some ways we can help our children to achieve learning flow:

1. **Remove distractions** - According to Csikszentmihalyi's book *Flow*, no flow is possible when the task at hand has to

compete for attention in a chaotic or noisy learning environment. Factors such as a TV, smartphone, computer, music, or other distracting sounds can keep learners from reaching flow. Simply eliminating these elements can facilitate concentration on the main priority, i.e., the learning process. If noise cannot be avoided completely, consider the use of noise-canceling headphones.

2. **Set clear goals** - Csikszentmihalyi goes on to share how clear goals are crucial to reaching flow and improving motivation. When our learners know exactly what they're working to accomplish and the process required to reach this goal has been broken down into small, achievable milestones, they will be more motivated to dive in and get started. Once they see progress happening, they will be encouraged to keep going and more likely to reach a flow state along the way.

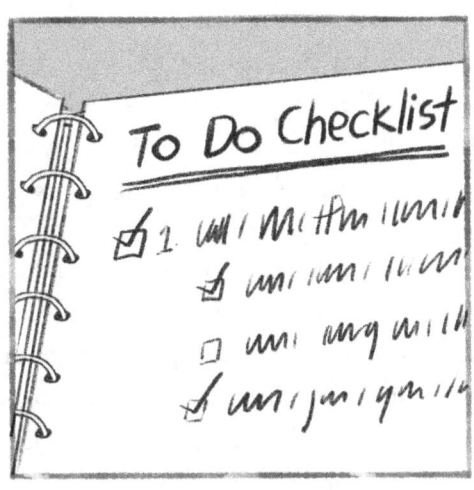

*Figure 13: A To-Do Checklist*

3. **Tap into intrinsic interests** - When learners are in flow, their motivation is fully intrinsic. External rewards are not needed to keep them going or to keep them focused. They're fully engaged in the learning process through their own initiative and desire to dig deeper and discover further. With this in mind, we can help our learner's experience flow by encouraging the pursuit of their natural interests. Their interest in a topic is likely to only grow as they understand more about it. If you're working to teach something that is not automatically of intrinsic interest, find ways to connect the subject to something that is intrinsically motivating to your learner.

4. **Identify the right challenge level** - Flow is most often achieved when a learner's skills are rightly matched to the task at hand or when a student feels well equipped to handle the project or subject before them. Csikszentmihalyi notes that "Flow happens when a person's skills are fully involved in overcoming a challenge that is just about manageable, so it acts as a magnet for learning new skills and increasing challenges." In other words, it's important to keep our tasks at an optimum difficulty level. If the learner finds the task too easy, flow can be achieved by gradually increasing the difficulty, or new skills can be learned to address extremely challenging tasks.

5. **Emphasize control** - Remind your child that they have what it takes to achieve flow and to learn the subject before them. Our children will inevitably struggle, but with our support and gentle reminders of their capacity and capability, they will come to realize success through persistence. They'll need to be constantly assured and encouraged when it comes to their own learning, especially when they're in the driver's seat.

6.  **Manage momentum** - Achieving a flow state requires momentum. In other words, one should not expect to be in a state of flow immediately once they start studying. It can take 15-20 minutes of concentrated work before one can enter a state of flow, which can last from 30 minutes to a few hours. Additionally, we can work to create an environment where learning momentum is sustained due to all these combined elements at work synergistically.

We've now established the foundation for effective learning strategies by covering the key components of motivation, beliefs, and optimization in our Learning Tree trunk. Moving forward, we'll build upon this foundation and pivot to focus specifically on the learning strategies that will help our children to be more successful and to achieve learning flow more often.

## ACTION PLAN

- Have you personally experienced a state of flow while working or learning? As you help your child to understand learning flow, consider sharing your personal experiences with them to illustrate what flow looks and feels like.

- Since flow is most often achieved when a learner is intrinsically motivated, has a high sense of control belief, or has skills aligned to the task they are working on, consider which subjects your child is intrinsically motivated to learn—encourage them to pursue these subjects **while reinforcing the conditions** for flow to occur.

- Encourage your child to be mentally immersed in their learning experiences. Prevent and remove possible distractions. Create a learning environment where your child would feel that "time flies so fast."

[1] Making Process Improvements Stick - Harvard Business Review

[2] The Ultimate Guide to Process Optimization by Shelly Madden - Wrike

[3] Wittman, J. "The Forgetting Curve." California State University, Stanislaus (2018).

[4] van der Schuur, W. A., Baumgartner, S. E., Sumter, S. R., and Valkenburg, P. M. (2015). „The consequences of media multitasking for youth: A review." *Computers in Human Behavior* 53, 204-215.

[5] Judd, Terry. "Making sense of multitasking: Key behaviors." *Computers & Education* 63 (2013): 358-367.

[6] Kokoç, Mehmet. "The mediating role of attention control in the link between multitasking with social media and academic performances among adolescents." *Scandinavian Journal of Psychology* 62, no. 4 (2021): 493-501.

[7] van der Schuur, Winneke A., Susanne E. Baumgartner, Sindy R. Sumter, and Patti M. Valkenburg. "Exploring the long-term relationship between academic-media multitasking and adolescents' academic achievement." *New Media & Society* 22, no. 1 (2020): 140-158.

[8] Cooper, Harris, Barbara Nye, Kelly Charlton, James Lindsay, and Scott Greathouse. "The effects of summer vacation on achievement test scores: A narrative and meta-analytic review." *Review of Educational Research* 66, no. 3 (1996): 227-268.

[9] Alexander, Karl L., Doris R. Entwisle, and Linda Steffel Olson. "Lasting consequences of the summer learning gap." *American Sociological Review* 72, no. 2 (2007): 167-180.

[10] Kuhfeld, Megan. "Surprising new evidence on summer learning loss." *Phi Delta Kappan* 101, no. 1 (2019): 25-29.

[11] The secret strength that fuels Stephen Curry and the Golden State Warriors - ESPN.com

[12] Wittman, J. "The Forgetting Curve." California State University, Stanislaus (2018).

[13] The Pomodoro Technique - Francesco Cirillo https://francescocirillo.com/products/the-pomodoro-technique

[14] Choe, Danbi. "Parents' and adolescents' perceptions of parental support as predictors of adolescents' academic achievement and self-regulated learning." *Children and Youth Services Review* 116 (2020): 105172.

[15] Williamson, Vickie M., Deborah Rush Walker, Eric Chuu, Susan Broadway, Blain Mamiya, Cynthia B. Powell, G. Robert Shelton, Rebecca Weber, Alan R. Dabney, and Diana Mason. "Impact of basic arithmetic skills on success in first-semester general chemistry." *Chemistry Education Research and Practice* 21, no. 1 (2020): 51-61.

[16] Wang, Qian, Yi Ding, and Qiong Yu. "Working memory load and automaticity in relation to problem-solving in college engineering students." *Journal of Engineering Education* 107, no. 4 (2018): 636-655.

[17] Roembke, Tanja C., Eliot Hazeltine, Deborah K. Reed, and Bob McMurray. "Automaticity as an independent trait in predicting reading outcomes in middle-school." *Developmental Psychology* 57, no. 3 (2021): 361.

[18] Logan, Gordon D. "Automaticity, resources, and memory: Theoretical controversies and practical implications." *Human Factors* 30, no. 5 (1988): 583-598.

[19] Schneider, Walter, and Richard M. Shiffrin. "Controlled and automatic human information processing: I. Detection, search, and attention." *Psychological Review* 84, no. 1 (1977): 1.

[20] Liu, Qimeng, Xiaofeng Du, Shuxin Zhao, Jian Liu, and Jinfa Cai. "The role of memorization in students' self-reported mathematics learning: a large-scale study of Chinese eighth-grade students." *Asia Pacific Education Review* 20, no. 3 (2019): 361-374.

[21] Warriors' Steph Curry breaks down art of draining half-court shots. https://www.nbcsports.com/bayarea/warriors/warriors-steph-curry-breaks-down-art-draining-half-court-shots

[22] How to Get into the Flow State by Steven Kotler - https://www.youtube.com/watch?v=XG_hNZ5T4nY

[23] *Flow*, Harper Collins Publishers - https://www.harpercollins.com/products/flow-mihaly-csikszentmihalyi

[24] Claremont Graduate University - https://www.cgu.edu/people/mihaly-csikszentmihalyi/

[25] Sumaya, Isabel C., and Emily Darling. "Procrastination, flow, and academic performance in real-time using the experience sampling method." *Journal of Genetic Psychology* 179, no. 3 (2018): 123-131.

[26] Wu, Renshuang, Eugene Scott Huebner, Jianhua Zhou, and Lili Tian. "Relations among positivity, positive affect in school, and learning flow in elementary school students: A longitudinal mediation model." *British Journal of Educational Psychology* 91, no. 4 (2021): 1310-1332.

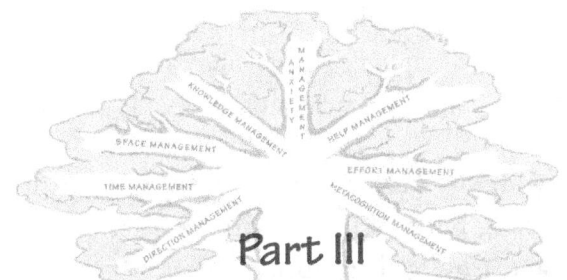

# Part III
# LEARNING STRATEGY MANAGEMENT
## The Tree Branches

## Introduction to Learning Strategy Management

Several years ago, I set a goal to become more fit. I knew I needed a big challenge to push me and keep me motivated, and so I set my sights on swimming across the English Channel. I knew a project of this magnitude—to train to swim more than 18 miles in cold, open water—would help me reach my fitness goal. I recognized I would have to put in hours of practice every week, spend extra time with swimming coaches, and master new skills and techniques along the way. With an appreciation for the health benefits that can result from regular exercise and my love for learning new things, I relished the enormity of the task before me.

From my years working in education and encouraging students to chase their dreams, I recognize the benefits of setting goals. In my case, not only would my swim training help me achieve a higher level of fitness, but the new strategies I would learn and adopt in order to accomplish such a feat would be valuable to me from a personal perspective, as well as an athletic one. I would develop new levels of self-discipline and mental strength, qualities that would be transferable to other areas of my life.

As our children grow and develop, they too will benefit from the practice of setting big goals for themselves—goals that will challenge them and require them to learn new skills. Endless learning opportunities will arise throughout the life of our children, and they will have the option of either completing the minimum requirements to get by or embracing the fullness of what these new experiences have to offer. As parents, we are in a wonderful position to open the eyes of our children to the possibilities of learning. When they believe they can develop new talents through hard work and effort and that they can become more dynamic, vibrant versions of themselves in the process, they will come to perceive the holistic value of learning new skills. They will see that it's not just about the skill itself. It's about the added benefits that can come from challenging oneself to do, learn, and accomplish things that are hard and outside our comfort zones.

This recognition, that the skills we acquire in one area of life will hold value in another, can be an important lesson to learn. We all want our children to develop attitudes and traits that will make them stronger, more capable adults—skills such as the ability to work well with others, not to give up when things get hard, to be an encourager to those around them, and to maintain a good work ethic. What we may not consider is that these skills can be developed in a number of ways, and they are transferable once they're adopted.

Consider then, with every activity your child agrees to pursue, what other life skills are also being learned along the way and how are they transferrable? As you open their eyes to the value of setting big goals, help them to also see how the pursuit of these goals will contribute to something bigger—including their overall growth and personal development. Guide them in understanding the value of learning and how time spent in practice or in pursuing new, challenging activities is never wasted. With this perspective, even if you dedicate a lot of time to helping your child develop a skill (swimming, for instance), if they give it up later in life (in college or as an adult), it can still be considered time well spent. The greater goal is for them to develop a love for learning, to push them to try new things with a belief in their ability to grow, and to help them develop life skills that are valuable and transferable to other areas of their life.

In the chapters to come, we'll introduce eight areas of learning strategy management, including direction, time, space, knowledge, anxiety, help, effort, and metacognition management. It will be helpful to recognize how to connect and apply these strategies to every area of your child's life, so they can see the applicability of these strategies in their overall improvement and development as a person. While each of these strategies has its own specific purpose, they also support each other and are interconnected. The regular application of these strategies will help them in their academic pursuits as well as in their athletic and artistic endeavors.

While each of these strategies is uniquely important to your child's development to become the wisest learner, the key to success will come through your ability to help them identify which strategies to use based on the opportunity before them. As we present these strategies, we'll make suggestions (based on research) on how to achieve the best outcomes based on the situation and the unique needs of your child. Research studies, which we will cover in detail in the following pages, show that each of these learning strategies when applied singularly cannot predict a higher GPA but when applied together can produce significant results. The consideration of all of them, working together, is important.

The individual nature of each child's learning process must also be kept in mind. With all the ideas we present, it's helpful to remember that each child is unique. Only through trial and error will you truly determine what works best for your child. Similarly, if you have multiple children, the same strategies won't work for every child. Our statistics and research can provide guidance, but we encourage you not to overlook what you know to be true about your child. For best results, pair your keen parental instincts with our recommended learning strategies in ways that are most helpful for *your* unique child.

To help you digest and better understand all eight strategies, we've divided them into three groups based on which part of the learning process they serve.

1. **Pre-learning** will be discussed in Chapters 7-9 and 14, which includes direction, time, and space management. This is where we address how to help your child develop skills that will set them up for success.

2. **In-learning** will be covered in Chapters 10-14 and includes knowledge, anxiety, help, and effort management. Here we'll address skills that can improve learning while it's happening.

3. **Post-learning** will be addressed in Chapter 14, which covers metacognition management. We'll discuss how your child can reflect on their learning process and pivot to improve.

As your children apply these strategies, they will experience lower cognitive load, increased automaticity, and a more regular occurrence of flow while learning. As a result, they'll become stronger students who are more capable of higher-level learning. Your children will earn better test scores, maintain a higher GPA, and learn more material at a faster rate.

While this is all very exciting, don't press the expectation of immediate results. The development of good learning skills and strategies will take time. Consider the story of the boy who encountered a cocoon and, with his childlike innocence, thought he could speed up the caterpillar's metamorphosis. He poked and prodded at the cocoon, thinking all the caterpillar needed was someone to help him out. In reality, what the caterpillar needed most of all was time and the opportunity for his metamorphosis to naturally occur.[1]

*Figure 14: A Butterfly Emerging From Its Cocoon*

Similarly, there will be plenty of instances where your child's learning development cannot be forced or unnaturally advanced. Give your learner time and space to grow. As you do, keep in mind that as your children continue to apply regular effort toward developing these skills, their work *will* pay off over time. With patience and regular practice, the desired result will be achieved. With that in mind, let's begin our discussion of the first strategy—direction management.

---

[1] The Boy and the Butterfly: The Struggle Makes Us Stronger - https://www.lifeandwhim.com/first-moments-blog/2018/the-struggle-makes-you-stronger

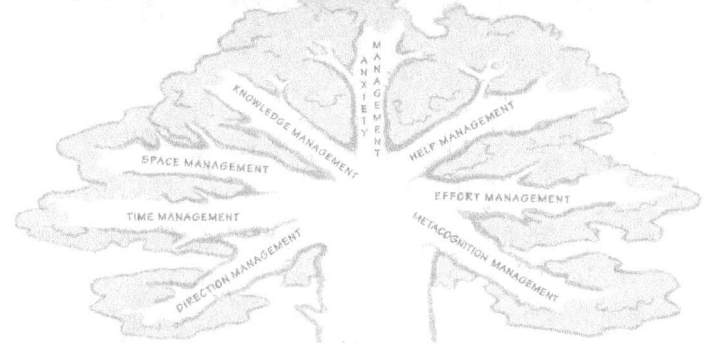

# CHAPTER 7

# DIRECTION MANAGEMENT

Those of us who were drivers before the age of the internet and smartphones will remember what it was like to study a paper map or plot our course of direction *before* leaving for a new destination. If we wanted to know how to get somewhere, we needed clear directions—step-by-step notes of where to turn, what roadside markers to look for, and a reasonable estimation of how long it would take us to get there.

In 2005, all of that changed. Google Maps was launched as a new solution to help people "get from point A to point B."[1] Today, with a cursory glance at the map on your phone, you can determine how long a trip will take, how much traffic to expect, and an estimated time of arrival. The way we travel has been irrevocably altered; today, more than one billion people worldwide use Google Maps every month.

While the way we access directions may have changed, our dependency on reliable maps and step-by-step driving instructions has never faded. We now rely more on our phones to provide the guidance we need, but should we ever drive through a dead spot, lose a phone signal, or run out of battery, we'll want to have a backup paper map close by. The reality is that without good directions—be they digital or analog—we'd all be lost.

In much the same way, every child needs a clear understanding of where they're headed as they embark on their learning journey. A child's ability to set specific, quantifiable goals regarding their learning is what we refer to as direction management. Their ability to set good, meaningful goals will determine how successful they'll be in reaching those goals. Without good direction management—including a precise destination in mind and a detailed list of the steps they will follow to get there—a learner can lose their motivation, become disoriented, or give up before they finish.

As part of my training to cross the English Channel, I signed up for a six-mile open-water race. Sighting skills, or the ability to keep track of the direction in which you're headed, are important for open-water swimming. Without the lanes and markers of a swimming pool, it can be easy to lose your way and head in the wrong direction. At this point in my training, I had not yet mastered this ability. But thankfully, with this race, I was promised that a guide would accompany each swimmer. So while this would be a big challenge, I was comforted by the idea of having a companion to keep me from swimming off course.

The night before the race, there was a big storm and when I showed up at the starting line, I saw all the markers and buoys that should've marked the path had been blown out of place by the storm's high winds. Worst of all, without explanation, the promised guide was nowhere to be found. I hated the idea of dropping out, so even though I was reluctant to, I decided to go ahead with the race. Unfortunately, as the race went on without markers or guides to direct my path, I found myself swimming in circles. More than once, I ended up back at the starting line, having taken a wrong turn. I finally managed to finish the race, but I was in last place and my six-mile race had turned into seven and a half. Without clear directions or a guide to lead the way, I'd been forced to work harder than I needed to just to finish.

Long-distance swimmer Florence Chadwick[2] faced similar difficulties as she attempted to be the first woman to swim the 26 miles between Catalina Island and Palos Verde on the California coast. Approximately 15 hours into her swimming journey, she encountered a dense fog. She could hardly see the boats riding alongside her. She kept swimming for another hour but became discouraged, with her physical exhaustion overpowering her will. She called it quits before reaching the shore. Once in her rescue boat, she could finally see that she was only a mile away from her destination. She was so close! At a news conference the next day, Florence shared, "All I could see was the fog.… I think if I could have seen the shore, I would have made it."

The situation is much the same for our children with their learning development—without goals and a road map to guide them, they can drift off course. Conversely, with a clear destination in mind, they are more likely to stick to their plans and accomplish their goals. Strong goal-setting is a key part of our pre-learning discussion, as your child will have a better chance of succeeding in their academic development if they have a clear idea of what they are aiming to achieve. Research has shown that detailed, well-written goals can result in stronger academic performance;[3, 4] the more specific the goals, the greater the student's likelihood to reach them. Additionally, good goal-setting can indirectly help a learner in other ways. For example, as they see their goal-setting leading to higher grades, their motivation and self-efficacy will increase as well.[5]

Research also points out that if goal-setting is going to be effective, children need to be highly **involved** in the process. Preferably, they will take the initiative to set their own goals. If children feel a sense of ownership over their goals, they are more likely to take responsibility for what needs to be done to reach those goals. That responsibility can drive performance and lead them to dedicate more time and effort to their work. In the next section, we'll discuss some specific ways parents can encourage good goal-setting behavior in their children.

## RESEARCH RECAP:

- When learners *write down their goals*—and when the goal is well written, detailed, and clear—they are more likely to reach their goal and *find overall academic success*.

- *Success leads to more success*—as students see their goals pay off in the form of higher grades, this will lead to an increase in motivation and self-efficacy too.

- Learners must feel *personal ownership* over their goals before they will take responsibility to put in the work necessary to reach them.

Let's consider three specific ways we can help our children to focus and hone in on the right goals for their learning journey:

1. **Framing** - This is when a learner sets parameters around their goal to make it more specific and quantifiable. A child needs their goals to be very clear and precise; any confusion can muddy the waters about what they are trying to achieve. They also need specific targets that can be easily measured. This means, rather than saying "do your best" or "be the best version of yourself," tell your child specifically what it looks like when they do their best or how they can be the best version of themselves. If a goal is not specific enough, it's hard to measure. If the goal is to get an A+ or a B-, that is measurable and specific and will help your child to see exactly what they are aiming for.

   With framing, it's helpful to keep in mind that there's more than one way to set a goal and the method used can alter the results. When I work out using an elliptical machine, for example, I experience different results based on the kind of goal I set. Sometimes, I set a time goal to work out for an hour. Other times, I set a distance goal or an exertion goal. When the aim is to keep going for a specific time period, my final distance may be shorter, as I may slow down when I get tired. By contrast, when trying to achieve a specific distance, I may reach that distance in a shorter amount of time because I know I can get there faster if I push myself harder. When tracking my heart rate, I will optimize my workout based on the elevation I want to see in my heart rate. In each case, the results are different.

   For our learners, it's important for them to understand this distinction about goals—not all goals are the same and the kind of goal they set can produce different behaviors and outcomes. For instance, they can establish immediate or future goals or a mix of the two. Our learners can set goals for the month or year ahead, as well as lifelong goals about what they want to accomplish. A larger, long-term goal may need to be broken down into smaller goals to make the overall achievement more attainable.

A commonly used technique for structuring goals and dividing them into manageable components is the S.M.A.R.T.[6] method—formulating a specific, measurable, achievable, relevant, and time-bound goal. The S.M.A.R.T. goal concept was conceived by George Doran, Arthur Miller, and James Cunningham in their 1981 paper titled "There's a S.M.A.R.T. way to write management goals and objectives." This is how S.M.A.R.T. goals can aid in achieving educational objectives:

Here's how S.M.A.R.T. goals can be helpful for reaching learning goals:

- **Specific** - The more concrete a plan a child has about how they will reach their proposed end result, the more likely they will be to get there. Referencing back to our story about driving directions, the more detail a driver has, the better equipped they will be to reach their destination without missing a turn or passing a key landmark. If you know what's coming, you can be better prepared. Similarly, specific, detailed goals will break down the process in a way that feels more manageable, all while prepping your learner, as much as possible, for what's to come.

- **Measurable** - When your child can tangibly track their progress, they'll be more likely to stay motivated, even if they hit a speed bump along the way. Measurements can help them to remember where they started and identify how much progress they've made. With a bigger goal, it can be helpful to have smaller increments of measurement that will help you reach the larger goal, as well as a clear marker of when the goal has been fully attained.

- **Attainable** - If a goal doesn't feel possible, this can have adverse effects on a learner, frustrating them and causing a loss of momentum. Conversely, a dream or plan that's too easy will lack effectiveness. There's a sweet spot to be found in goals that challenge our learners just enough so they feel they have to work hard to see results, all while not demoralizing or overwhelming them.

- **Relevant** - The key here is that a child feels their goal is important and needed, particularly to them. They need to perceive the value of what they are working to accomplish and have a sense of purpose for their effort.

- **Time-bound** - It's helpful to set a reasonable timeframe for when a goal will be completed. Many children thrive when they have clearly set expectations, they know how long they will be working to reach each step of a process, and they have a promising estimation of when their project will be done. If there's no target stopping point, anyone, particularly children, can lose their drive to keep going.

By ensuring a goal meets each of these five criteria, a learner will more likely have the focus, motivation, and clarity they need to achieve their goal. For our learners, their goals can be the much-needed fuel that will keep them working hard and reaching for success.

2.  **Planning** - This refers to the road map for how a goal will be achieved. It's the step-by-step outline for how your learner will get from where they are now to where they want to be when they reach their goal. But it's a little bit more than *just* a plan.

    In the business world, the development of a strategic plan is something often done annually and involves the leadership of a company coming together to define its vision for the future as well as the organization's goals and objectives. Similarly, while our children's version of their strategic plan should include a detailed listing of their goals and how they plan to reach them, it can be helpful for them to also include their vision for who they want to be in the future. In essence, this can be their opportunity to define *why* they want to reach the goals they've identified. At a future point, when they get discouraged or face challenges, it will likely be their bigger vision, their "why," that draws them back on track and keeps them motivated.

3.  **Orientation** - Orientation is about knowing the "position or status" of a learner during the learning process. It's a periodic checkpoint to determine one's distance and trajectory from the set goal. For example, a parent might find his child struggling to learn certain math concepts despite the child's best efforts and even after proper framing. Orientation will allow the parent to determine possible causes, such as the child might not

have adequately mastered certain foundational concepts, the child's interest is veering away as a result of his attention being diverted toward an online game he's playing with friends over the weekend, or the child is having anxiety attacks due to certain pressures. Wherever the source might be, it's important for parents to have a clear understanding of their child's position or orientation as they're learning.

As parents, we must help our children orient their plans toward completing tasks that will leave them feeling stronger or that provide them with a sense of purpose. When working toward something they believe in, they'll be more driven to give the project their best effort and less likely to quit. Mark Zuckerberg, founder and CEO of Facebook, has shared how early on, when the company was going through a difficult season, he was encouraged to reconnect with what he believed to be the mission of the company. To do so, he traveled for almost a month "seeing people and seeing how people connected."[8] Zuckerberg shares that his interactions allowed him to capture a vision of how important it was for everyone in the world to connect with each other. He recognized that Facebook could be the platform through which such a connection could happen. This vision reinforced his belief in the work he was doing and helped him to push through the hard times they were facing.

With constant practice, orientation can be a great ally. It will be quite useful, especially during times of uncertainty or struggle. Consider the story of Olympic swimmer Michael Phelps[7] who, in 2008, had to swim blind for 175 meters out of a 200-meter race. His goggles were so full of water that he couldn't see a thing, yet he still won gold and broke the world record. His story illustrates how with the right orientation and an identifiable, clear goal, it's possible overcome the toughest of setbacks and uncertainties.

With the evident value to be gained from strong directional management skills, here are some ways you can help your child develop this skill:

1. **Engage their writing interests:** An article from the University of Arizona[9] on the importance of writing well shares that "If your writing is not fully developed, it could indicate that you have not fully matured your thoughts. Improving your writing skills will improve the way you think about your topic and help you explain or discuss it with others." The discipline of putting one's thoughts on paper can lead to a more well-thought-out, complete, and detailed idea. Writing forces us to clarify our thoughts and helps us to think through the details involved with a proposed plan. Additionally, as stated earlier, goals that have been written down are more likely to result in a strong academic performance. In fact, the more effectively a child can present their ideas in writing, the more likely they are to succeed in reaching a learning goal.

   By encouraging your child to sit down and write out their goals and plans, you are setting them up for a greater chance of success. At first, and especially with younger learners, it will be important for you to help them through this process. You can do this by reading their drafts and providing feedback on how to more clearly express their thoughts. Once their goals are documented, be sure to save what they've written in a place you can all remember, so they can refer back to it as they progress toward their achievement.

2. **Ensure the goals are their own:** Eli Straw, founder of Success Starts Within,[10] writes, "Taking personal responsibility for our lives is very important to our success and overall well-being. When we set goals, we are giving ourselves something to work for. The goal is our own making, which means accomplishing it will be by our own result." A child must feel ownership over their goals if they're going to engage and maintain their drive to work toward them.

Artyom shares that when his son was in first grade, his teacher set goals for each student. The students would have to sign and agree to complete the goals during the school year. Unfortunately, since the teacher set these goals, his son lacked clarity on what he'd agreed to, and he never felt a personal connection to the goal. He did what the teacher asked of him, but he wasn't incentivized to own the goal and only felt frustration toward the assignment.

A goal that lacks personal attachment and ownership is doomed to fail. As you encourage your child to set goals, be sure the goals are *their* goals and not yours. Help them to identify learning achievements that uniquely interest them and then guide them in setting small steps and bigger milestones that will help them to accomplish their dream. If it's ultimately *their* dream, you'll be able to remind them of that when they struggle and help them to reconnect with their initial interest in reaching the goal.

Additionally, a common concern we've heard from parents is how to handle when children are fickle, especially when they struggle to stick with a goal, even if they set it for themselves. Based on her experience as an educator and assistant principal, Primal Dhillon[11] writes that autonomous goal-setting "will instill awareness in children of their own agency." She also notes that "ownership leads to involvement." With those ideas in mind, consider these strategies for helping your children stick to their goals:

- **Prioritization:** Support their efforts to focus on what they deem important. By setting goals based on what they value most, our children will be more naturally inclined to stick with them. Encourage them to list the two or three things that matter most. Use that list as a launching pad for goal-setting. Based on the Pareto 80/20 principle,[12] which states that for many outcomes, roughly 80% of consequences come from 20% of causes, it will be helpful to identify the 20% that should be done in a day, week, or month that will make the most impact in terms of achieving 80% of their goals.

- **Prevention:** Plan ahead with a premortem to help your child identify and anticipate barriers to their success. Discuss ways they can overcome or remove them. Ask questions such as "What do you think your biggest distraction will be?" or "How do you plan on overcoming that?"

- **Participation:** Collaborate with your child to establish a reward system that will encourage success. Also, it's helpful to praise effort instead of outcomes. Say, "I think you worked very hard to reach your goal. Your effort is very motivating!"

Dhillon also encourages parents to model behavior that demonstrates what it looks like to stick to a commitment. If you set a goal for yourself, follow through on it. Treat your own tasks with the respect you hope to see from them. Parents can essentially be influence agents when it comes to their children's goals. The younger the child, the deeper the influence level. For example, when parents expose their children to sports or hobbies, there'll be a higher chance of their child developing goals related to those activities. Exposing children to certain people can also have the same effect. Regular exposure to talented musicians, for instance, can influence a child's interest in pursuing a musical goal.

3. **Encourage them to develop a strategic plan and vision:** Just as a strategic plan can help an entire business operation to rally around a united idea and vision for the future, providing a framework and clear guidelines for how to work together, a strategic plan and vision can provide our learners with boundaries and a specific road map to follow, solidifying what needs to be done to reach their goals. Helping your learner to set a vision for who they want to become will feed their intrinsic motivation. They will be able to identify the reason for their work and be more personally tied to the project.

A strategic plan will need to include short-term steps to reach a long-term goal. Encourage them to think through the minutiae of each step and to include details about their plans that will be easy to follow and remember. The short-term steps will provide your child with small wins that will motivate them and their progress. Each small win should be celebrated, as it's the collective amassing of these mini goals that will eventually lead to them reaching their bigger, ultimate goal.

Artyom shares that when his son's school set the goal for him to improve his reading speed and comprehension, they worked together to break that big goal down into these smaller steps:

- His son would read aloud to either Artyom or his wife for 15 minutes every day. This would be additional reading outside of their son's assigned homework.

- His son would choose the book to ensure it was a text he was interested in.

- They would continue this practice for three months and then reevaluate his reading fluency after that period of time.

Tangible rewards, which can shift the focus to extrinsic motivation, were not needed to keep him going. Rather, the celebrations he received for sticking to his goals were verbal praises from Artyom and his wife. Through their positive attitude and encouragement, they helped him to stay focused by pointing out improvements in his reading ability.

A good strategic plan will be quantifiable. Help your learner to identify how they will know when they've completed each step and set trackable markers for success. The specificity of their measurements will provide clarity to help them to visualize their end game and will also ensure they know when they've achieved a successful result.

Consider using a sample sheet, such as the one provided in Figure 15, to help your child detail steps to their strategic plan in a way that follows the S.M.A.R.T. goal-setting system. Using a sheet like this one, your child can list their plans and corresponding actions along with specific dates for when they will complete the actions. This will help them to create measurable milestones for achieving their goals.

# SMART GOALS SHEET

**SPECIFIC**

**MEASURABLE**

**ATTAINABLE**

**RELEVANT**

**TIME**

*Figure 15: SMART Goals Sheet*

# ACTION PLAN

- Set aside time for you and your child to dream about the future. Share your long-term vision for yourself and your family with them and help your child think about their future self too. Dreaming about who they want to become will inform the kinds of goals they need to set to get there.

- Spend some time reflecting on your own experiences with goal-setting. Identify times when you have set goals and worked hard to achieve them. Share these stories with your child as you encourage them to set goals for themself. If goal-setting is never something you've personally tried, then consider setting a new goal for yourself along with your child—it can be something you both experience together!

---

[1] A look back at 15 years of mapping the world, Elizabeth Reid, https://blog.google/products/maps/look-back-15-years-mapping-world/

[2] Florence Chadwick, https://biography.yourdictionary.com/florence-chadwick

[3] Schippers, Michaéla C., Dominique Morisano, Edwin A. Locke, Ad WA Scheepers, Gary P. Latham, and Elisabeth M. de Jong. "Writing about personal goals and plans regardless of goal type boosts academic performance." *Contemporary Educational Psychology* 60 (2020): 101823.

[4] Dotson, Ronnie. "Goal setting to increase student academic performance." *Journal of School Administration Research and Development* 1, no. 1 (2016): 45-46.

[5] Sides, Jacklyne D., and Joshua A. Cuevas. "Effect of goal setting for motivation, self-efficacy, and performance in elementary mathematics." *International Journal of Instruction* 13, no. 4 (2020): 1-16.

[6] Setting Goals, https://cce.bard.edu/files/Setting-Goals.pdf

[7] "My Goggles Filled Up With Water"- Michael Phelps Swam Blind for Over 175m to Achieve One of His Biggest Career Achievement, https://www.essentiallysports.com/us-sports-news-swimming-news-my-goggles-filled-up-with-water-michael-phelps-swam-blind-for-over-175m-to-achieve-one-of-his-biggest-career-achievement/

[8] A story of the Mystic Neem Karoli Baba and How He inspired Steve Jobs and Zuckerberg, https://metrosaga.com/mystic-neem-karoli-baba/

[9] The Importance of Writing Well & How to Grow as a Writer, https://www.uagc.edu/blog/the-importance-of-writing-well-how-to-grow-as-a-writer

[10] Importance of Goal Setting, https://www.successstartswithin.com/blog/importance-of-goal-setting

[11] The Case Against Setting Goals for Children, https://medium.com/the-ascent/the-case-against-setting-goals-for-children-243a58411542

[12] Pareto Principle (The 80-20 Rule), https://www.simplypsychology.org/pareto-principle.html

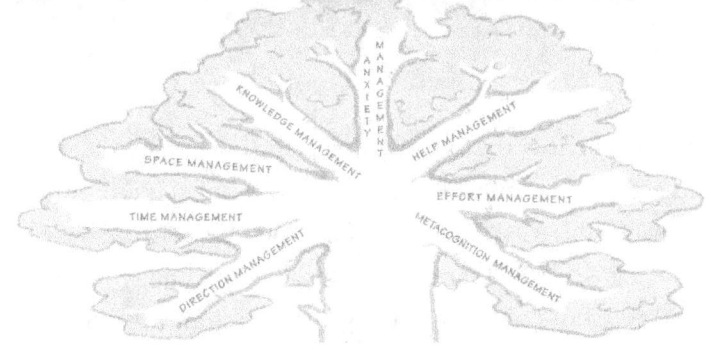

# CHAPTER 8

# TIME MANAGEMENT

If you've ever taken a trip to Disney World or Disneyland, you know what I mean when I say that a great deal of planning goes into this vacation. While advanced preparation is a must for almost any form of family travel, particularly when young children are involved, a trip to Disney requires a whole new level of planning. Not only should you think through which parks you want to visit each day, but if you hope to enjoy the rides, you must sign up weeks in advance for the right tickets to get a step ahead in the lines. Early risers will want to arrive as soon as the gates open for a chance to walk through the parks with fewer people around. Night owls looking to catch a fireworks show will want to coordinate some time back in their rooms for a rest or a break at the pool so their family has the energy they need to head back to the park after dark. Good planning skills and, as we like to call it, proper time management are a must for families hoping to make the most out of this experience.

Time management is the ability to plot out how you want or need to spend a period of time. While this can certainly pertain to elaborate trip planning, it's more commonly experienced in regular day-to-day life scheduling. Planning in advance for how you want to progress throughout a day with the goal of reaching a specific point in a project by dinnertime requires one to estimate how long it will take to complete their various tasks or activities.

As this idea relates to our children and their learning experience, time management means having the ability to estimate how much time it will take to learn something. Our learners must master this skill in order to determine how to make the most of a series of hours of study or how to calculate the amount of time it will take them to complete a homework assignment. As they plot a course through their studies, they'll want to consider how much new information they need to cover during a set study session, how deep they want to dive into a topic, and how to manage their time so they'll be adequately prepared for their next exam or paper.

Many children who experienced online schooling during the COVID pandemic felt the need for time management most acutely when asynchronous learning became a required part of their homeschool experience. Without the structured schedule of the schoolroom, these students were required to manage parts of their learning time on their own, with the expectation that they would complete and turn in assignments by a certain deadline. For many families, this was a new and challenging experience that necessitated more focus than before on establishing good at-home time management patterns.

Even as we've moved past that short but tenuous season of intense at-home learning, many lessons learned in that time have stuck with us, including the value of establishing good rhythms around managing our time. Research supports the value of good time management as well. A study by Britton and Tesser[1] found that good time management skills were a better predictor of long-term academic success than a student's scores on their SAT test. While tests measuring aptitude tend to be strong predictors of success, this study demonstrates that when a learner determines how to manage their time in a way that is productive and effective, they can still come out ahead academically, as session after session of well-spent study will result in a positive cumulative effect over time. This is one of the reasons we listed time management in this pre-learning portion of our discussion on strategies, as the development of this skill will most certainly set your child up for academic success throughout their life.

Two additional studies by Valle[2, 3] considered how time management influences academic performance. The first found academic achievement to be positively associated with the amount of homework a learner completed—the more homework completed, the better the child's GPA. Digging into this idea a bit deeper, we see that the better a learner is at planning and effectively managing their time while doing their homework (so that homework time is focused, goal-oriented, and less likely derailed by distractions), the more work they will be able to complete. This regular, productive study time results in higher GPAs.

The second study by Valle found that fast learners and hardworking students alike, when applying good time management skills, experience higher academic achievement. It was concluded that if a child needs more time to learn in order to fully master a subject and they have good time management skills (meaning, they're able to carve out time for more productive study), this, in turn, leads to better grades. These learners are able to budget their time according to their academic needs in order to meet their goals.

While it's clear from these studies how important it is for a child to discern how to effectively spend their study time, there's another key aspect of time management that shouldn't be overlooked. For learners of all ages, periods of rest and recovery *between* learning sessions are just as vital as the study time itself. Particularly for long-term memory and retention, our learners' minds need the chance to pause, reflect, and evaluate a new idea before the complete ingestion of that idea can take place. With this in mind, consider these three Rs of time management, which we believe can lead to an optimal learning experience:

- **Routine:** Good time management doesn't always equate to more time spent working. Rather, with good routines, more can be accomplished in each session of study. With focused, regular patterns of study time, learners will become more familiar with the amount of time needed to accomplish a learning task and, as a result, become better at managing their time.

  Additionally, establishing a routine involves maintaining a good rhythm for how to complete an activity. For example, when I was training for open-water swimming, one of my coaches taught me to make sure my legs were constantly moving, even as I was trying to focus on my arm strokes. She mentioned that sustaining a rhythm, whether two-beat, four-beat, or six-beat, will help me develop muscle memory to ensure that my legs are constantly kicking. It's almost like having background music playing as I work on my swimming technique during drills.

Learning routines for children can have the same effect as my leg movements did for my swimming. For this reason, I encourage you to monitor, encourage, and explain to your children the importance of having established routines. When they're tempted to take a shortcut, such as skipping or shortening a study session or attempting a faster but less effective learning strategy, their routines will help to keep them on track. Routines reduce the inner struggle of whether or not to go through the learning motion, rather their dedication to their routine will keep them on the path to reaching their goals.

- **Reflection:** In our hurried pace of life, it's common for us to rush from one thing to the next, simply in an effort to keep up. But if we want our children to experience deep, lasting learning, they will need time to pause and contemplate everything their minds are taking in. Only with periods of reflection can a learner truly consider the complexities of a science experiment or wonder at the way a new book is unfolding.

These reflection times may not happen without encouragement from you, so make time and space for this to occur. Prompt your child to think about something they've just learned by asking them questions about the new information. Aim to keep this discussion conversational; the less it feels like a formal Q&A session, the better. Talk them through the strengths and weaknesses of a new idea or encourage critical thought by offering a differing opinion on the subject. Encourage them to write down their ideas and feelings about a newly learned topic as well. Your guidance will model for them how to reflect on their own in the future.

- **Rest:** Young, developing brains need time to process everything they've learned throughout the day. Sleep provides essential space and time for learners to ingest what they're studying and reenergize for the next session. Additionally, establishing a sleep routine can lower a student's cognitive load by giving the brain time to rest and process what they've just seen and heard.

Numerous research studies have illustrated the connection between a well-rested mind and academic achievement. One study by Curcio[4] considered the sleep patterns and daytime functioning of high school students, finding that students with higher grades reported more total sleep and earlier bedtimes on school nights. A second study by Stefansdottir[5] showed that inconsistent sleep duration had a negative effect on exam performance. The same negative effect was found for students with late bedtimes—the later they went to bed, the worse they performed. A third study by Seoane[6] had similar findings, with poor sleep quality and daytime sleepiness having a negative impact on students' academic performance.

It's important to note that rest doesn't just pertain to sleep. In fact, research[7, 8] highlights several other valuable ways our bodies can take a break from study time, including mental rest periods or short bursts of activity. A 20-minute break of unstructured time away from one's studies can result in increased rigor when returning to work. Breaks that are coupled with physical exercise and some relaxation were shown to improve rigor *and* reduce later fatigue.

The key takeaway from these studies is that a good sleep routine, consistent periods of mental rest, and even breaks for physical activity are essential for our learners. As we've stated before, modeling from you, first, is key. Show your child how you prioritize sleep, take breaks, and rest mentally from work. They will be more inclined to follow your lead.

## *RESEARCH RECAP:*

- *Good time management will result in higher academic achievement.* In fact, good time management skills can be a better predictor of long-term academic success, even more so than SAT scores.

- Better *planning* and effective *management of homework time* will result in a *higher GPA.*

- *Regular rest will lead to more productive study sessions.* A good sleep routine, periods of mental rest, and breaks for physical activity are essential for our learners.

To help your child understand the value of good time management, it can be beneficial to discuss with them the idea of trade-offs. When they make a choice to spend their time in one way, this keeps them from being able to do other things. Their choices ultimately come down to what they value. The activities of higher importance to them will take precedence over activities they deem less valuable. They'll have to develop a good sense of the importance of their schoolwork, likely based on the goal-setting we discussed in the last chapter, in order to prioritize study time. With their values aligned with their goals, they'll be more interested in structuring their time in a way that allows them to achieve their goals.

NBA basketball player Ray Allen provides a great example of how it can pay off to prioritize good, productive routines in order to reach a goal. Allen, who is widely considered one of the greatest three-point shooters of all time (in my opinion, second only to Steph Curry), cites his dedication to his routine as the secret to his success. Allen shares that "there were countless mornings I woke up in freezing, snowy Milwaukee, my back still aching from the game the night before, and asked myself: Why not, just this one time, give yourself a break and stay in bed for another hour? What's the harm? No one will ever know. Only I would know, and if I skipped one time, I might skip another, and another, and would soon feel the difference come the fourth quarter when my team needed me the most and the usual lift in my legs wouldn't be there. It's one thing to miss a free throw or a jump shot because, well, you miss; that happens. It's another to miss because you don't put in the work. That should never happen."[9]

Of course, like all of us, there were days when Allen would have loved to skip practice. And while we all do need breaks and rest, our children must learn to decipher between good rest and procrastination or excuse-making. When they have a big goal to accomplish, they'll need to push through their dips in motivation to reach it. A good routine can help with that. In Allen's case, he had big goals that kept him focused. He wanted to be an accomplished basketball player and he knew that in order to successfully be there for his team when they needed him most, he couldn't slack off on his training. His goals helped him to prioritize his time and routines, even in the face of enticing alternatives (such as sleeping in!).

One issue that often hinders learners from good time management is procrastination (illustrated in Figure 16).

*Figure 16: Procrastination in Action*

When it comes to procrastination, a habit we should help our children to avoid whenever possible, there are nuances worth noting. Consider the findings from one research study,[14] which investigated the association between academic performance, procrastination, and a student's learning flow while completing a research paper. While the study didn't find a connection between procrastination and flow—as almost all of the students, both the ones who achieved flow and the ones who didn't, waited until two days before the paper was due to start—it did present the idea that there can be two kinds of procrastinators: ones who are either passive or active. With the majority of the students procrastinating to start, there were still some who were able to achieve flow and, as a result, earned higher grades on their papers. Those students were propelled by active procrastination. Their waiting till the last minute galvanized them to work harder and kick into a higher gear, leveraging their adrenaline to finish well. Students who experienced passive procrastination were paralyzed and frozen over the limited time they had left to complete the project. In turn, they did not perform well under pressure.

Keep in mind that while these active procrastinators still achieved good grades, this should not be considered advocacy for waiting till the last minute to study. As we highlighted earlier in the optimization chapter, last-minute cramming can pay off thanks to the recency effect, but it does not ensure long-term, sustained learning. Encourage your child to work on an upcoming project little by little each day, leading up to the due date, to avoid the need for last-minute cramming. Even with the possibility of active procrastination kicking in, which can result in a one-time good grade, this is not a recipe for quality learning over time. Rather, diligent, ongoing effort will allow them to finish their project in a calm, thoughtful manner and will result in a more positive overall learning experience.

In light of all we've now discussed on the importance of good time management, here are some practical ways you can help your learner to establish better routines in this area:

1.  **Time management requires self-discipline.** As with most of the points we've discussed in this book, this idea is best demonstrated to our children through our example of discipline, routine, and wise time management. We cannot expect children to be disciplined if we're not exhibiting these qualities ourselves. Once we've established regularity in our own routines, we can then press our children to stick to theirs as well.

    And while, as parents, we can provide a lot of guidance and influence in this area, ultimately our children must develop a personal sense of discipline to prepare for the time later in life when we won't be around to ensure they stick to their routines and time management practices. With regularity, practice, and dedication, eventually our children will develop their own personal sense of discipline.

2.  **Prioritization is key.** It's crucial to begin with a clear understanding of what matters most. Otherwise, there's a high chance that too much time will pass in which clear priorities are not set, leading to unachieved objectives. To determine the right set of priorities, begin with the end in mind (what's the goal your child is working toward?) and work backward. Establish

a short-term set of priorities that will build toward the bigger goal.

Prioritize short-term scheduling by encouraging your child to make a daily to-do list they can follow. Assist them in establishing everyday objectives to advance their long-term goals. Help them to determine what should be accomplished at the end of each week. This will give them a clear plan of what needs to be accomplished in the here and now.

3.  **Recognize that there'll be trade-offs.** Time is a finite resource. Discuss with your child how, if they set aside time to do one activity, it means they're deciding not to do something else. Parents can help here by their example and in how many activities they schedule for their child. It's easy to overschedule your child with the mindset that they can be master artists, athletes, *and* academicians.

Before getting trapped by the need to do a little bit of everything, take a step back and consider the principles and premises of how you're managing your time and your child's time. Remember that if they are overbooked, there won't be time for rest. Also, keep in mind their goals. Help them to choose activities that support these goals, so they won't get sidetracked. Help them to pick and choose the right activities for the limited time they have each day. In this way, you'll lead them toward a smarter way of using their time.

4.  **Identify when and how to apply good time management.** It's important to determine the best time of day to study based on an acknowledgment of when your child will do their best learning. Pay attention to whether they study best, in the morning or the evening—consider when they get the most run-down and tired and when their brain seems to come alive with activity. Parents can greatly help in this regard, particularly when the children are young.

    It is also important and beneficial to recognize the best day of the week for study time. For example, when I was in grade school, I always made sure that Saturday mornings were available for me to catch up on my Monday through Friday work. This was a prime time for me to do my advance studies, a topic we'll be discussing in subsequent chapters. Carving out these optimal learning times can be one of the most effective strategies for wise learning.

    Good parental modeling and guidance are critical for our children as they work to establish their own time management practices. Making productive use of time for study is not often a skill that comes naturally for children. They need our guidance in developing this very important skill. Especially when they are younger, our input is essential. And if they establish these patterns early on, there's a better chance they will become a fixed and ongoing life practice.

# ACTION PLAN

- Set aside some time to consider your current time management practices and identify opportunities for improvement. Weigh how you are with managing your own time and work to make any needed improvements before you consider how to help your child.

- The value of effective time management is often best considered in hindsight. When you recognize your child practicing good time management strategies, let them know, and then point out the positive outcomes that result from their productive use of time. Similarly, if you notice that your child has bad time management practices, help them reflect on bad practices they can change.

---

[1] Britton, Bruce K., and Abraham Tesser. "Effects of time-management practices on college grades." *Journal of Educational Psychology* 83, no. 3 (1991): 405.

[2] Valle, Antonio, Bibiana Regueiro, José C. Núñez, Susana Rodríguez, Isabel Piñeiro, and Pedro Rosário. "Academic goals, student homework engagement, and academic achievement in elementary school." *Frontiers in Psychology* 7 (2016): 463.

[3] Valle Arias, Antonio, Isabel Piñeiro Aguín, Susana Rodríguez Martínez, Bibiana Regueiro Fernández, Carlos Freire Rodríguez, and Pedro José Sales Luís de Fonseca Rosário. "Time spent and time management in homework in elementary school students: A person-centered approach." *Psicothema* (2019).

[4] Curcio, Giuseppe, Michele Ferrara, and Luigi De Gennaro. "Sleep loss, learning capacity and academic performance." *Sleep Medicine Reviews* 10, no. 5 (2006): 323-337.

[5] Stefansdottir, Runa, Vaka Rognvaldsdottir, Kong Y. Chen, Erlingur Johannsson, and Robert J. Brychta. "Sleep timing and consistency are associated with the standardised test performance of Icelandic adolescents." *Journal of Sleep Research* 31, no. 1 (2022): e13422.

[6] Seoane, Hernan A., Leandra Moschetto, Francisco Orliacq, Josefina Orliacq, Ezequiel Serrano, María Inés Cazenave, Daniel E. Vigo, and Santiago Perez-Lloret. "Sleep disruption in medicine students and its relationship with impaired academic performance: a systematic review and meta-analysis." *Sleep Medicine Reviews* 53 (2020): 101333.

[7] Comparison of rest-break interventions during a mentally demanding task, https://www.ncbi.nlm.nih.gov/pmc/articles/PMC6585675/

[8] "Give me a break!" A systematic review and meta-analysis on the efficacy of micro-breaks for increasing well-being and performance https://journals.plos.org/plosone/article?id=10.1371/journal.pone.0272460

[9] Excerpt from *From the Outside: My Journey Through Life and the Game I Love*, by Ray Allen

[10] The 5 Types of Note-Taking Methods You Need To Learn, https://theglobalscholars.com/the-5-types-of-note-taking-methods-you-need-to-learn/

[11] Shi, Yinghui, Huiyun Yang, Yi Dou, and Yong Zeng. "Effects of mind mapping-based instruction on student cognitive learning outcomes: a meta-analysis." *Asia Pacific Education Review* (2022): 1-15.

[12] Gagic, Zvezdan Z., Sonja J. Skuban, Branka N. Radulovic, Maja M. Stojanovic, and Olivera Gajic. "The Implementation of Mind Maps in Teaching Physics: Educational Efficiency and Students' Involvement." *Journal of Baltic Science Education* 18, no. 1 (2019): 117-131.

[13] Adodo, S. O. "Effect of mind-mapping as a self-regulated learning strategy on students' achievement in basic science and technology." Mediterranean Journal of Social Sciences 4, no. 6 (2013): 163-163.

[14] Citation: Sumaya, Isabel C., and Emily Darling. "Procrastination, flow, and academic performance in real time using the experience sampling method." *Journal of Genetic Psychology* 179, no. 3 (2018): 123-131.

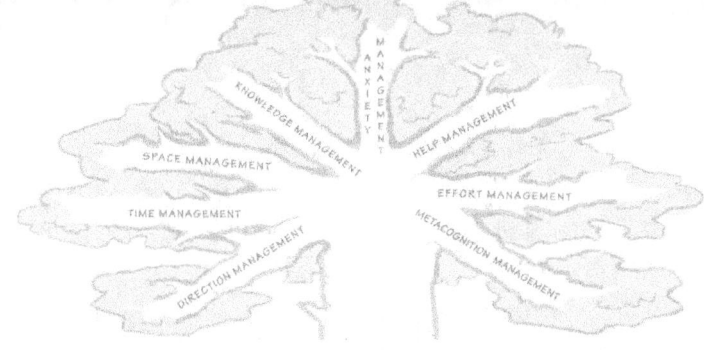

# CHAPTER 9

# SPACE MANAGEMENT

As a grade school and high school student, one of the most valuable habits I practiced was the intentional structuring of my learning environment. I found that if I set aside time on Saturday mornings to prepare for the week to come, my mind would feel more organized and ready to learn as a result. My preparations would look something like this—I'd clear my table or desk of clutter that had accumulated the week before, filing away documents I'd need to reference again in the future and throwing away papers or other items that were no longer needed. I'd ensure that books required for the coming week were pulled out and easily accessible. I'd sharpen my pencils. These practices prepared me to do what I loved to do every Saturday morning, that is, study material in advance to prepare for the lessons that my teachers would discuss the following week. (Note that studying the material in advance refers to a specific learning strategy that will be discussed in more detail in Chapter 10 of this book.)

I was fortunate to have parents who respected my need for a dedicated space to study. Additionally, our home had enough room for me to have an area that I could claim as my specific learning area. I had a place for my books, access to good supplies, a quiet environment, and adequate lighting.

By contrast, my wife has shared that while growing up, it was always difficult for her to establish an environment conducive to study. Her home was often noisy, there were many distractions, and with several older brothers with whom she shared a room, it was hard for her to identify a space that was all her own. This made it nearly impossible for her to carve out times of quiet reflection and focus—which are vital to a child's ability to absorb and consider what they are learning. In truth, it was a miracle that she was able to study at all! The result was that she struggled to learn as a grade school and high school student.

Processing and retaining information is difficult when one is constantly distracted. For my wife, it was only after she went to college and pursued her graduate studies that she flourished as a student. I do believe this was not a coincidence, as she finally had her own space to study, with minimal distractions. She eventually became an outstanding early childhood educator.

Ensuring your child has a study environment conducive to learning is a fundamental strategy adopted by the Wisest Learners™. Many learners struggle, as my wife did, to identify a place in their home where they can be productive and focused on their studies. For some families, space is truly an issue. It simply isn't possible for every child to have their own dedicated desk. But as we'll discuss in the pages to come, even in the case of a smaller home, there are still ways to work with your learner to ensure they're set up for success.

An article published in 2015 by Peter Lewinski[1] outlines the most important factors for space management: light, noise, color, room temperature, and arrangement. We'll consider the main points of each of these elements below.

1. **Lighting:** The key idea with lighting is that it should be "just right," as in the Three Little Bears nursery rhyme. Lewinski's overview found there to be no differences in learning that took place under warm or cool white light. As long as there is *enough* light and the light isn't so glaring as to be a hindrance, then it is conducive to productive learning.

2. **Noise:** Lewinski shared that 40 decibels were the upper threshold for optimal learning—anything louder was found to be distracting. For reference, a normal conversation volume would be held at 75 decibels. This brings to mind the often-raised question of whether or not it is helpful to have music or a podcast playing while studying. Based on Lewinski's findings, music playing in the background can be accommodated as long as it's turned down very low. Having said that, a totally quiet environment is ideal. If sound cannot be avoided, we suggest instrumental or classical music that doesn't contain words, as they will compete for the learner's attention.

3. **Color:** A study published in 2001 by Stone[2] suggested that the color of an environment can affect and detract from a learner's ability to complete more difficult tasks, and the color red was consistently shown not to be good for learning or test taking. Conversely, blue and green can produce a calming effect and are considered better colors for a productive learning environment.[3] Note, though, that there are also works that found little

relationship between color exposure and cognitive task performance and mood in high school students, at least in the short run. Nevertheless, it is important to consider the color of the environment in which your child will be studying. The color can contribute to the overall ambiance of the learning space and can lead to increased focus and motivation.

4. **Room temperature:** The temperature of a room plays a significant role in how comfortable a child feels while studying. The ideal temperature is one that is hardly noticeable—neither too cold nor too hot. A 2002 study by Earthman[4] showed that temperatures between 68 and 74°F—20 and 24°C—are most conducive to comfort and, by extension, learning.

5. **Room arrangement:** Lewinski summarized that learners are most happy with their study environment when they have a comfortable chair and a nice view of the outdoors. Keep in mind that it's helpful to have seating that is inviting enough for a child to spend an extended amount of time in, possibly encouraging them to study longer, but not so comfortable that it could induce sleepiness. Similarly, a view of the outdoors that shows a peaceful, natural scene is favorable, but an outside view that is noisy or busy can be a distraction.

*Figure 17: A Good Study Space*

## RESEARCH RECAP:

- If you're looking for a room color that is favorable to learning, you can't go wrong with **green and blue**.

- **Room lighting and temperature should be "just right"** rather than extreme in either direction. It's important to have enough lighting and for the temperature to be set between 68 and 74°F.

- **A quiet, peaceful setting is ideal.** Zero background noise (or music) is the best choice. The second best option is non-distracting background music (at a soft and low volume).

- **An outside view of a garden or the beach can enhance learning**, as long as there are minimal distractions such as a busy and noisy street or vehicular and pedestrian traffic.

Making an effort to designate a singular, special space for your child to spend their study time is a worthwhile endeavor. A suitable environment provides a better learning foundation. There will be more catalysts and opportunities to achieve the flow state, develop motivation and effective beliefs, and establish effective lifelong learning habits. Many children, especially those with siblings, relish the idea of having something uniquely theirs. Denoting such a space that is particularly for study will reinforce to them the importance of their learning. If it's possible, find ways to make this learning space special to them. Provide them a way to hang their own art nearby, or allow them to pick out the pencils or notebooks they will use. This will further their sense of ownership over this part of your home.

I recognize that many homes cannot spare a room, desk, or area that is dedicated solely to learning. Some siblings may have to share a space, and other children may do their homework at the kitchen table. While this can certainly create challenges, there are ways to facilitate many of the above-mentioned elements of space management. For instance, if your child is studying in a busy kitchen, provide them with noise-canceling headphones. If siblings are prone to bickering, specifically identify the boundaries of each child's space and, if possible, have them face in different directions. Identify times during the day that are designated study times, during which you keep the TV off, turn the radio down, and strive to maintain a quiet, peaceful atmosphere. Encourage siblings to coordinate work times, when possible, so everyone can be operating simultaneously to keep noise levels down and concentration on studies high. To further minimize distractions, always ask older children to leave their phones in another room, with the volume turned down, while they are focused on their studies.

The ideal learning setting is one that is used with regularity. So whatever your home can accommodate, the goal is to establish spaces that invite your child to sit quietly, reflect on what they've learned, and prepare for the new schoolwork to come. Implement as many of these strategies as possible, and through trial and error, you'll discover how to establish the right learning space for your child that works within the bounds of your home's unique and specific circumstances.

# ACTION PLAN

- If your home can accommodate the space, set aside a desk or table designated as a learning station for your child. Ensure it is comfortable enough (but not too comfortable!), has good lighting, and is removed from the distractions of TVs, video games, or cell phones. Encourage your child to complete their homework and studies in this spot, so they will come to identify it as a space dedicated to learning.

- Work with your child to regularly organize and declutter their study area. This will promote focus and reduce distractions.

- If a separate space is not possible, find one area of your home that can be their regular spot for learning. Even if it is the kitchen table, stick to a space that they can connect to as their place to study. Help your child or children to schedule when their studying will take place so that others in the house can respect that as a quiet time in the home.

- Establish a learning culture where distractions during your children's study time are recognized as detrimental to optimal learning. Regularly check in with your child and other family members to see how the study space is working and make adjustments as needed. Be open to compromise and try to find a solution that works for everyone.

[1] Lewinski, Peter. "Effects of classrooms' architecture on academic performance in view of telic versus paratelic motivation: a review." *Frontiers in Psychology* 6 (2015): 746.

[2] Stone, N. (2001). "Designing effective study environments." *Journal of Environmental Psychology* 21, 179–190. Doi: 10.1006/jevp.2000.0193

[3] "Cognitive performance and emotion are indifferent to ambient color " by Christoph von Castell, Daniela Stelzmann, Daniel Oberfeld, Robin Welsch, and Heiko Hecht - https://onlinelibrary.wiley.com/doi/abs/10.1002/col.22168

[4] Earthman, G. (2002). "School facility conditions and student academic achievement," in Williams Watch Series: Investigating the Claims of Williams v. State of California, Los Angeles, CA: UCLA's Institute for Democracy, Education, and Access. Available at: http://www.escholarship.org/uc/item/5sw56439 [accessed October 1, 2002].

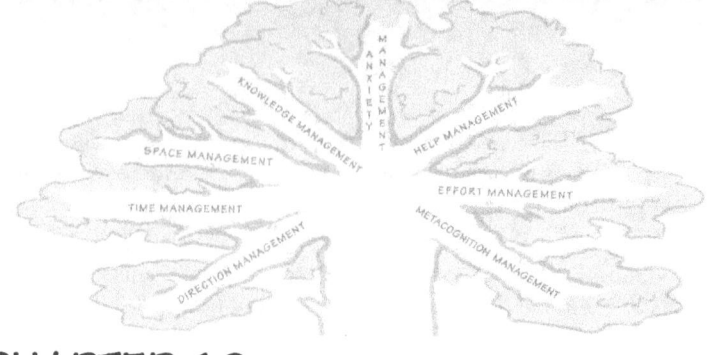

## CHAPTER 10

# KNOWLEDGE MANAGEMENT

When I was training to become a long-distance, open-water swimmer, an adventure I've shared in Part III Learning Management, I had little swimming experience but worked with coaches to create a workout plan and practiced for two hours every day, six days a week, to swim across the English Channel. I learned from coaches from Australia, the Philippines, the UK, and the U.S. who implemented different training strategies, with some being more effective than others. Some drills were intended to boost my speed in freestyle, while others were designed to improve my cardio for endurance swimming.

In the same way, as our children work to learn new things—whether they're aware of it or not—they'll use a variety of techniques to do so. Just as some of the swimming drills I learned were more useful for certain skills-building goals than others, our research shows that certain learning practices can be better than others. Some are gold-standard practices, while others only deserve a silver or bronze ranking.

In this chapter, we'll discuss knowledge management, which is the initialization, acquisition, development, and/or reinforcement of new skills and information. We'll unpack how to optimize several learning strategies related to knowledge management, including

1. Recall and Elaboration

2. Mixed and Periodic Learning

3. Advance Studies

We'll equip you, and your child, with proven, gold-standard practices for gaining and retaining new skills and information. We'll then discuss how your child can most efficiently move those newly acquired assets from their short-term into their long-term memory baskets. Let's begin by discussing the most effective strategies for knowledge management.

**Recall and Elaboration**

**Recall** involves actively retrieving and reproducing information that's been previously learned. Recall requires a learner to actively engage with the material as they're learning in order to more effectively store it in their long-term memory. This active engagement better equips your child to retrieve the information later on.

Consider your child's experience when studying a lesson on how the United States, under the leadership of General George Washington, launched the American Revolution. As your child reads and learns about this war, it will be helpful for them to memorize facts about when the Revolution took place, the key players involved, and the locations of all the major battles. It will also be important for your child to think critically about the whole story, consider the political and economic conditions of the time, and dissect the meaning surrounding this pivotal world event. There are several ways for your learner to apply the strategy of recall in order to retain all these details about the American Revolution. Let's consider a few best practices:

- **Rote memorization** is the most basic, fundamental practice for remembering facts and details and it's a good basis for facilitating recall. In the case of our American Revolution example, rote memorization would involve a repetitive review of the key names, dates, and locations related to this war so that this information can be retained and later retrieved. In a similar way, rote memorization would be engaged to help a child memorize multiplication facts or the chemical elements that make up the periodic table.

When in college, I worked for a company that trained me to perform extraordinary rote memory stunts as a demonstration for the educational courses they offered. These courses taught memory techniques for learning numbers or concepts. As a part of my sales pitch, I'd visit schools and have students write on the board a 100-digit number. I'd memorize the number forward and backward after looking at it for less than a minute. The audience would be so impressed, and as a result, many students signed up for their courses! Here are some techniques for rote memorization:

- **Association** is the practice of connecting words or concepts in a way that will make them easier to remember. With my course, I adopted a system where every number represented a letter and every group of numbers represented a word. For example, I'd connect the number 22 with the word "nun" because two represents "n" in my memory. Then, I'd connect 34 with the word "mare" because three represents "m" and four represents "r" in my memory. The more I could associate numbers with words, the easier it was for me to remember. Because numbers are more abstract than words, I was able to make the abstract more concrete.

- **Mnemonics** involves the use of rhymes, songs, acronyms, and visual imagery to facilitate recall. Colors of the rainbow (ROYGBIV) is an example of using acronyms. Learners can often remember a song about the days of the week or the names of the continents if this information is recited as words to a catchy tune. This is a technique I use to this day to help me remember concepts and ideas.

- **Exaggerated storytelling** is when you tie an over-the-top story with the concept that's being learned. The more I could relate the numbers I was memorizing with a fun, exciting, or exaggerated story, the easier they were to remember. I'd put together a word association such as "a mare was fencing with a nun" or "a nun was playing chess with a mare."

Rote memorization is a great practice for short-term memory, but it doesn't always lead to information being transferred into long-term memory. Think of it as a great foundational building block for starting memory practices. It's best for memorizing facts but not for the development of critical thinking. The following tactics will help to further store ideas in long-term memory and open the door to more creative thoughts and comprehension, as well.

- **Mental Recall**. After reading a passage, several pages, or a chapter (depending on the complexity of the topic), your child should pause, close their book, and possibly walk away for a time to consider what they've just read. They must take time to ensure they truly understand the information. This time and space will give your child a chance to digest what they've learned.

- **Journaling**. Keeping a learning journal, where your child can write down their thoughts and reflections after reading a lesson, can provide a way for them to organize information in a meaningful way, making it easier to remember and recall later on.

- **Pause and Reflect**. The practice of pausing to reflect and writing key points will help your child to recognize areas of weakness in their learning where additional effort is needed. This is when it can be helpful for your learner to go back and highlight key terms and phrases that will reinforce what they need to know. Highlighting is when a learner calls attention to or emphasizes certain material by underlining it or marking it with brightly colored ink (see Figure 18). Highlighted terms and phrases and journaled notes can be helpful references for a child to revisit and reread as they work to better understand and commit their studies to memory.

A note about highlighting: learners often make the mistake of *over-highlighting* a text. As a result, nothing stands out as important. Children must learn to be more selective in what they highlight—focusing only on *key terms and phrases* that will be valuable to them to remember when they work to recall the information later on.

A 2022 study by researchers at the University of Santiago and the University of California[1] considered the effectiveness of learner-generated highlighting versus instructor-provided highlighting. The learner-generated work improved memory, but it didn't improve comprehension. Conversely, instructor-provided highlighting improved both memory and comprehension. The difference between the learner and instructor highlighted text was that the instructors knew to focus only on the key terms and phrases that would trigger memory recall later. The learners highlighted too much, which led to highlighting that was ineffective and not useful. The main point for learners to remember is that overuse of this tactic will almost entirely cancel out its value. Encourage your students to ask for input from you or an instructor if they feel they're over-highlighting.

*Figure 18: Highlighting Texts in a Book*

A 2011 study out of Purdue University[2] found recall practices to be very effective in promoting conceptual learning about science, in particular, because when done properly, recall prompts a learner to assess comprehension repeatedly. The mechanism behind the efficiency of recall is relatively complex. When we try to recall something from memory, we need to first figure out how we organized that information in our mind and then use that organization to retrieve specific details. Doing this repeatedly, or practicing recalling the information, can make it easier for us to remember the information in the future by making the cues we use to recall the information more specific and helpful. Practicing retrieval helps us better understand the connections between different pieces of information, making it easier for us to retrieve them. It provides time and space for learners to reason and make conclusions about what they are studying.

Recall also opens the door for deeper, more lasting memories to develop because as fundamental facts about a topic are squirreled away over time, a child's brain then has a greater capacity to consider the subject critically and, as a result, to connect with it on a more personal level. In the case of the American Revolution example, as your child files away the facts of the war, over time, their brain will not have to work so hard to remember those details. As a result, they have more room to consider other aspects of this historical event. As we covered in our earlier discussion on optimization, lower-level learning such as rote memorization frees your child's working memory and executive capacities to think about more complex matters that are built upon that basic information.

Taken together, recall can strengthen the neural connections in the brain and make the information easier to access and recall in the future. By recalling information, learners are not only reviewing what they have learned but also applying and integrating it into their knowledge base, which enhances their understanding and retention of the information. Additionally, recalling information often requires effort and attention, which also contributes to the strengthening of the memory trace or the change in the brain that occurs when something has been coded into our memory. Overall, recall is a crucial component of effective learning and memory formation.

Recall is an effective way for learners to build long-term memory. However, it's a strategy that requires discipline on the part of your learner, something they will likely have to develop over time. The tendency of an unseasoned learner will be to take shortcuts, but the wisest learner will recognize the value of applying more time-consuming but ultimately higher-value strategies of recall.

Now that we have established the different tactics for recall, let us proceed to another knowledge management strategy called **Elaboration.** This is a learning strategy that involves actively connecting new information to prior knowledge or experiences in order to create more meaningful and memorable associations. It's a process of actively engaging with new information and thinking about how it relates to what you already know. This can help to make the new information more meaningful and easier to remember.

There are several different elaboration strategies that can be used to learn new information. Some examples include:

- **Making connections:** Encourage your child to link new information to what they already know and understand; relate new material to other experiences or concepts they've learned.

- **Generating examples:** Prompt your learner to think of specific examples that illustrate the new information or to imagine scenarios in which they might use the information.

- **Summarizing:** Ask your child to create a brief summary of the new information, in their own words, as a way of reinforcing the main points and making them more memorable.

- **Visualizing:** Encourage your learner to create mental images or generate pictures of the material in their mind. Encouraging them to visualize the relationship between concepts will make the information more memorable.

Consider again our example of learning about the American Revolution. To memorize important events from the American Revolution using elaboration, a child could try the following techniques:

- **Making connections:** Encourage your child to relate the events of the American Revolution to things they have experienced in their own life. For example, they might compare the fight for independence to a time when they stood up for what they believed in. Or they could attempt to see the American Revolution in the context of other historical events. They could compare it to other wars of independence, such as the French Revolution or the Haitian Revolution.

- **Generating examples:** Encourage your child to ask questions about the events of the American Revolution and think critically about the information they have learned. Ask questions such as "What emotions would a person be feeling during a time of war and upheaval?"

- **Summarizing:** Motivate your child to retell the events of this war in their own words and to visualize what it would have been like to be there. Ask them to turn the events of the American Revolution into a story. Ask questions such as "How accessible were food supplies?" and "What would people involved in the conflict be eating?"

- **Visualizing:** Encourage your child to imagine the events of the Revolution as if they were happening right in front of them.

Ask questions such as "What was the weather like at the time of the year when this war started?" and "What would the soldiers have worn?"

Discussing a lesson in this way will make the events more engaging and meaningful. Your child will be more likely to remember important details and the key players involved. As a result, they'll more successfully store it in long-term memory.

**The combination of Recall and Elaboration** is one of the best ways for your child to strengthen their long-term memory and gain an overall better understanding of what they're learning. By engaging in regular recall exercises— reflecting on a lesson, journaling their ideas, and highlighting keywords—and then adding the practice of elaboration, your child will be positioned to have a more complete, in-depth understanding of a subject.

### Periodic and Mixed Learning

**Periodic learning** involves spreading the study or practice of material over time, rather than cramming learning into a single session. This technique is based on the spacing effect, the phenomenon in which people tend to retain information better when it is presented and reviewed over time, rather than being learned all at once.

The spacing effect works by taking advantage of how our brains process and store information. When we first encounter new information, our brains process it in a short-term memory system, which is limited in capacity and duration. However, when we encounter the same information again in the future, our brains process it in a different way, by transferring it to a long-term memory system, which is more durable and permanent. This process of transferring information from short-term to long-term memory is called consolidation, and it is what makes the spacing effect possible.

The optimal time between learning sessions when using the spacing strategy is dependent on the specific learning goals, the type of information being studied, and the personal learning preferences and abilities of a learner. However, research suggests that spacing intervals should be long enough to allow some time for forgetting to occur but not so much time that information is completely forgotten. A general guideline is to space study sessions by one to three days. For longer-term retention of information, spacing intervals can be increased to several days or even weeks. The key idea behind spacing is to find a balance between creating opportunities for retrieval and reinforcement—which helps to strengthen memory—and avoiding the loss of information due to disuse.

By spreading out study sessions, learners have better memory consolidation. They will recall information during a study session happening later in time, i.e., accessing their long-term memory more, which leads to better retention and understanding of the information. Periodic learning has been found to be particularly effective for the long-term retention of information such as facts, vocabulary, and procedures, as well as complex concepts.

The 1978 study conducted in the United Kingdom known as the "Spacing Effect Study," or the "Postal Worker Study,"[3] aimed to investigate the effects of spacing and massing (also known as cramming, wherein a child groups together study time into fewer, longer sessions) on learning. In the study, four batches of postmen were trained to input alphanumeric code data using a standard typewriter keyboard. The first group received training for four hours per day for four consecutive days, the second group received an identical amount of training but spaced over eight days with two hours per day, the third group received two hours of training per day for four consecutive days, and the fourth group received the same amount of training as group three, but it was spaced over eight days with one hour per day.

Results showed that the group who received training two hours a day spaced over eight days performed significantly better on typing tests compared to the group who received the same amount of training in a shorter, massed format. The results of this study support the idea that spacing out study sessions leads to better learning and retention compared to massing study sessions. Note also that the study suggests that *both* the spacing of study sessions and the amount of material studied are important factors in learning and retention. This is because it was found that a larger amount of material over a longer period of time is more effective for learning and retention compared to studying less material over the same period of time. Additionally, periodic learning can help reduce forgetting by providing opportunities for learners to actively retrieve and practice the material. This is in contrast to massed learning, which is not optimal because the brain needs breaks to process new information or knowledge.

Periodic learning sessions provide children an opportunity to consider what they've failed to remember since their last session. Learners can test themselves as a way to gauge their mastery of the subject by writing down a list of challenging, thought-provoking questions during their first study session. Then, a week or a month later when they come back to review, they can check in with those questions again to see how much they still remember and where additional study is needed.

Consider the comparison between massed learning and spaced learning in the context of planting a garden. If you plant all your seeds in one spot and water them all at once, the seeds will likely become waterlogged and not grow properly. On the other hand, if you space out your seeds and use the same amount of water but spaced over regular, longer periods of time, the seeds will have a better chance of growing into healthy plants. Similarly, when a child crams the learning of all their lessons, it's like planting all their seeds in one spot, while spacing out study sessions and reviewing the material regularly over a longer period of time is like planting seeds spaced out and watering them regularly. The latter approach allows for a more effective and sustainable process of learning and retention, just as the latter gardening approach allows for healthier plant growth.

An important note is that periodic learning sessions shouldn't involve a simple rereading of the material. Learners have a tendency to improperly approach rereading. The common mindset is that simply rereading a text is good enough. While rereading can provide some short-term value, the act of rereading *alone* is not a productive strategy. The recency effect will trigger the illusion of learning, giving your child the impression that they've learned the material, when in fact it's not yet been planted in their long-term memory bank. Instead of basic rereading, keep in mind that these sessions will be exponentially more impactful when the principles of Recall and Elaboration are applied.

**Mixed learning** is a technique in which learners study different topics or skills in a layered or "interleaved" order rather than focusing on one topic or skill at a time. This means that instead of studying all of one topic before moving on to the next, learners switch back and forth between different topics or skills during a study session (see Figure 19). For example, a student might work on chapter one of math, then chapter one from literature, and then go back to chapter two of math again rather than moving on to chapter two of literature. The goal of interleaved learning is to actively engage the learner in switching between different topics or subjects, which can improve the retention and transfer of the material.

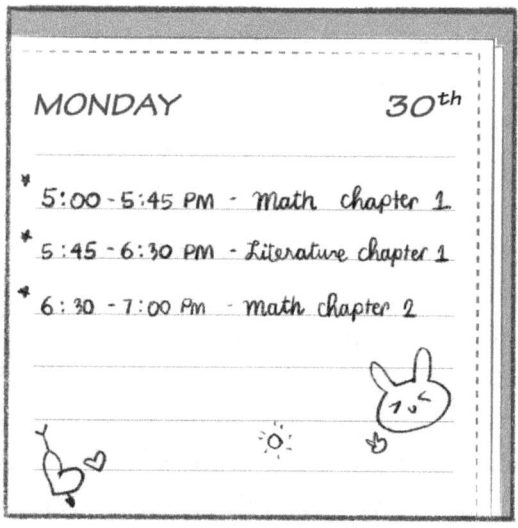

*Figure 19: Mixed Learning Schedule*

This is a key principle of mixed learning. By taking breaks from studying the same material, switching to different topics, and then returning to the original material, the brain has to work harder to retrieve or recall the information, leading to improved understanding, retention, and stronger memory traces in the brain.

Additionally, interleaved learning can help promote the transfer of information to new contexts, which is essential for practical problem-solving and applying knowledge in real-world settings.

Mixed learning is rooted in the awareness that knowledge is complex. This is a concept we discussed in our Chapter 5 discussion on beliefs. Every aspect of our hyper-connected world speaks to the layered nature of knowledge, and in a similar way, the subjects your child is learning are infinitely interconnected and integrated. The study of biology, for example, also requires a certain level of math and reading abilities. You can't do one without the other. For this reason, it can be helpful to encourage your child to mix and integrate their studies—considering, for instance, the math, language, and reading skills required to complete their science work.

A 2001 study on mixed learning, published in the *Journal of Experimental Psychology*,[4] found that while blocked learning sessions did help with short-term memory, when students were tested 24 hours later, those who learned in a blocked manner performed very poorly when compared to students who followed a mixed learning schedule. An additional interesting finding was that when students were asked how they'd perform, blocked learners were much more confident that they would perform better, and mixed practice students assumed that they would perform poorly. So blocked learning creates an illusion of learning or an illusion of good performance, which turns out to not be true.

Mixed learning is more successful relative to blocked or siloed learning because it requires learners to actively retrieve and apply previously learned information, rather than simply repeat the same information over and over. This active retrieval process helps to strengthen and consolidate memory, making the information more accessible and easier to recall in the future. Note, however, that it is not the retrieval per se that drives the process in mixed learning but specifically retrieval of information that has become slightly forgotten due to one's involvement with other, non-related material. This process of retrieving slightly forgotten information, as described by the Ebbinghaus Forgetting Curve we discussed earlier, helps to reinforce and consolidate memory, making the information more accessible and easier to recall in the future. This is what makes mixed learning so successful in comparison to blocked or siloed learning.

Mixed learning also helps to prevent the phenomenon of "interference," which happens when new information blocks old information. When learners study different topics or skills in a blocked or siloed manner, new information may interfere with the old information and make it harder to recall. By studying different topics in a layered or mixed manner, learners are forced to actively retrieve previously learned information, which helps to prevent interference and improve retention.

Additionally, mixed learning allows children to better transfer their learning to new and varied problems or situations. When children only focus on one topic or skill at a time, they may find it difficult to apply their knowledge to new or different problems. By switching back and forth between different topics or skills during a study session, learners are exposed to a greater variety of problems and situations, which can help them to better transfer their ideas to new and varied contexts. This improves critical thinking skills and can help your child handle challenges with creative thinking more adeptly. When a complex question is posed in an exam, for example, a child will feel less anxiety over their ability to answer correctly if they've already trained their brain to handle concepts that involve complexity. They'll be able to pull from their experience of creatively considering how things are interconnected and be able to consider all the possibilities of how to answer the question.

Spiral curriculum teaching, a pedagogical (educational) approach ingrained in the Singapore school system, does a good job of mixed learning. This teaching style allows students to experience all of the sciences every year and better understand how one is connected to the other. Students learn multiple science disciplines, such as biology, chemistry, and physics every school year with increased difficulty. This contrasts with a linear curriculum, where subjects are typically taught once and in a sequence, with each new topic building on the previous one. For example, in mathematics, topics are taught in a specific order such as arithmetic, geometry, algebra, and so on. The effectiveness of the spiral curriculum approach can be seen in the results, as Singapore schools regularly excel by global education standards such as PISA.[5]

This concept is one that our children can use to strengthen physical and mental muscles since mixed learning has been found to be particularly effective when learning math and science *and* in sports training. If your child is working to improve their skills as a basketball player, for instance, they'll benefit more if they practice shots from a variety of angles, as opposed to only shooting from one spot again and again. Similarly, when a child is in a study session focused on math, it can be helpful for them to mix their learning by taking breaks to focus on other subjects too. A two-hour study session that includes math, spelling, and science can be more mentally challenging and beneficial than a two-hour session solely focused on math.

An important benefit of **periodic and mixed learning** is that these practices will counter the recency effect. Remember that the recency effect is tied to how we tend to recollect the most immediate information we've learned more accurately. This creates the illusion of learning. The practices of mixed and periodic learning force your brain to remember information over longer periods of time, keeping your mind engaged with the subject you're learning and increasing your ability to plant ideas in your long-term memory bank. These are powerful methods for countering learning illusions.

The final knowledge management strategy to be discussed in this section is related to the work that a learner does ahead of time to prepare for a class or lecture. This is called Advance Studies or Preview Learning. At the beginning of Chapter 9, in our discussion on space management, I shared a habit I developed during my school years where I would spend a few minutes every Saturday morning preparing for the week to come. I'd study material in advance to get ready for the lessons my teachers would discuss the following week. This practice gave me a huge learning advantage. Since I'd already gone through the initial hurdle of becoming familiar with the material before it was taught, I was freed up to deeply process on what the teacher was presenting and exercise more critical thinking about the subject.

In an article about study strategies, author Angela Zanardelli Sickler[6] shares that "within 24 hours before a lecture, it's imperative to preview the material to be covered. This step rarely takes longer than 30 minutes, especially once you're familiar with how to properly preview information." Sickler goes on to say that students bypassing this step will experience the content firsthand during the class. Learners can often get overwhelmed or lost during the class presentation and in a scramble to catch up, take messy or incomplete notes. This scramble can sometimes lead students to simply tune out the lecture, as they feel it's just too hard to keep up with all they're hearing.

A well-cited work by Barbara Wakimoto[7] showed significant improvement in learning for students who had an overview of what was to come before an actual lecture. After studying 700 students, Wakimoto found a 21% increase in performance when the material had been studied ahead of time.

The habit of preparing for a class beforehand may seem daunting to a student at first. But even just a short amount of preparation can pay off. The more your child practices this behavior and experiences the positive results of productive class lectures and a stronger grasp of the material, the more inclined they will be to continue the practice.

Now that we have established the many facets of knowledge management, below is our recommended approach to establishing good study routines:

- **Understanding that time is limited, work with your child to narrow down and choose which subjects they will apply the principles of Knowledge Management—Recall and Elaboration, Mixed and Periodic Learning, and Advance Studies.** In an ideal world where time is infinite, one can choose to do frequent reviews of all subjects or lessons. But since this isn't the case, it's important to identify which subjects or lessons should receive more time and attention.

- **Help your child to allot time to establish good routines, to ensure the work of Knowledge Management is happening.** For example, if the selected topic is fractions, have your child study fractions in advance so when their teacher presents the lesson, they'll be able to reinforce their understanding of fractions. After a week (and then after a month), have your child review the same lesson again.

- **Accept that trade-offs will inevitably happen.** A child likely won't be able to apply all these strategies to every subject. By choosing one subject or lesson over another, a decision has been made *not* to choose another.

- **Strive to encourage your child to be *internally* motivated in applying all the principles of Knowledge Management, so as to prevent possible burnout.**

As you consider the limitations of your child's time, energy, cognitive load, and flow, it makes sense to get them in the habit of practicing and hopefully mastering only the gold-standard practices of knowledge management—the ones that will deliver the best results within the bounds of your child's ability. When your child is able to master the study techniques outlined in this chapter, the resulting improvement in learning proficiency will be immense. These fundamental yet dynamic disciplines will equip your child to exponentially advance their learning capability and expand their capacity to remember more information in a lasting way.

## ACTION PLAN

- Help your child to understand and appreciate the value of applying all the knowledge management strategies we've covered in this chapter, including recall, elaboration, periodic and mixed review, and advance studies.

- Work with your child to establish effective and suitable study routines (review this chapter for our recommended approach).

- Each of these learning habits requires time and discipline, and it may be overwhelming to implement them all at once. If that's the case, help your child to approach one at a time, adding a new practice once they've effectively mastered the previous one.

[1] Ponce, Héctor R., Richard E. Mayer, and Ester E. Méndez. "Effects of Learner-Generated Highlighting and Instructor-Provided Highlighting on Learning from Text: A Meta-Analysis." *Educational Psychology Review* 34, no. 2 (2022): 989-1024.

[2] Karpicke, Jeffrey D., and Janell R. Blunt. "Retrieval practice produces more learning than elaborative studying with concept mapping." *Science* 331, no. 6018 (2011): 772-775.

[3] Baddeley, Alan D., and D. J. A. Longman. "The influence of length and frequency of training session on the rate of learning to type." *Ergonomics* 21, no. 8 (1978): 627-635.

[4] Simon, Dominic A., and Robert A. Bjork. "Metacognition in motor learning." *Journal of Experimental Psychology: Learning, Memory, and Cognition* 27, no. 4 (2001): 907.

[5] Schleicher, Andreas. "PISA 2018: Insights and Interpretations." OECD Publishing (2019).

[6] Study Strategies for Before, During, and After Class by Angela Zanardelli Sickler - https://www.facultyfocus.com/articles/teaching-and-learning/study-strategies-class/

[7] Moravec, Marin, Adrienne Williams, Nancy Aguilar-Roca, and Diane K. O'Dowd. "Learn before lecture: A strategy that improves learning outcomes in a large introductory biology class." *CBE—Life Sciences Education* 9, no. 4 (2010): 473-481.

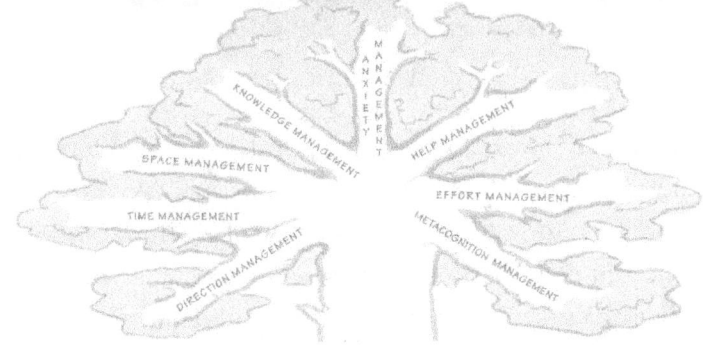

## CHAPTER 11

# ANXIETY MANAGEMENT

In May 2000, a new reality TV phenomenon called *Survivor* was released by CBS. A group of contestants, or "castaways," as the show prefers to call them, were left in Sabah, Malaysia, on the northern coast of the island of Borneo. The castaways are required to produce for themselves food, fire, and shelter and to compete against each other in a series of challenges that test their physical capabilities. One by one they're voted out by fellow castaways. Building strong alliances with others or winning competitions can protect them from elimination. The last person standing wins a million-dollar prize.

This show has proven to be immensely popular. As of the publication of this book, it has run for 44 seasons and has been nominated for 63 Emmy Awards. It has consistently been one of the top 20 most-watched shows on television. It also capitalizes on our collective fear of being rejected by our peers. Those who don't win the favor of their fellow castaways are literally kicked off the island!

While none of us *wants* to experience this level of rejection, viewers seem to resonate with the anxiety that the castaways' experience and are drawn into watching the spectacle of it all play out week after week. I noticed that a good number of castaways were skilled in anxiety management notwithstanding the difficult environment. They have the unique ability to find mental and emotional balance in high-stress situations.

Dealing with anxiety is a topic that is top of mind for many people. Back in 2018, well before concerns of a pandemic had entered the collective consciousness, Barnes & Noble reported a surge in sales of books about stress and anxiety.[1] A few years later, the World Health Organization reported a 25% increase worldwide in the prevalence of anxiety due to fears over COVID-19.[2] The current top-selling books on anxiety include titles such as *Unwinding Anxiety, Practicing Mindfulness,* and *What to Do When You Worry Too Much.* A best-seller for parents of teens is *Helping Your Anxious Teen.*[3]

For our learners, anxiety is often felt over test taking. Testing triggers performance concerns and worries over not passing. This anxiety has deep evolutionary roots, dating back to a time when people would agonize over having their tribe evaluate their performance and the consequences that would result if they failed; a plotline that is noticeably identifiable in the show *Survivor.*

A child of one of Artyom's acquaintances, who is 12 years of age, possesses exceptional intellectual abilities and displays boundless energy and a thirst for knowledge. Despite his academic aptitude, the child struggles with an elevated degree of test-related stress. This anxiety has caused him to struggle with memory and recall, making it difficult for him to remember what he has learned in class. As a result, he becomes anxious and worried when it's time to take a test or do a class presentation.

Test anxiety is quite common among students of all ages and the reasons for it can include any of the following:

- Academic pressure: Children may feel overwhelmed by the demands of schoolwork, grades, and expectations from teachers and parents.

- Social anxiety: Children may worry about fitting in with their peers, making friends, or being rejected.

- Separation anxiety: Children may experience distress when separated from parents or caregivers, especially when starting school for the first time.

- Fear of bullying: Children may be afraid of being bullied or teased by other students, which can lead to anxiety in school settings.

- Previous negative experiences: Children who have had traumatic or negative experiences in school, such as being bullied or punished, may develop anxiety about going to school.

One study by Charles D. Spielberger and his team in the late 1970s[4] found that individuals with test anxiety are more likely to see testing situations as threatening and to experience elevated levels of anxiety and worry during evaluations, compared to those who do not experience test anxiety. In other words, test anxiety is a type of anxiety that is specifically related to testing or evaluation situations. It's a common form of anxiety that can affect people of all ages but is especially common in school-aged children and adolescents.

Test anxiety can manifest in a variety of ways, including physical symptoms such as dizziness, nausea, and rapid breathing, as well as cognitive symptoms such as difficulty concentrating, racing thoughts, and negative self-talk. It can interfere with a person's ability to perform well on tests and can have negative impacts on academic success.

*Figure 20: A Child Experiencing Anxiety*

Test anxiety has been reported in 10-40% of grade school children,[5] while pronounced test anxiety in college students has a prevalence rate of between 10-50%.[6] If no interventions are implemented, test anxiety has been shown to persist over time,[7, 8] which naturally leads to poorer academic performance and worse grades on standardized tests,[9] weaker working memory,[10] or even dropping out of school.[11]

An analysis conducted by Isabelle Plante and her colleagues was published in the *British Journal of Educational Psychology* in 2022[12] and it examined the relationship between academic achievement and test anxiety in students. The researchers discovered that mathematical performance at the end of elementary school predicted test anxiety at the start of high school. However, this relationship was not straightforward or linear. In other words, students who had very low or very high math achievement scores (whose test scores were 20% above the average) were all at higher risk for test anxiety. These results point to the important fact that test anxiety does not necessarily happen only in students who have lower grades, but rather, it can affect students across achievement profiles. I saw this occur with one of my top students who, because of their test anxiety, resorted to cheating in order to keep their high grades.

And yet, as distressing as it may be, testing is an unavoidable fact of life for our children. The learning progress cannot be traced without some sort of feedback loop that objectively evaluates the achievements and improvements they should be making. Structured multiple-choice and open-question tests follow students throughout their schooling years. According to a report conducted by the Council of the Great City Schools,[13] up to 112 standardized tests are performed over 12 years of school. This number likely doesn't include smaller-scale pop-up quizzes, practice tests, reports, verbal checkups (e.g., in language classes), and other forms of student evaluation that are performed every semester in every class.

Managing test anxiety is of critical importance since tests mean entrance exams, grades in school, etc., which can result in being accepted or not accepted into a good college or university, getting or not getting a good job, and so on. Tests follow us all our life, and we must all learn to manage this kind of anxiety.

## RESEARCH RECAP:

- Test anxiety is a type of anxiety that is specifically related to testing or evaluation situations. It's a common form of anxiety that can affect people of all ages but is especially common in school-aged children and adolescents.

- Without intervention, test anxiety can lead to poorer academic performance, worse grades on standardized tests, weaker working memory, or even a school dropout.

- Test anxiety can affect students across achievement profiles but the right interventions can make a difference.

For parents with learners who have test anxiety, there *is* hope. Research has shown that with the application of the right strategies and practice, your child can overcome the challenges of test anxiety. One such study confirming this idea was published in 2019 in the *Journal of Anxiety Disorders*. This meta-analysis, conducted by Christopher Huntley and his colleagues,[14] considered 44 randomized controlled trials involving 2,209 university students to assess the effectiveness of interventions for test anxiety in improving academic performance. The study found that interventions significantly reduced test anxiety and improved academic performance. In other words, the right interventions can make a difference! Below are several effective ways to help your learner deal with test anxiety.

1.  **Make testing a regular part of learning:** Create opportunities for your children to test themselves, or you can test them while they're reading or studying. When testing becomes the norm, and your learner sees that it's okay to make mistakes, then it

will become much easier for them to manage test anxiety in a classroom setting. The leap from testing during study time to the actual test will feel less scary.

2. **Practice relaxation techniques:** Work with your child to develop relaxation techniques to help them manage their anxiety before and during a test. Exercises such as deep breathing, progressive muscle relaxation, or visualization (the practice of using one's imagination to experience a peaceful setting or experience) can all be very helpful. Try out various methods at home, well *before* a test, to see which works best. Remind your child to use these techniques if they experience anxiety *during* a test.

3. **Study regularly and prepare well:** Encourage students to consistently apply the learning strategies offered in this book so they can feel better prepared for a test. Thorough and regular implementation of good study habits will create a sense of control and mastery that can help reduce anxiety.

4. **Create positive learning conditions:** A supportive and nurturing home environment will promote self-esteem and can give your child more confidence when approaching a challenge such as a test. Additionally, when your child knows you'll have their back, no matter how they perform, they'll feel safe about openly communicating their fears and concerns with you and their teachers.

5. **Set realistic goals:** Encourage students to set attainable goals and avoid comparing themselves to others, as this can increase anxiety.

6. **Get plenty of sleep and exercise:** Encourage students to get plenty of rest and to move their bodies often, as both activities can help reduce stress and improve overall well-being.

7. **Reframe negative thoughts:** Teach students to challenge and reframe negative thoughts and beliefs about testing, such as "I always fail tests" or "Tests determine my worth." Help them to replace those ideas with positive, supportive thoughts such as "I can do this!" or "This test doesn't reflect my worth." Encourage them to call these positive phrases to mind if they begin to experience anxiety during an exam.

8. **Work with a mental health professional:** It's important to remember that these techniques work well with children whose test anxiety is not above the clinical level of anxiety. If your child has formed a serious anxiety disorder, contact a mental health professional, such as a school counselor or psychologist, as soon as possible to develop an individualized plan for managing test anxiety.

Our top recommendation is to address test anxiety with the suggestions above *before* a test occurs. However, should your child still experience anxiety *during* a test, below are a few additional suggestions for them to apply:

- **Practice deep breathing:** Taking slow, deep breaths can help calm the body and reduce feelings of stress and anxiety.

- **Focus on the present:** Remaining focused on the task at hand and not on worries about the future or past mistakes can be calming and reassuring.

- **Manage physical symptoms:** When feeling physical symptoms of anxiety, such as sweating, shaking, or racing heartbeat, try to stay calm and focus on your breathing.

- **Use visualization:** Imagine yourself successfully completing the exam and visualize yourself feeling calm and confident.

- **Read the instructions carefully:** Make sure you understand the instructions for the test, and if you're unsure, don't be afraid to ask for clarification.

- **Pace yourself:** Don't try to rush through the exam. Take your time, read each question carefully, and try to stay calm.

- **Get organized:** If you feel overwhelmed by the exam, try to break it down into smaller, manageable tasks and prioritize the questions you feel most confident about.

While it may be helpful for adults to understand that test anxiety is in our nature, that's often not reassuring or helpful to children. When working with your child, help them to see that overcoming test anxiety can be done through control beliefs. Reassure your child that *they* have control, *they* have the ability to overcome their anxiety through better preparation. *They* have the power to change their situation.

When my daughter was facing a big test, I'd work with her to ensure her control beliefs were reinforced. This was an important step toward helping her understand that she could increase her skill through hard work. I'd then reinforce my encouragement with task value, helping her to see the benefit of performing well on a test. This would trigger her intrinsic motivation to study hard before the test. As a final step, I'd let her know that if she gave her best effort she'd be rewarded by me (with ice cream or a fun activity) for her hard work, not necessarily her final grade. Close communication with your children and the implementation of practices such as these can empower them to manage their test anxiety and approach each new school challenge with more confidence.

## ACTION PLAN

- Help your child establish regular routines leading up to a test based on the best practices highlighted in this chapter.

- Work to foster a nurturing and loving home environment where your child feels supported, no matter the outcome of their testing.

- Remind your child that with hard work, they *can* make a difference in their grades. But also, good grades aren't the only goal. Giving their best effort is the top priority.

---

[1] 'An anxious nation': Barnes & Noble sees a surge in sales of books about stress by Rachel Siegel - https://www.washingtonpost.com/business/2018/08/02/an-anxious-nation-barnes-noble-sees-surge-sales-books-about-stress/

[2] COVID-19 pandemic triggers 25% increase in prevalence of anxiety and depression worldwide - https://www.who.int/news/item/02-03-2022-covid-19-pandemic-triggers-25-increase-in-prevalence-of-anxiety-and-depression-worldwide

[3] The Best Books About Anxiety of 2022 - https://psychcentral.com/reviews/best-books-about-anxiety

[4] Spielberger, C. D. (1978). The State-Trait Anxiety Inventory: Its theoretical and empirical foundations. In C. D. Spielberger and I. G. Sarason (Eds.), *Stress and Anxiety* (Vol. 5, pp. 3-20). Washington, DC: Hemisphere Publishing Corporation.

[5] Plante, I., Lecours, V., Lapointe, R., Chaffee, K. E., and Fréchette-Simard, C. (2022). "Relations between prior school performance and later test anxiety during the transition to secondary school." *British Journal of Educational Psychology* 92(3), 1068-1085.

[6] Bischofsberger, L., Burger, P. H., Hammer, A., Paulsen, F., Scholz, M., and Hammer, C. M. (2021). "Prevalence and characteristics of test anxiety in first year anatomy students." *Annals of Anatomy-Anatomischer Anzeiger* 236, 151719.

[7] Weems, C.F., Scott, B.G., Graham, R.A. et al. "Fitting Anxious Emotion-Focused Intervention into the Ecology of Schools: Results from a Test Anxiety Program Evaluation." *Prevention Science* 16, 200–210 (2015). https://doi.org/10.1007/s11121-014-0491-1

[8] Yeo, L.S., Goh, V.G. and Liem, G.A.D. "School-Based Intervention for Test Anxiety." *Child Youth Care Forum* 45, 1–17 (2016). https://doi.org/10.1007/s10566-015-9314-1

[9] von der Embse, Nathaniel, Dane Jester, Devlina Roy, and James Post. "Test anxiety effects, predictors, and correlates: A 30-year meta-analytic review." *Journal of Affective Disorders* 227 (2018): 483-493.

[10] Owens, M., Stevenson, J., Hadwin, J. A., and Norgate, R. (2014). "When does anxiety help or hinder cognitive test performance? The role of working memory capacity." *British Journal of Psychology* 105(1), 92-101.

[11] Cizek, G. J., and Burg, S. S. (2006). *Addressing Test Anxiety in a High-Stakes Environment: Strategies for Classroom and Schools.* Corwin Press.

[12] Plante, I., Lecours, V., Lapointe, R., Chaffee, K. E., and Fréchette-Simard, C. (2022). "Relations between prior school performance and later test anxiety during the transition to secondary school." *British Journal of Educational Psychology* 92(3), 1068-1085.

[13] Hart, Ray, Michael Casserly, Renata Uzzell, Moses Palacios, Amanda Corcoran, and Liz Spurgeon. "Student Testing in America's Great City Schools: An Inventory and Preliminary Analysis." Council of the Great City Schools (2015).

[14] Huntley, Christopher D., Bridget Young, James Temple, Melissa Longworth, Catrin Tudur Smith, Vikram Jha, and Peter L. Fisher. "The efficacy of interventions for test-anxious university students: A meta-analysis of randomized controlled trials." *Journal of Anxiety Disorders* 63 (2019): 36-50.

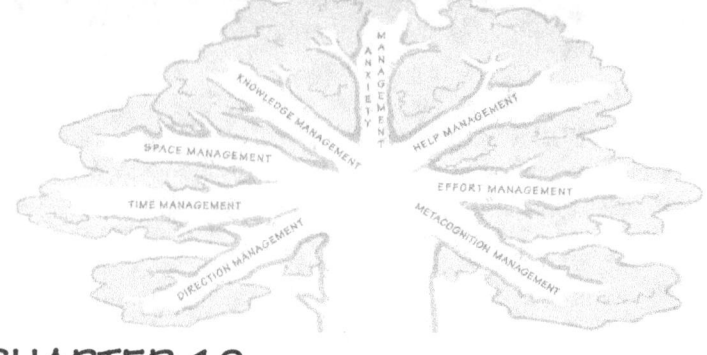

# CHAPTER 12

# HELP MANAGEMENT

If we get lost hiking in the woods, trail markers are typically in place to help us find our way. In the absence of such guides, a map or compass can be relied upon to get us back on track. A map highlights the different paths we can take and obstacles we might encounter along the way, while a compass helps us determine the right direction in which to go.

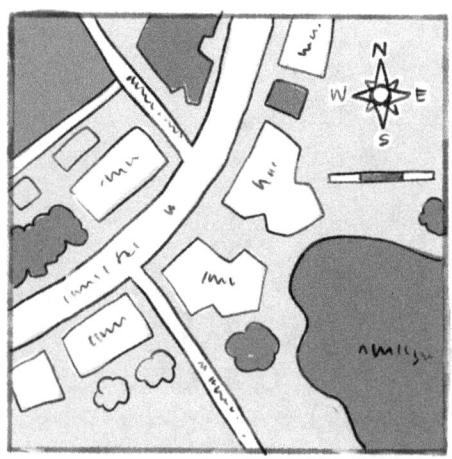

*Figure 21: A Map as a Guide*

Similarly, when learning a new subject, children can find themselves feeling lost or uncertain about the direction they should take—how to make sense of the material they're reading or how to retain it in the best way possible. When their path is unclear and they aren't comprehending new material or they don't know how to tackle a challenge, they need access to the right support and guidance. They need help management or an understanding of when and how to ask for help in order to find their way to success. Our children need to understand:

1. The best way to learn according to their unique and particular needs

2. How to manage the limitations and constraints of each form of help management

Our children must learn *when* to ask teachers, parents, or peers for help. They need to know *who* to ask, *what* to ask, and *how* to ask for help. By equipping our learners with effective help management strategies, we provide them with the tools they need to navigate their learning journey.

My wife once had a preschooler who was really struggling in math, when suddenly he started to get all his homework 100% correct. The teachers were amazed, but they were also curious. They wondered what intervention was helping this child. What was the magical ingredient to his rapid turnaround? The truth was revealed one day in class, as the student called out to the virtual assistant Alexa for help. As it turns out, the "help" this student was getting was from Alexa. The teachers were so tickled to find out the truth but knew they had to also address this issue with the child, and his parents, for the future. This child knew he needed help, but clearly, he didn't know *who* was best to seek help from.

When I started training for my swimming goal, I knew I needed help and guidance, so I engaged the services of a strength and conditioning coach. I needed someone who could let me know if I was lifting weights properly to optimize my sets and prevent injury. When I decided to join open-water races, I once again knew I needed the help of a coach. My swim coaches would tell me what I was doing right and wrong so my swimming techniques would improve for better swimming efficiency. In both instances, I knew *what* to ask for, as well as *how* and *when* to ask for it, and as a result, both my workout and swim coaches helped me achieve better results.

Studies conducted by Lim and a team of researchers[1] show that when you account for a child's intelligence along with other learning strategies such as time, knowledge, and space management, help management is able to explain more variation in achievements such as GPA. In other words, when help management is added to other strategies, learners perform better and attain better grades. Just as I knew how, who, what, and when to ask for help with my training, it's important for our learners to understand the importance and value of seeking help, as it can lead to an improvement in their ability to learn and retain information.

It's also critical that help is given the right way because the help you give or offer may be counterproductive, such as when it's given with a disparaging tone, in anger, or with a demeaning spirit. Let me explain. As a parent, there were times when I needed to help my daughter for various reasons, but how I did it wasn't always the best. My help would sometimes be delivered with a harsh tone or an unkind attitude, something I would later regret. My intention was to help her, but my words and actions fell short. When we're providing help, we must find ways to check our approach, forcing a pause to right our mindset before we act, if necessary. Help delivered with a calm mind and spirit is always more beneficial. Remember that our children can see through our demeanor, tone, and body language. They may not take our help to heart if it's delivered with impatience or an unwilling spirit.

If help isn't provided the right way, a child can develop the wrong mindset toward help management. If it is delivered with a harsh tone or a mean spirit, they can come to resent the help or will ignore it. For it to be effective, help management must be given with the following principles in mind:

1. **Scaffolding:** In construction work, scaffolding is erected to aid in the repair or building of a structure. Similarly, scaffolding refers to providing a learner with the proper support or tools to figure out how to develop learning structures they can reuse in the future. A learner should still be responsible for his or her own learning but help should be provided in a way that *supports* their efforts. Whenever help is excessive or given too early, or if it is even given too late, when the student has become too demotivated to work, a learner can become lazy and may lose out on the chance to improve their study skills.

   Actor and author Matthew McConaughey tells a story in his book *Greenlights*[2] about a poetry contest he once entered in the fifth grade. As he was sharing drafts of his poem with his mom, she made the suggestion that he should turn in a well-written poem that had already been published by another author. When he protested, she responded, "Do you like the poem?" and "Do you understand the poem? Then it's yours!" McConaughey went on to enter the published poem in the contest...and he won! While the end result may seem positive—winning the contest—if the goal is for your child to learn how to write poetry, then you likely can see that there are better ways to *support* your learner's efforts to do so.

For similar reasons, as a school administrator, I established a policy that homework at our school would not be graded. This policy was partly due to a tendency for some parents to step in and provide excessive help so that their children would receive higher grades. When some parents would overstep and help too much with homework, it was usually because they weren't aware that what they were doing was ultimately not helping their child. By removing the grading component, the pressure for higher grades was removed as well. Any inclination toward excessive intervention was reduced, which, in turn, empowered the students to learn more based on their own efforts. As a result, the children had a more effective homework experience.

2. **Self-awareness:** Both the helper and learner will benefit from being self-aware of the learning process as it progresses. A helper must know when to hold back and when to step in and provide support. The learner will also benefit from developing this skill, knowing when to ask for more help and when to keep trying on their own. Just as giving help too early can be counterproductive, likewise, if help is provided *too late*, a child can become demotivated and give up.

3. **Collaboration:** There is a social component to seeking help that should be kept in mind. Help management necessitates that a learner is in contact with their teacher, a parent, or a friend—someone who is able to help them. Just as there is value in participating in group sports or other activities where learning is happening together, a child can benefit from working with others, especially when they are in need of help.

Peer learning can provide a rich context for learning and development. When peers work together on a task, they can share their knowledge and expertise, challenge each other's ideas, and provide feedback and support. Peer learning can also promote social and emotional development by fostering relationships, communication skills, and a sense of belonging.[3]

When I used to manage a tech startup, I noticed that my IT teams would join forums to help them find solutions to technical issues. When they didn't have the answer to a problem, these forums, which were composed of other tech practitioners, helped them find various solutions and gave them helpful insights.

Additionally, let's consider two studies published in 2013, one by Shiro Sakaiya and a team in Japan, as well as one published in the Cambridge University Press by Leonhard Schibach and team. Both found that interactive learning environments, such as peer learning, can significantly increase students' intrinsic motivation to learn.[4,5] The inclination to continue social interactions and the heightened anticipation for future peer-learning activities can be traced back to the brain's reward-related pathways. When these pathways are stimulated through social engagement, they may lead to an increase in dopamine production. This biochemical response reinforces the desire for ongoing interaction and creates a sense of excitement for future collaborative learning.[6,7]

Educators often refer to the difference in how and when help is administered as either being executive or instrumental. When help is given too early—when the teacher, tutor, or parent circumvents the learning process and too quickly steps in to provide support—this is considered help that is executive in nature. When help is given in the right way and at the right time, then it is considered instrumental.

When my daughter was still in high school, she struggled with certain math concepts and I hired a couple of tutors to assist her in grasping the subject matter. I noticed that her tutors sometimes gave her the answers too soon. They didn't give her a chance to work through the problems on her own, to struggle and wrestle with the process of finding an answer. By doing so, they didn't truly help her to develop the conceptual learning foundation she needed. On the other hand, whenever her tutor *did* take the time to ask her good questions and to make her think through the homework problems on her own, without giving away the answer too soon, she was able to strengthen her learning foundation.

In our introduction to Part III Learning Strategy Management, we shared the story of the boy who encountered a cocoon and thought he would help the butterfly by cutting open its confinement with a pair of scissors. What the boy didn't know was the butterfly *needed* to struggle to get out of the cocoon in order to **fully develop**. By helping too much, he actually hurt the butterfly. Likewise, some struggle is critical for our children.

They must try, on their own, to work to learn and understand a concept. Only once they've experienced a few failed attempts should we intervene and provide **strategic** support. For help to be effective, it must be instrumental.[8,9]

In each of the above scenarios, there was a right and a wrong way to provide help. The key is for help to be provided at the right time and in the right way, so that it is most effective and helpful for the learner. Too much help given too soon or too late will be detrimental and not effective. But when it's given with the ideas of scaffolding, self-awareness, and collaboration in mind, it will help our children to grow and develop the skills they need to be stronger, better-equipped learners.

## RESEARCH RECAP:

- *Help management is most effective when it's used alongside other learning strategies* such as time, space, and knowledge management. In essence, help management makes these other strategies even more useful.

- *For help to be effective, it must be instrumental*, not executive.

- *When help is given in the right way and at the right time*, children will be able to *strengthen their learning foundation*.

With an awareness of the need for and value of seeking help in the right way, here are some practical ways we can support our learners in this effort.

1. **Practice patience:** As we've stated, intervention is only helpful when it is instrumental—after a child has a chance to struggle and work through a problem on their own. Sometimes the "help" needed should come in the form of a hint, not a full takeover. As parents, we must practice patience and refrain from helping too much or too soon. Remind your learner that the help you give is meant to be scaffolding, or framing, for how to eventually problem solve on their own.

2. **Model help-seeking behavior:** Children learn by observing and imitating the behavior of others. Parents can model effective help management by asking for help when they need it and being open to receiving help from others. Help-seeking can be demonstrated when you reach out to your mom for help with a Thanksgiving recipe or if you face challenges with a car repair and need to call a trusted mechanic for advice. Let your child in on these experiences so they can see how you work through big and small difficulties with the help of a friend or family member.

3. **Teach them to identify their needs:** Children must learn to identify when they need help and what kind of help they need. Parents can support this by asking open-ended questions and encouraging children to talk about their thoughts and feelings.

4. **Teach them to ask for help:** Children need to learn how to ask for help effectively. This means using appropriate language,

being clear about what they need, and being open to receiving support.

5. **Encourage them to seek help from a variety of sources:** Children can benefit from seeking help from a variety of sources; just be sure they're reaching out to the *right* sources; in other words, not Alexa! Discuss with your child a list of good options such as teachers, parents, peers, and other trusted adults. Encourage your child to explore different options and find what works best for them.

6. **Offer positive reinforcement:** Reinforce your child's efforts and successes in seeking help and working through problems. Celebrate their achievements and encourage them to continue seeking help when needed.

7. **Encourage independence:** While it's important to provide support and assistance when needed, it is also important to encourage children to work through problems on their own. This will help them develop their problem-solving skills and increase their confidence in their ability to handle challenges.

If you see that your child is hesitant to ask for help from you or a teacher, it's important to create a supportive learning environment where they feel comfortable seeking help when needed. Here are some strategies that can be helpful in doing so:

- **Build a positive and trusting relationship** with your child. This can be done by being approachable, nonjudgmental, and showing genuine interest in your child's learning.

- **Normalize asking for help.** Explain that it is okay and natural to ask for help and that everyone needs help sometimes.

- **Provide opportunities for your child to receive help** from a teacher or parent. This can be done by providing after-school tutoring or office hours with the teacher.

- **Use feedback and assessment** to identify areas where your child needs help. Regular check-ins can provide space for your child to ask for help if they're struggling.

- **Empower your child** to take ownership of their learning and encourage them to determine when they need help. Encourage them to come up with a plan to address the areas where they need additional support.

*Figure 22: A Conversation Between Parent and Child*

If your child has become *too* dependent on receiving help, there are ways to address this behavior as well. Start by setting clear expectations and gradually reducing the amount of help you provide. It's also important to reinforce positive behaviors and praise your child when they make an effort to work through problems on their own. Over time, your child will learn that they're capable of solving problems independently and will become more confident in their abilities.

In general, it's important to empower your child to take ownership of their learning and encourage them to determine when they need help. However, if they're consistently struggling and not asking for help, it may be appropriate for parents and teachers to step in and offer guidance or support. Parents and teachers should use their own judgment to determine if the child needs help or support in a particular area.

Artyom has shared how, over the years, he's noticed that the most successful students are often the ones who are willing to ask for clarification when there is something they don't fully understand. While some students will struggle to work with the notes they have, give up, or even guess an answer, the students who are willing to push back when something isn't clear are the most likely to truly grasp the subject. These students won't wait until the end of an exercise to ask for help, rather, they'll stop a discussion to clarify their point of confusion. Raising your hand in front of everyone and being willing to speak up and admit that you don't understand something can be socially challenging. But in order to understand a topic, sometimes, students must be willing to do that. The critical lesson in all of this is for our learners to be brave enough to know *when* to raise their hand and ask for help, self-aware enough to know *what* and *who* to ask, and trained in *how* to ask the right questions that will support their work without giving too much away. By supporting our children with these help management strategies, we're effectively equipping them to succeed academically.

## ACTION PLAN

- The first step toward teaching your child a new practice is usually through modeling. Don't be afraid to let your child know when you don't understand something, and let them know what you're doing to get help.

- Talk to your child about who they can go to for help. Identify peers, teachers, and other trusted sources who are available for them to reach out to when in need.

- When you see your child asking for the right kind of help in the right way, let them know! Encourage them to continue to do so in the future.

---

[1] Lim, Chee, Habibah Ab Jalil, Aini Ma'rof, and Wan Saad. "Peer learning, self-regulated learning and academic achievement in blended learning courses: A structural equation modeling approach." *International Journal of Emerging Technologies in Learning (IJET)* 15, no. 3 (2020): 110-125.

[2] *Greenlights* by Matthew McConaughey https://greenlights.com/

[3] Vygotsky, L. S., and Cole, M. (1978). *Mind in Society: Development of Higher Psychological Processes.* Harvard University Press.

[4] Sakaiya, S., Shiraito, Y., Kato, J., Ide, H., Okada, K., Takano, K., and Kansaku, K. (2013). "Neural correlate of human reciprocity in social interactions." *Frontiers in Neuroscience* 7:239. doi: 10.3389/fnins.2013.00239

[5] Schilbach, L., Timmermans, B., Reddy, V., Costall, A., Bente, G., Schlict, T., et al. (2013). "Toward a second-person neuroscience." *Behavioral and Brain Sciences* 36, 393–462. doi: 10.1017/S0140525X12000660

[6] Guionnet, S., Nadel, J., Bertasi, E., Sperduti, M., Delaveau, P., and Fossati, P. (2012). "Reciprocal imitation: toward a neural basis of social interaction." *Cerebral Cortex* 22, 971–978. doi: 10.1093/cercor/bhr177

[7] Schilbach, L., Wohlschlaeger, A., Kraemer, N., Newen, A., Shah, N., Fink, G., et al. (2006). "Being with virtual others: neural correlates of social interaction." *Neuropsychologia* 44, 718–730. doi: 10.1016/j.neuropsychologia.2005.07.017

[8] Martín-Arbós, Sergi, Elena Castarlenas, and Jorge-Manuel Duenas. "Help-seeking in an academic context: A systematic review." *Sustainability* 13, no. 8 (2021): 4460.

[9] Schenke, Katerina, Arena C. Lam, AnneMarie M. Conley, and Stuart A. Karabenick. "Adolescents' help seeking in mathematics classrooms: Relations between achievement and perceived classroom environmental influences over one school year." *Contemporary Educational Psychology* 41 (2015): 133-146.

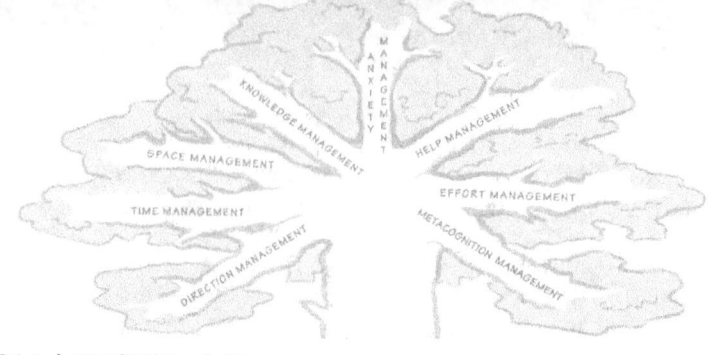

# CHAPTER 13

# EFFORT MANAGEMENT

Born in Orlando, Florida, NFL running back Chris Johnson gained prominence for his speed as a track and field athlete, but his real dream was to become a professional football player.[1] Raised by a single mom, Johnson shared with *I Am Athlete*[2] that he grew up in "the hood" and was driven to make something of himself to improve his life.

A broken leg sustained during his senior year of high school caused Johnson to miss numerous football games, taking him off the radar of pro scouts. Compounding his issues, Johnson's grades were poor. Without a serious effort to turn things around, he was at risk of losing his NCAA eligibility and ability to play college ball.

Josh Staph[3] says that it was at this point that Johnson's determination to succeed truly kicked in. His desire to achieve a professional career in sports "motivated him to attend night classes until 9 p.m. each day to bolster his weak grades." In the same article, Johnson shares that "where I'm from, there are a lot of dudes with talent who [don't] make it. I always knew working hard was one of the most important things [I could do]."

East Carolina's head coach John Thompson offered him a scholarship as long as Johnson was willing to continue to work on his academics. Johnson made the most of this opportunity, keeping his grades up, and by his senior season at East Carolina, he was leading the nation in all-purpose yards. At the 2008 NFL Combine, Johnson was again given a chance to prove himself. He wowed everyone by setting the Combine record in the 40-yard dash with an incendiary 4.24 seconds. As a result, he was the first-round draft choice of the Tennessee Titans. Once he earned his chance to play in the NFL, Johnson never stopped giving his all. During his pro career, he played for 10 seasons, amassing 9,651 rushing yards and scoring 55 touchdowns. He was named NFL Offensive Player of the Year and First-Team All-Pro.

Johnson found success as a professional football player after years of dedicated effort. Facing one uphill climb after another, Johnson persistently pushed himself to overcome obstacles to achieve his dream. Whether it was fighting back from an injury or buckling down to pull up his grades, Johnson was able to put forth the effort he needed to when it counted.

What enables someone like Johnson to persevere when others fail and fall victim to their circumstances? Our research shows that effort management plays a big role. Effort management is a person's ability to persist in achieving one's goals.[4] It also refers to an individual's ability to regulate the amount of effort and concentration they apply to a task based on its level of difficulty and importance.

A child's ability to manage their effort can play a critical role in determining their academic success. When a child can learn to sustain focus and motivation, even when faced with challenging or tedious material, they'll have a better chance of overcoming the difficulties of learning a new subject.

Several key skills are tied to the development of effort management, including resilience, willpower, self-control, and delayed gratification. Let's consider how to think about each of these practices in the context of our discussion and then consider how each is uniquely connected to the development of your learner's effort management.

- **Resilience** refers to the ability to endure, bounce back, or rapidly recover from challenges or adversities; it's when someone can display toughness in the face of misfortune or change.[5] In Chris Johnson's story, a clear thread of resilience can be seen. His ability to rebound in the face of challenges is what set him apart. It's what enabled him to be successful. He'd been a kid with little opportunity, but he had the resilience to overcome the hand life had dealt him.

- **Willpower** is the individual's capacity to resist immediate temptations and exert control over undesirable thoughts, emotions, or impulses. Like resilience, willpower refers to a person's ability to persevere when faced with difficulties.[6] Recent studies on willpower have found that a person's mindset about willpower is self-fulfilling.[7] If you believe your willpower will be easily depleted, it will be. Conversely, if you believe you'll be energized by resisting temptation, then your use of willpower will leave you feeling motivated to keep going. In other words, willpower is a muscle you can build with regular use and practice.

- **Self-control** is the ability to control oneself, specifically regulating emotions and desires, or controlling how they are manifested in behavior, particularly when faced with challenging circumstances.[8] An example of self-control is when a learner chooses to study for a math test instead of chatting with friends or watching a new movie. Self-control is key in school settings because learners may recognize the importance of academic work for their future but don't enjoy it at the moment and can get easily distracted by other, seemingly more interesting activities.

- **Delayed gratification** refers to the ability to resist the temptation for an immediate reward and instead wait for a larger, more valuable reward in the future. The benefits of delayed gratification were demonstrated in a well-known Stanford marshmallow experiment[9] that started in the 1970s. In this study, children were offered a choice between one small but immediate reward (a single marshmallow) versus two small rewards (multiple marshmallows), which they'd receive if they waited 15 minutes. Follow-up studies revealed that children who exhibited greater patience in delaying gratification for a superior reward demonstrated enhanced life outcomes, as indicated by their SAT scores,[10] educational attainment,[11] body mass index (BMI),[12] and other life measures.[13]

While all four skills—resilience, willpower, self-control, and delayed gratification—are related to effort management, they each play a different role. Consider, for example, how each skill would be important for the effort management of an athlete training for a marathon.

- A high level of **self-control** will enable the athlete to refrain from eating unhealthy food. Even though junk food is something he enjoys, he recognizes that if he wants to do well in his race, he should avoid eating foods that will make him sluggish or slow.

- His restraint with sweets also highlights the runner's awareness of the importance of **delayed gratification**. The treats might be nice at the moment, but the joy of succeeding in his race is the higher value gratification he's holding out for.

- During training, if he were to suffer a knee injury, his **willpower** would enable him to resist the temptation to quit training. Whenever he's having negative thoughts about working to overcome his injury, so he can heal and get back to race training, his willpower will kick in and pull him through.

- Healing and bouncing back from an injury will develop his **resilience**, not only as a runner but as a person, as well. His resilience will set him up to become a unique kind of athlete, one who overcomes adversity and succeeds in the face of challenges.

The strengthening of each of these skills is directly tied to the development of effort management. The more a learner can improve their aptitude in each of these areas, the more their effort management will grow. As a result, their likelihood of success when learning gets tough will improve too.

Through our modeling and direct instruction, our children can learn and experience the benefits of stronger resilience, greater willpower, consistent self-control, and sustained delayed gratification. As a result, they will develop the ability to focus on long-term goals and to persevere through challenges and setbacks in order to achieve those goals. They will develop a perspective where they see failure and obstacles as chances for learning and personal development rather than as reasons to quit. The regular practice of each of these skills will build toward the overarching development of effort management, or the ability to persist, sustain focus, and keep going even when faced with challenging or tedious school subjects.

There are a number of ways to teach children the skills of effort management. Playing board games is an excellent option. By waiting for their turn and resisting the temptation to make impulsive moves, children learn self-control and delay their gratification. Additionally, when children lose at board games, they learn resilience, how to cope with disappointment, and how to bounce back from setbacks.

Other activities, such as learning a musical instrument or mastering a new sport, can help children develop willpower and resilience as these activities require ongoing work and persistent effort, especially in the early stages when the activity is wholly unfamiliar and new. These activities require many hours of practice time, which helps children learn to focus on long-term goals and delay immediate gratification since they will have to say no to doing other things while they are practicing.

Finally, active participation in sports is a powerful way to develop both effort management abilities and resilience. Artyom remembers being part of a wrestling club in high school. Many students came to train and learn about this demanding sport. However, the training was not for those lacking resilience, as it demanded rigorous effort, unwavering dedication, and substantial hard work.

At the start of the school year, a group of around 80 students would join the club, but within a few weeks, the number would decrease as the training became more challenging. Only some 20 athletes who had the willpower and resilience to push through remained by the end of the year. Artyom remembers how his coach, Eric Hensen, used to remind young athletes during the most difficult parts of the training and weight loss phases that "if you can survive this, you can survive anything in life." And he was right. Research demonstrates that active sports participation can improve one's resilience and effort even outside of the gym setting.[14]

*Figure 23: A Wrestling Match*

Effort management will develop best when your child exercises these strategies alongside the foundational principles of the Wisest Learners™, including motivation, beliefs, and attitude. Intrinsic motivation supports effort management, such as when a child grinds through a tough workout, pushes hard to comprehend a new idea, or sticks it out to see a project through until the end. When I was still building my skills as a swimmer, for example, I'd often ask myself *why*—why was I doing another race, why did I need to keep practicing? My intrinsic desire to become a better swimmer helped me remember why I was swimming. It allowed me to persist when things got hard. There were times I was so discouraged and wanted to quit, but my intrinsic motivation kept me going. I persisted because I wanted to set a good example for my daughter, students, and family. I told myself that I would finish something I started, notwithstanding the challenges.

Keep in mind that a learner can have willpower based on both intrinsic and extrinsic motivation, but intrinsic is always the better of the two. For example, a child who is intrinsically motivated to learn a new skill, such as playing a guitar or reading, will show more willpower, self-control, and resilience when faced with challenges. They will keep practicing even when it's difficult because they enjoy the process and find it rewarding. On the other hand, a child who is extrinsically motivated to learn the same skill (e.g., because their parents promised them a treat or a toy) may give up more easily when faced with challenges, especially if they feel that the promised reward is not worth the effort required to learn the skill. This is because their motivation is tied to external rewards rather than personal interest or enjoyment. As discussed previously, intrinsic motivation, compared with extrinsic motivation, empowers the learner to boost their willpower, self-control, and resilience.

While extrinsic motivation can do the same, intrinsic motivation goes further and digs deeper.

When it comes to beliefs, an idea discussed back in Chapter 5, a learner with a healthy belief believes in their ability to accomplish a task or achieve a goal. They trust they possess all the necessary tools to succeed, and they just need to work hard, stay focused, and put their minds to achieving their goals. These healthy beliefs will only improve a child's effort management, as healthy beliefs increase the likelihood that a child will persist when things get difficult. Much like Chris Johnson, who leveraged his belief in his ability even when his circumstances were challenging and he had to work hard to prove himself, your child can lean on their healthy beliefs about their ability in order to successfully master a new subject.

Whenever any of us tries to learn something new, it's inevitable that we'll encounter challenges. So will our children as they work to learn a new subject. This is something I struggled to understand many times as a child. When I tried to learn to play guitar, for instance, I'd feel the pain in my fingers and start developing calluses from practice. But I didn't believe in my ability to learn musical instruments. I was unable to persist through the pain. As a result, I gave up too quickly with guitar lessons, before I had the chance to experience the reward of developing this skill. Therefore, developing the ability to persist through challenges and persevere in the face of obstacles is the right attitude for the wisest learner. Being able to embrace the struggle and recognize that it is a natural and necessary part of the learning process can help individuals develop the proper attitude of resilience and ultimately achieve greater success in their educational pursuits.

Another foundational principle covered in Part II has close ties to effort management, and that's the principle of self-efficacy. As you may remember, self-efficacy is a learner's belief in their ability to be successful. Much like willpower has self-fulfilling qualities, so too is the connection between self-efficacy and effort management. The more a child exercises the skill related to effort management—the more they develop their resiliency, self-control, and willpower—the stronger their self-efficacy will become and the more positive their learning outcomes will be. As they see the benefits of putting off short-term fun in order to study, exercising their self-control, and delaying gratification, they will find their knowledge and skills improving, which will manifest in better learning outcomes and most likely higher grades. As they improve in their learning journey, they will have more confidence in their ability and be encouraged to study more. Similarly, the more they practice willpower and resiliency, pushing through to complete a difficult task, the more they will build their confidence in their ability, experience the rewards of doing so, and the more likely they will be to repeat this effort again in the future.

Many have a tendency to give up too easily when things get tough. My coach told me that many people sign up for gym memberships at the start of each year, but most have stopped exercising by the time the year is over. Children, in particular, are prone to giving up when they're unable to do something the first time they try it. But everyone can do better with practice, and we can overcome our natural inclination to quit. It starts with modeling. As children see their parents practicing the skills of effort management, when they see us exhibiting resilience, willpower, self-control, and delayed gratification, they will likely witness the benefits of doing so too. This is why it's critically important for us to not only model effort management but to communicate with our children along the way. Explain to your learners what you're doing and why. Let them see that it's hard, but let them witness the rewards, as well.

We've now highlighted numerous positive outcomes that can come with the development of effort management, but the flip side of the story is important to touch on, as well. When effort management is underdeveloped, there can be crippling consequences,[15] such as the following:

1. **A tendency to quit school:** Studies have shown that a lack of skills related to effort management, such as resilience, can lead to higher school dropout. The good news is that the opposite has also been proven true. The development of effort management can *prevent* school dropouts.[16]

2. **Increased stress and anxiety:** Children who lack effort management may become easily overwhelmed by stress and anxiety. They may struggle to cope with difficult situations and may be more prone to experiencing anxiety, depression, or other mental health issues.

3. **Social difficulties:** Children who lack resilience may struggle to make and maintain friendships and may have difficulty resolving conflicts with peers. They may also be more likely to engage in risky behaviors or exhibit aggressive or impulsive behaviors.

- Effort management is a strategy that can be developed and strengthened with practice.

- We aren't born with a finite amount of resiliency, willpower, or self-control, but rather, the more our learners practice these skills, the more strength they will gain in each area.

- Delayed gratification and self-control will enable our learners to focus on long-term goals and persevere through challenges in order to achieve those goals.

The negative side effects of poor effort management likely motivate you more to support your child in developing this strategy. In order to assist your efforts, here are a number of best practices to follow.

1. **Break tasks down into smaller, manageable parts:** When children face a large, daunting task, it can be easy for them to feel overwhelmed and lose motivation. By breaking the task into smaller, more achievable parts, children can experience a greater sense of control and enhance their ability to sustain effort effectively.

2. **Set achievable goals:** Goals that are too challenging can be demotivating, while goals that are too easy may not provide enough challenge. Encourage your child to set goals that are achievable but require some effort and challenge to accomplish.

3. **Provide regular feedback:** Regular feedback can help children understand what they're doing well and what they need to work on. This can help them sustain motivation and effort as they work to improve their skills.

4. **Encourage self-reflection:** Prompt your child to reflect on their learning process and what strategies are effective for them. This can help them develop a greater awareness of their own strengths and weaknesses and make adjustments to sustain their effort.

5. **Encourage intrinsic motivation:** Internally motivated learners are more likely to sustain effort and persist in the face of challenges. Motivate your child to find joy and meaning in the learning process itself, rather than relying on external rewards or praise.

6. **Celebrate effort, not just achievement:** Praise your child's effort and hard work, even when they don't achieve the outcome they were hoping for. This can help them see the value in resiliency, willpower, self-control, and delayed gratification, even when success is not immediate.

7. **Support your child without solving every problem:** Rather than fixing every minor issue your child faces, allow them to discuss how they feel and find solutions on their own. If your child is struggling with a particular subject at school, resist the urge to simply do the work for them. Instead, support your child's effort to find a plan for improvement. Helping your child develop strategies to succeed on their own will build their confidence in their abilities.

8. **Help your child to identify and manage strong emotions:** Acknowledge their feelings and provide support while also encouraging them to find constructive ways to cope.

9. **Build your child's self-compassion:** Teach them to be kind to themselves, especially when they face disappointment, failures, or mistakes.

10. **Help your child develop problem-solving skills in age-appropriate ways:** For instance, if your child encounters a situation at school where another child behaves unkindly or says hurtful things, brainstorm how to respond better the next time they encounter a similar situation.

11. **Find positive role models for your child who have faced similar challenges:** This could be an older friend or family member who has experienced a similar situation and can offer practical advice.

Developing your child's skills in effort management will not happen overnight. However, with consistent good modeling and lots of encouragement from you, you'll see a shift in mindset over time, leading to better control of thoughts, feelings, and actions toward reaching their goals. Consistency is key, especially when showing your learners how to practice resilience, willpower, self-control, and delayed gratification. The more they see you exercising these habits, the more they will be likely to follow your path.

Remember to lean on the learning foundation of the Wisest Learners™ as well, such as your child's healthy beliefs, intrinsic motivation, and self-efficacy, as building strength in one area will only support the others. These practices will take hold over time and build momentum, ultimately equipping your learner to reach their full potential and lead successful life.

## ACTION PLAN

- Develop a rhythm in your home that engages the practices outlined in this chapter. Follow these action steps to further support and reinforce the good practices of effort management.

- Start simple: With all the good strategies in this book, it can be overwhelming knowing where to start. Begin small by clearly discussing important behaviors, such as goal-setting, self-reflection, and problem-solving, and establishing simple rules that will step-by-step help your child develop their ability to handle each strategy.

- Establish routines: Regular schedules can help children become more familiar with their day-to-day activities and can help to develop their effort management abilities.

- Incorporate physical activity: Don't let the big picture overburden your child. Give them plenty of mental and physical breaks. Alternating learning activities with movement can help children focus and regulate their behavior.

[1] Life Lessons from the World's Greatest Athletes by Dr. W.D. Panlilio

[2] Chris Johnson: Talks Near Death Experience, Embracing Culture & Life After NFL - *I Am Athlete*. https://www.youtube.com/watch?v=1V2AuKJaah8

[3] Chris Johnson's Speed Workout by Josh Staph, https://www.stack.com/a/chris-johnsons-nine-speed-building-exercises/

[4] Inzlicht, M., Shenhav, A., and Olivola, C. Y. (2018). "The effort paradox: Effort is both costly and valued." *Trends in Cognitive Sciences* 22(4), 337-349.

[5] Resilience definition: https://www.merriam-webster.com/dictionary/resilience

[6] American Psychological Association. "What you need to know about willpower: The psychological science of self-control." Washington: APA (www.apa.org/helpcenter/willpower. pdf) (2012).

[7] The mindset that brings unlimited willpower by David Robson - https://www.bbc.com/worklife/article/20230103-how-to-strengthen-willpower

[8] Self-control definition: https://www.oed.com/

[9] Zacharia, Janine. "The Bing 'Marshmallow Studies': 50 Years of Continuing Research." (2015).

[10] Mischel, W.; Shoda, Y.; Rodriguez, M. (26 May 1989). "Delay of gratification in children." *Science* 244 (4907): 933–938.

[11] Ayduk, Ozlem N.; Mendoza-Denton, Rodolfo; Mischel, Walter; Downey, Geraldine; Peake, Philip K.; Rodriguez, Monica L. (2000). "Regulating the interpersonal self: Strategic self-regulation for coping with rejection sensitivity." *Journal of Personality and Social Psychology.*

[12] Schlam, Tanya R.; Wilson, Nicole L.; Shoda, Yuichi; Mischel, Walter; Ayduk, Ozlem (2013). "Preschoolers' delay of gratification predicts their body mass 30 years later." *Journal of Pediatrics.*

[13] Shoda, Yuichi; Mischel, Walter; Peake, Philip K. (1990). "Predicting adolescent cognitive and self-regulatory competencies from preschool delay of gratification: Identifying diagnostic conditions." *Developmental Psychology*.

[14] Norris, G., and Norris, H. (2021). "Building Resilience Through Sport in Young People With Adverse Childhood Experiences." *Frontiers in Sports and Active Living* 3, 663587.

[15] Ayala, Juan Carlos, and Guadalupe Manzano. "Academic performance of first-year university students: The influence of resilience and engagement." *Higher Education Research & Development* 37, no. 7 (2018): 1321-1335.

[16] Hupfeld, Kelly. "A review of the literature: Resiliency skills and dropout prevention." *Scholar Centric* (2010).

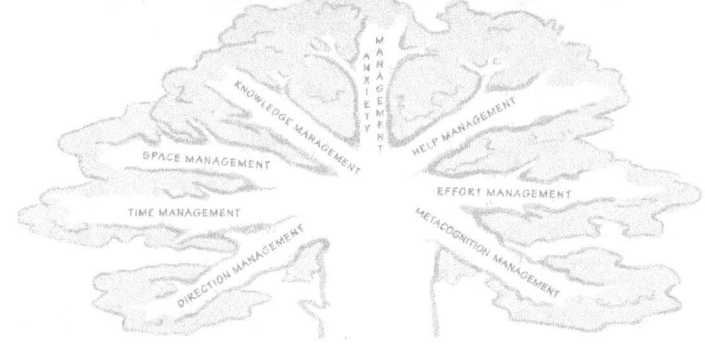

# CHAPTER 14

# METACOGNITION MANAGEMENT

Over the last several years, my daughter has pursued her under-graduate degree at a college in Sydney, Australia. At times, she's struggled with the feeling that she wasn't making the most of her learning experience. She knew some of her study habits were falling short of what they should be. So now, as she begins her master's program studies, I'm encouraging her to reflect on her undergraduate experience. I've suggested that she make a list of the things she felt she'd handled well along with a list of the habits that she knew were not resulting in her most productive work. My hope is to help her identify which practices to repeat and see where she can improve. I'm lending my guidance in an effort to help her prepare, so she can lay the groundwork for a more optimal learning season in graduate school.

As parents, this is often our role—the encourager, pointing our learners in the right direction and providing gentle reminders about where and how they can improve. There have been times when my daughter has felt overwhelmed by the complexities of what she's learning. The work that lies ahead of her can feel impossible, and this can lead her to lose hope and motivation. Sometimes, she can work through these feelings on her own, with space and time to consider her goals and motivation, knowing that I'm there if she needs guidance and support. Other times, I need to step in to provide encouragement and help her refocus. I remind her why she chose this field of study to begin with, revisiting the long-term goals and dreams that drew her to this program. I prompt her to pause, breathe, and take one small step at a time as she embarks on learning a challenging new subject. I remind her that what she's learning will come with practice and that she is capable of learning the subject if she puts in the work. She just can't let herself quit prematurely or she'll fail to see her hard work come to fruition. In other words, I work to address her intrinsic motivation and control beliefs.

When my daughter takes time to practice these thought processes about her learning and to consider how she can improve, this is a clear example of metacognition management in action. Metacognition is the ability to think about your own thinking. It's like having a tool that helps you manage your thoughts and actions so you can become a better learner and problem-solver. When our children use metacognition, they reflect on their learning process, figure out what they already know, what they need to learn, and how to learn it. They also monitor their progress, check their understanding, and adjust their learning strategies as needed.

Another way of describing metacognition management is someone standing back and taking a bird's-eye view of oneself. It's an awareness of one's thought processes and an understanding of the patterns behind them. It involves asking oneself questions such as "How am I doing?" or "How did I do?" as it relates to a task or the understanding of a new subject. It's the ability to think about one's own thinking. It speaks to a higher order of thinking that includes the ability to plan, monitor, and evaluate one's own learning and problem-solving processes. This is important work for our learners, especially as they mature and become more independent in their studies.

Metacognition management involves two main components:

1. **Thought management:** This includes understanding one's own thoughts, feelings, and beliefs about learning. Our learners can use this knowledge to make better decisions about how to approach a learning task, how to monitor their progress, and how to regulate their emotions and motivation.

2. **Process management:** This involves analyzing one's use of different strategies and techniques that need to be adopted in order to learn more effectively. For example, your child might have initially focused on highlighting and rereading but decided to prioritize recall and elaboration strategies for a deeper understanding of the assigned reading. She might also use strategies like self-testing, self-explanation, or goal-setting to monitor her progress and stay motivated.

Metacognition management is the linchpin strategy that unites all the strategies we've discussed so far. If you think of all the learning strategies as fingers, then metacognition management is the thumb that connects and brings them together. The human thumb is opposable, meaning that it can be moved to touch each of the other four fingers, which allows us to grasp and manipulate objects with great precision. Our opposable thumb allows us to perform precise motor actions by providing us with a high degree of control over our hands and fingers. In a similar way, metacognition allows us to monitor and regulate our own thinking and learning processes, which can help us to stay on track and achieve our learning goals with greater precision.

I recently came to have a new appreciation for my thumb. As a result of my swimming regimen, my right thumb had become weak and sore. I couldn't use it for basic things such as carrying a book. I even struggled to pick up a piece of luggage! I had to undergo therapy to help it operate properly again. Before my injury, my thumb was nearly an afterthought—it's just one finger after all, so it shouldn't have such an impact. I certainly didn't credit it as an integral part of my daily functioning ability. But my thumb allows my hand to do things like grasp or move items. Without my thumb, my four other fingers struggle to do many functions that I easily do with my thumb. My thumb allows my four other fingers to be at their best. Consider this: it is much harder to grasp and hold a book with just your forefingers as opposed to using your hand with your thumb.

Similar in importance to our thumbs, metacognition management is the key strategy that brings together all the others, and without it, our children will fail to reach their full learning potential. It's the strategy that consolidates the foundational principles and learning strategies. It enables our children to elevate their learning process and achieve long-term success. It is especially crucial in equipping our children to become more independent, self-regulated learners. By developing their metacognitive skills, they will be able to take charge of their own learning and become more confident and successful in school. The moment our learners master metacognition is the point at which they will reach optimal learning.

Research has shown that metacognition management can have an impact on learning over the long term. Research work by Ohtani[1] indicated that metacognitive skills contribute unique variance to academic achievements beyond what can be explained by general intelligence alone. This research also found there to be a relationship between academic performance and metacognition that is consistent across age groups, including elementary school students and secondary school students. This suggests that training children to adopt the habits of metacognition management can lead to improved academic performance in students of all ages. De Boer[2] and colleagues' research found metacognition to have a positive effect on academic performance over periods of time, highlighting the importance of investing energy and focus into the development of this strategy as a way to support your child's ongoing, lifelong pursuit of knowledge.

Metacognition management strategies are particularly noticeable and useful when considered in the context of three stages of learning—as children begin setting goals and planning for how to be successful (the preparatory phase), as they monitor progress (the performance phase), and as they reflect on their learning (the appraisal phase). Consider the following examples for how to support your learner in each of these stages:

1. **Preparatory:** This is the phase in which planning should take place in preparation for a task or learning assignment. This stage of learning is crucial as it lays the groundwork for the other two. It's the point at which learners ask the question "What can I do to prepare well before I start my learning?"

   For example, a basketball player knows that his goal is to make baskets in order to score points and win a game. A player in the preparatory stage will be asking himself, "What kind of shooting drills do I need to do in order to score more points?" and "How can I better prepare myself for a game?"

   Similarly, when a student is preparing for an exam, metacognition management can involve setting specific goals for what they want to achieve on the exam, breaking down the material into manageable chunks, and creating a study schedule to ensure they have enough time to review all the material before the exam. It also involves taking proactive steps to set oneself up for success in the learning process. This can include deciding how to allocate time and resources and determining the order in which to tackle tasks.

   Much of what I encouraged my daughter to do ahead of her graduate studies would fall under the category of preparatory, pre-semester planning. I was guiding her in how to set herself up for success in the semester to come.

   Preparatory work is the important first step in deciding which strategies should be engaged once learning is taking place. For example, as a child looks over their upcoming schedule and their list of classes, it'll be important for them to consider which of the strategies they should use to most effectively retain the material they will learn. They may need to engage the strategy of  or help management, depending on how comfortable they feel with the topic. Before they sit down to begin their studies, they will want to consider if they've optimized the strategy of space management. Being aware of all the strategies at their disposal is a key component to their best learning.

Our learners will need to determine which subjects are their top priority. Their time is limited, and it won't be possible to apply every learning strategy to every subject. So, they will need to choose where to devote more effort. Also, keep in mind that the strategies in this book do not operate well in silos. At times, certain strategies will need to be prioritized, but they all must work together for top performance effectiveness.

One way to highlight the importance of this preparatory stage is to offer a view of what happens when students fail to properly prepare for their studies. When learners lack the necessary skills and strategies to plan and prepare effectively, they may experience a range of negative outcomes, such as:

○ Procrastination: Without clear goals and a plan of action, learners may find it difficult to get started on a task, which can lead to delays in completing the work.

○ Poor time management: Without a well-organized study schedule or an understanding of how to allocate time effectively, learners may struggle to balance competing demands on their time, such as extracurricular activities and social obligations.

o   Overwhelming workload: Without prioritizing tasks or breaking down large assignments into manageable chunks, learners can feel overwhelmed by the volume of work they need to complete, which can lead to feelings of anxiety.

o   Lack of direction: Without clear goals or a plan of action, learners may feel directionless and unsure of what they need to accomplish, which can lead to a lack of motivation and engagement in the learning process.

With the proper preparation, learners can avoid these issues and have a much more engaging, interactive, and enlightening learning experience.

2.   **Performance:** This is the stage in which learners should pause while learning or studying to assess if they should continue or change their adopted learning strategies. Learning has begun, and as it continues, a child should be ready to monitor how things unfold so they can make pivots or tweaks to their process if and when things don't go as planned.

At this point in the learning process, learners should be able to monitor their progress and identify if their strategies are working or not. Frequently, performance monitoring involves asking oneself questions such as "Do I understand the main points of this reading?" or "What are the key points I need to remember from this lecture?" Self-questioning helps learners to identify whether the selected and/or practiced learning strategy is working well and is leading to better memory of the learned material and where they may need to adjust their learning approach.

Keep in mind that there is no definitive answer to *when* during the performance phase this reflection should happen. Factors like learner profile, material complexity, time allotment, learning goals, etc., will need to be considered. As a rule of thumb, learners should focus on practicing one or at most two strategies per lesson or session to provide sufficient focus.

We would propose that learners set a deadline for evaluating learning strategies, such as two to four weeks, and focus on implementing and giving the current strategy a chance to evolve until the deadline is reached. Once the deadline is reached, they can then use metacognitive strategies to evaluate their progress and assess whether the strategy should be fine-tuned. However, in those two to four weeks, they should forget about switching strategies and should ignore any doubts about the current strategy, thus giving it a chance.

By not making any strategy changes in the first two to four weeks, the learner will avoid the issue of spending too much time questioning and switching strategies, which can lead to frustration and abandonment of metacognitive approaches.

After the deadline, learners can reflect and evaluate the effectiveness of their strategy and make adjustments as needed. This approach promotes a balance between actively monitoring performance and avoiding excessive self-doubt and strategy switching, allowing learners to fully engage with their learning process while still making progress toward their goals.

Some helpful performance monitoring strategies to consider are the following:

- **Reflection:** Reflection is a key component of metacognition, and learners can use it to evaluate their own learning strategies. They can ask themselves questions like "How well did my learning strategies work for me?" and "What could I do differently to improve my learning outcomes?" By reflecting on their learning process, learners can identify areas where their current strategies are working well and areas where they need to make changes.

- **Creative visualization:** Learners can imagine themselves using different learning strategies and evaluate how effective they are. By using creative visualization, learners can tap into their imagination and gain new insights into their own learning process.

- **Feedback:** Learners can also seek feedback from others, such as teachers, peers, or tutors, on their learning strategies. They can ask questions like "What do you think of my approach to studying?" or "Are there any areas where you think I could improve my learning strategies?" By getting feedback from others, learners can gain valuable insights into their own strengths and weaknesses and make adjustments accordingly. Research has shown that effective feedback can promote metacognitive awareness[3], self-regulation[4], and learning outcomes.

- **Self-monitoring:** Learners can use self-monitoring techniques to evaluate their own learning strategies. For example, they might keep a learning journal, where they record their study habits, what worked well, and what did not. By reviewing their journal regularly, they can identify patterns and trends in their learning process and make adjustments as needed.

- **Peer assessment:** Learners can work in groups and assess each other's learning strategies. By observing and evaluating their peers' learning strategies, learners can gain new insights into their own learning process and identify areas where they need to make changes.

  o **Experimentation:** Learners can experiment with different learning strategies to see what works best for them. For example, they might try different study techniques, such as using flash cards, taking notes, or creating mind maps, and evaluate their effectiveness. By experimenting with different strategies, learners can identify what works best for them and adjust their approach to learning accordingly.

---

[3] The ability to recognize, monitor, and understand one's own thinking processes, including knowledge of one's strengths and weaknesses in learning and problem-solving.

[4] The capacity to control and manage one's own thoughts, emotions, and behaviors to achieve specific goals and adapt to different situations effectively.

○ **Role-playing:** Learners can role-play as a teacher and evaluate their own learning strategies from the perspective of a teacher. For example, they can create a lesson plan for a concept they have learned and evaluate the effectiveness of their learning strategies as if they were teaching it to someone else.

○ **Mind mapping:** Learners can use mind mapping software to visually represent their learning strategies and evaluate their effectiveness. By creating a visual representation of their learning process, learners can identify areas where they need to make changes and see the connections between different concepts.

○ **Gamification:** Learners can create a game where they earn points for using effective learning strategies and lose points for using ineffective ones. By gamifying the learning process, learners can make it more engaging and motivating and identify areas where they need to make changes.

One thing to keep in mind is that performance monitoring strategies can differ depending on the nature of the material being learned. For example, a learner studying a complex mathematical concept may need to engage in more self-questioning and problem-solving activities to assess their understanding, while a learner studying a historical event may need to focus more on summarization and critical analysis.

Additionally, the performance stage can also involve metacognitive strategies for managing stress and anxiety during the learning process. Learners who experience anxiety or stress during assessments may benefit from implementing performance monitoring strategies such as deep breathing, positive self-talk, or visualization techniques.

3. **Appraisal:** This is the stage at which a learner should reflect on what they've learned after completing a task. This involves thinking about and analyzing one's own learning and thinking processes. For example, students might reflect on their study habits and ask themselves, "What worked well for me in this learning situation?" or "What might I do differently next time to improve my understanding?"

This phase involves taking action based on how well the child feels they were able to learn their material. It's not enough to simply reflect and assess one's progress and understanding; learners must also use this information to make adjustments and improve their learning strategies. This can involve changing study habits, seeking additional resources or support, or reevaluating goals and plans.

A significant part of the evaluation process is self-assessment, which is a reflection on one's own understanding of a particular subject or task. For example, a student might ask themselves, "Do I feel confident in my understanding of this material?" or "Have I improved my skills in this area over time?" Besides self-assessment, the appraisal stage can also benefit from external review. This involves seeking feedback about a particular subject from others, such as classmates, study partners, or someone with more expertise or experience, such as teachers, mentors, or parents. This can help identify areas where more work is needed and provide guidance on improvement.

Possibly the most objective way to appraise one's progress is self-testing. This involves evaluating one's own knowledge and understanding through practice quizzes or tests. Self-testing can help identify areas where more study is needed and track progress over time.

## 3 METACOGNITIVE STAGES

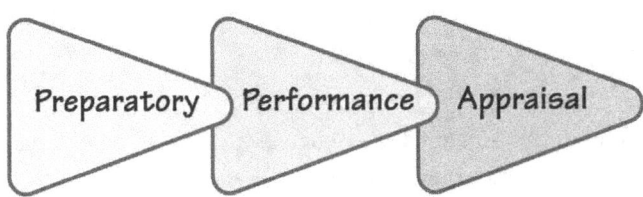

*Figure 24: The Three Metacognitive Stages*

Parents of younger children can use different analogies to convey the idea of the three metacognitive stages (Figure 24) of the learning process. By using analogies and age-appropriate language, parents can help their children understand the importance of planning before starting a task, paying attention to their progress along the way, and reflecting on what they've learned after completing the task.

When dealing with the three stages of metacognition, think of learning as a journey through an unfamiliar forest. In the preparatory stage, you gather all the necessary supplies for the journey, plan your route, and figure out what obstacles you might encounter along the way. This is like packing a backpack, making a map, and studying the terrain before you set out on your hike. In the performance stage, you start your journey and pay close attention to your surroundings. You take note of the plants and animals around you, how the weather is affecting your journey, and whether you're on the right path. This is like checking your map and compass, ensuring you're not lost, and adjusting your route if necessary. Finally, in the appraisal stage, you stop and take a break. You look back at your path and evaluate whether you've made progress, what challenges you faced, and what you've learned so far. This is like taking a breather, looking at the trail behind you, and reflecting on your journey.

## RESEARCH RECAP:

- The development of metacognition management skills can help learners to be more strategic and self-directed in their learning.

- Metacognition has a positive effect on academic performance over time and can support your learner's overall academic success and development.

- The relationship between academic performance and metacognition is consistent across age groups, suggesting that metacognition management training can be useful for improving academic performance in students of all ages.

- Metacognitive skills contribute unique variance to academic achievements beyond what can be explained by general intelligence alone, making this strategy a key aspect of successful learning.

For younger children who may not be ready to embark on all of the metacognitive strategies outlined in this chapter, I recommend starting by leaning more on the foundational principles of developing and encouraging intrinsic motivation, control beliefs, and self-efficacy. Parents can provide support through activities such as asking open-ended questions, encouraging self-reflection, and providing feedback. Parents can also plant the seeds of metacognition by making use of age-appropriate questions and stories. For instance, ask questions that will prompt your learner to consider why they are able to retain certain information or help them to think about what they did leading up to a class that helped them to be better prepared to receive instruction from their teacher.

Similarly, you can stimulate their interest by sharing stories of accomplished learners. Point out what steps they took to reach their level of success, identifying patterns in their life that benefited their ability to learn. These can be stories about historical or modern-day figures. For example, if you tell them the story of Benjamin Franklin, highlight how he went about his experiments; how did he stage his environment, rely on peer learning, or investigate a new idea? For modern-day examples, read stories together of U.S. presidents or other world leaders and look for clues about their learning habits, particularly those that your child can emulate. Remember that metacognition development is a gradual process that continues throughout a person's life and young learners will need support from parents, teachers, or caregivers to handle more complex metacognitive activities such as setting goals, reflecting on progress, and adjusting learning strategies.

By developing these metacognitive skills, children can become more independent learners, capable of managing their own learning process and making informed decisions about their own education. Both parents and teachers can play a role in helping young children to develop their metacognition management strategies by providing opportunities for them to engage in these types of activities and by helping them to become more aware of their learning processes. Here are some tips to help you support your child in the development of their metacognition management skills:

- **Encourage reflection:** Parents can encourage children to reflect on their learning by asking open-ended questions that require them to think about their own thinking. For example, parents can ask their children how they solved a math problem, what they learned from a book, or how they could improve a project. **Practical implementation:** After completing a homework assignment or reading a book, parents can ask their children to reflect on what they learned and how they could apply it to other areas of their lives.

- **Foster creativity:** Encourage children to engage in creative activities such as drawing, painting, writing, or playing music. These activities can help children develop metacognitive skills such as planning, self-monitoring, and self-evaluation. It can also help children express themselves and understand their emotions. **Practical implementation:** Provide your child with materials for creative activities and encourage them to explore their interests. Ask them to reflect on their creative process and to think about how they could improve their work.

*Figure 25: A Child Learning to Paint*

- **Play strategy games:** Playing strategy games with children can help them develop metacognitive skills such as planning, decision-making, and self-monitoring. Games like chess, checkers, battleship, or sequence can help children learn to think ahead and anticipate their opponent's moves. **Practical implementation:** Set aside time to play strategy games with your child on a regular basis. Encourage them to think aloud about their strategy and to reflect on what they could have done differently after the game.

- **Use reflective journaling (best for older children):** Encourage learners to keep a reflective journal where they write about their thoughts, feelings, and experiences. This can help children develop self-awareness and metacognitive skills such as self-monitoring and self-evaluation. **Practical implementation:** Provide your child with a journal and encourage them to write in it regularly. Ask them to reflect on their learning experiences, identify their strengths and weaknesses, and set goals for improvement.

- **Practice mindfulness (best for older children):** Mindfulness practices such as meditation, deep breathing, and yoga can help children develop metacognitive skills such as self-awareness, self-regulation, and self-evaluation. **Practical implementation:** Set aside time to practice mindfulness with your child on a regular basis. Encourage them to focus on their breath and to observe their thoughts and emotions without judgment.

- **Teach goal-setting:** Parents can teach children to set goals and monitor their progress toward achieving them. For example, parents can help their children set goals for academic, personal, or social development and work with them to develop a plan to achieve those goals. **Practical implementation:** At the beginning of each school year, parents can help their children set academic goals and create a plan to achieve them. They can check in with their children regularly to monitor their progress.

- **Foster critical thinking:** Parents can foster critical thinking skills by encouraging children to ask questions, evaluate information, and consider different perspectives. For example, parents can encourage their children to question assumptions, challenge their own beliefs, and think critically about the world around them. **Practical implementation:** During family conversations or when reading books together, parents can ask their children to consider different perspectives and think critically about the information presented.

- **Develop self-awareness:** Parents can help children develop self-awareness by encouraging them to think about their own emotions, strengths, and weaknesses. For example, parents can help children identify their emotions and understand how they affect their behavior and learning. **Practical implementation:** When children experience strong emotions, parents can encourage them to identify and name the emotion. They can help their children develop coping strategies to manage their emotions.

- **Build study skills:** Parents can help children build study skills by teaching them effective study habits and time-management strategies. For example, parents can teach their children how to prioritize tasks, create a study schedule, and manage distractions. **Practical implementation:** Parents can work with their children to create a study schedule that includes breaks and rewards. They can help their children identify the most important tasks and plan how to complete them.

- **Encourage curiosity:** From my experience, kids are utterly curious about everything. I often feel my goal as a parent is to not hinder their curiosity. You can do so by providing more space for their curiosity to run wild. Encourage their natural inclination to ask questions and explore new ideas. This can help them develop metacognitive skills such as critical thinking, problem-solving, and self-evaluation. **Practical implementation:** Provide opportunities to learn about new subjects and engage with different perspectives. Ask them to reflect on what they learned and how they could apply it in their own lives.

While metacognition management is an extremely important learning strategy, it's also arguably the hardest. The brain has to work double-time—learning a subject, applying strategies to acquire and retain knowledge, and then analyzing *how* you're learning. And yet, for your learner to truly optimize their learning, this is a strategy they must master.

Keep in mind the learning curve that comes with metacognition management and with the application of *all* the learning strategies covered within this book. Think of this work in long-term measurements—this is a five-year marathon, for example, not a five-day sprint. It will take time for children to understand, adopt, and maximize these strategies. This endeavor will not be accomplished quickly. Remove the expectation for immediate understanding or acceptance on the part of your child. It may take time for them to understand the value of these strategies. The ultimate goal is for these strategies to become so second nature that they can be self-applied and self-regulated by your learner.

As always, modeling, feedback, and ongoing communication with a parent or trusted teacher can help them see the importance and value of this strategy. As our children become more mindful of their learning process, they will become more intentional about it too. This intentionality and dedication to refining their process will inevitably lead to growth and improvement in their academic achievement, as well.

# ACTION PLAN

- **Create space for metacognition:** There must be time for your learner to think and reflect about why they're struggling in certain areas and succeeding in others. If your child is overscheduled and always tired, it will be harder for them to carve out this time and make it productive. If your child is overly committed, then work to remove activities that are not a priority, so they can focus on areas of greater importance.

- **Use metacognitive language:** Use metacognitive language with your child, such as asking them how they plan to approach a task or what strategies they might use to solve a problem. This can help them become more aware of their own thinking processes and develop their metacognitive skills.

- **Play "detective" with your child:** Help your child become a metacognitive detective by encouraging them to ask questions about their own learning process. For example, they could investigate why certain study strategies work better for them than others or why they struggle with a particular subject. Encourage them to collect evidence and draw conclusions based on their observations.

- **Start a learning journal:** Encourage your child to keep a journal where they can reflect on their learning process. They could write about what they have learned, what strategies they have used, and what challenges they have faced. This can help them become more aware of their own learning process and identify areas for improvement.

- **Cheer them on through challenging seasons:** Frequently, as your child is working on mastering a new subject or task, there will be dips in performance because there is something being learned that the student is struggling with it. But if they can push through the dips and metacognitively consider how to improve their process, they'll be able to overcome the obstacle and level up their ability.

[1] Ohtani, K., and Hisasaka, T. (2018). "Beyond intelligence: A meta-analytic review of the relationship among metacognition, intelligence, and academic performance." *Metacognition and Learning* 13(2), 179-212.

[2] de Boer, H., Donker, A. S., Kostons, D. D., and van der Werf, G. P. (2018). "Long-term effects of metacognitive strategy instruction on student academic performance: A meta-analysis." *Educational Research Review* 24, 98-115.

[3] Zhang, J., and Zhang, L. J. (2022). "The effect of feedback on metacognitive strategy use in EFL writing." *Computer Assisted Language Learning*, 1-26.

# EPILOGUE

As we reach the end of the book, I would like to share the story of our church pastor and his daughter. I chose their story because their journey resonates with the various learning precepts that we discussed in this book. I was quite inspired when I heard their family's story.

Hannah[5] grew up in a family where education was a priority. As a child, she had big dreams, and her parents explained the importance of education in reaching those dreams. They'd say, "If you want to chase your dreams, you need a solid education first." They never pushed her toward one career path, but they encouraged her to work hard at whatever she pursued.

Hannah often ranked at the top of her class at the all-girls elementary school she attended. While some of her friends struggled with their desire to study, her aspiration to "be somebody," the somebody of her dreams, was the intrinsic motivation that kept her

---

[5] This is a true story, but the names and some of the details have been changed to protect the identity of the subjects.

going. Reaching her goals and making her parents proud was her "why." They were the internal drivers that pushed her to study every challenging subject until she mastered it.

One significant situation threatened to derail the trajectory of her path. While Hannah was still in elementary school, she and her family were forced to leave their home country due to religious persecution. Hannah and her family escaped to another country, where they lived as refugees. It was a country where they were safe, but it wasn't their home. Hannah didn't know English yet (a common language spoken among refugees there), nor did she know the native language of this new country. She couldn't understand the world around her—street signs, restaurant menus, passersby on the street—everything felt foreign. Naturally, this all led to a great deal of stress and anxiety, but her greatest heartache was the change in school. Her struggle to catch on to English meant she couldn't keep up at the local refugee school. She went from a thriving school experience to a crippling and embarrassing season of starting over. She was a nine-year-old sitting with four-year-olds in language classes. She went from the top of her class to the bottom.

One night in bed, she overheard her parents talking and her mother crying. They were struggling financially, and they were worrying over whether they had let their children down. At that moment, Hannah empathized with their pain and felt the heaviness of their burden. She knew that as a nine-year-old, she couldn't do much, but it was a turning point for her all the same. She could have crumbled under the pressure and the sadness of the situation. Instead, she found a renewed motivation to work hard. She decided she would not let her struggles with school be an added worry for her parents. She became empowered by the motivation to once again make them proud of her hard work and dedication to her studies. As a result, Hannah renewed her intentions to pursue her education with her whole heart, as she had done in their home country.

From then on, she stayed up late studying. She read her English assignments, determined to learn the new language. At school, she asked her teachers to only speak to her in English. Her control beliefs and self-efficacy were high. She *knew* she had the ability to succeed. Little by little, she learned more every day. She went on to finish preschool through sixth grade in just three years. She also gained clarification about what kind of "somebody" she wanted to be when she got older. Driven by the hurt and injustices of her life up until that point—particularly due to the religious persecution her family experienced and the struggles of living as a refugee—she recognized a desire to pursue a degree in law. She longed to have the power and knowledge to stand up for what was right, to help others who were hurting, and to make a difference. Becoming a lawyer was a proxy expression of her intrinsic motivation to fight injustice. This planted in her a drive to attend a highly esteemed law school in the United States, where law schools are more often recognized internationally.

As she continued on through middle and high school, her dreams were called into question by other students who were threatened by her goals and determination to succeed. Since Hannah was a newer student and, in many ways, an "outsider," they would often exclude her and challenge her accomplishments. These students would accuse her of cheating in order to make good grades and would make fun of her desire to move to the U.S. to pursue a law degree. These confrontations crushed her spirit, but her parents encouraged her to press on. They reminded her that her dreams *were* possible with dedication and hard work. Their support gave her the motivation to keep going.

As parents, we're often the first and most influential role models for our children, and our support and encouragement can make a significant difference in their motivation to learn and succeed. In the case of Hannah, her parents had been ongoing providers of support when she faced challenges. They'd modeled perseverance when their family was enduring painful seasons of religious persecution and living as refugees. They were hard workers, shouldering financial burdens and persevering through difficult times. Additionally, their encouragement helped her overcome the setbacks she faced in school and motivated her to keep going. All of this laid a solid foundation for Hannah to build upon.

The support of her parents spurred Hannah on, and she continued to earn good grades. Her diligence allowed her to skip her junior year and graduate a year early at the age of 16. Hannah's story is a reminder to us all that the Parental Engagement Cycle (PEC), which we discussed early on, can be a useful tool for parents to stay involved in their children's learning journey. With consistent application of the PEC and with the nurturing of a child's interest in pursuing their dreams, the learning practices outlined in this book can become deeply ingrained in your young learner's mind, helping them to accomplish what they set their mind to.

At this point in Hannah's story, with high school complete, she was ready for the next step. In support of her dreams for law school and with a desire to relocate to a country where they could truly build a long-term home, her family worked with an agency to help them resettle in the U.S. Once more, she was shifting into a new environment, a new culture, a new normal. Thankfully, she knew the language, but everything else was once again different. Now 17, she got a job at a coffee shop in order to earn money and save up for college. Working the morning shift, she was often challenged by the differences between the more formal "British English" she'd learned as a refugee and the more informal English she encountered in the southern United States. Coworkers and patrons would become impatient with her inability to understand what they said, but if she'd learned anything over the years, it was to keep working hard and not lose belief in her ability to adapt to something new and hard. She recognized the task value of the work she was doing. She saw this job as an opportunity to stand on her own two feet. It also provided a fertile learning ground for her to acclimate to the new culture in which she'd landed.

As she came to understand the college system in the U.S., she realized she didn't have enough money to pursue a degree on her own, and her parents would not have the means to assist her financially. After much research, she applied for government financial aid, and the day before her semester's tuition was due, she was awarded a Pell Grant to cover her schooling.

Now in college, her motivation to excel and become a lawyer, a big dream which requires her to earn good grades, has driven her to maintain a 4.0 GPA. She is often recognized as an honors student. As of the publication of this book, she's completed her first two years of community college and will be transferring to Middle Tennessee State University in the fall of 2023. She has established a lifelong pattern as someone who finishes what she starts because of her high task value regarding whatever work she has committed herself to.

Over the years, Hannah has also come to recognize the importance of good study strategies. When listening to a lecture, she stays focused and in tune with what's being taught. After class, she'll review her notes, research anything that confuses her, and study the questions available after a lecture. She looks for ways to apply what she's learning. If a teacher is not engaging, she seeks out other lectures on the subject or reads books on the topic. When possible and time allows, she will prep and study ahead of time. For a subject that has a lot to remember, she'll periodically go back and review terms time and again to refresh her memory. It took practice and trial and error for her to identify which habits worked best for her, but the more she saw success with certain tactics, the more she leaned into those habits and experienced the benefits of her hard work and consistency.

*Figure 26: Hannah and Her Family*

Hannah's story highlights the wonderful payoffs that can come from dedicating oneself to a goal, overcoming challenges, and persevering in the face of seemingly insurmountable circumstances. It's a story full of pain and heartache, some of which will not be directly relatable to the upbringing your children will experience, but it's a story that we can all learn from and be inspired by. Hannah's belief in her ability matched with an ongoing effort to optimize her learning experience and intrinsic motivation to work hard (even in the face of overwhelming adversity) to chase the dream of becoming a lawyer, is admirable and worth emulating.

We began this book with the parable of "The Blind Men and the Elephant," a tale that considers the limitations of one person's experience, thereby highlighting the need for humility. It emphasizes how little we know and how much more we all have to learn. Hannah's story brings that idea full circle, inviting each of us to remain open and humble not only to learn from those around us but as parents to stay receptive toward the learning experiences of our children. Each of us has a lot to learn about how to help our children—where to step in and guide them and where to hold back and let their interests lead.

In both stories, there is a theme of perception and the limitations that come with our own perspectives. In the six blind men story, each blind man could only understand one small part of the elephant and so they each had a different perception of what the elephant was. Similarly, in Hannah's story, she faced limitations and obstacles that caused her to view her situation in a certain way. Her struggle with language and cultural differences as a refugee made her feel like an outsider, but through hard work and determination, she was able to overcome those limitations and achieve her dreams.

Both stories highlight the importance of recognizing our own limitations and biases and the importance of understanding the perspectives of others. It is only by seeing the full picture and by seeking to understand the perspectives of others that we can gain a deeper and more accurate understanding of the world around us.

Hannah's story and the parable of the six blind men also remind us that learning is a multifaceted experience. The learning process is layered and complex. It's important for us as parents to support and encourage our children's learning experiences while remaining receptive to their unique perspectives and ideas, including the specific dreams and desires they have that provide insight into what will intrinsically motivate them.

Hannah's parents played a crucial role in guiding and supporting her throughout her challenging journey as a refugee and as a student. They recognized the importance of education and encouraged Hannah to pursue her dreams despite the obstacles they faced as a family. They provided her with the guidance and support she needed while also giving her the freedom to explore and discover her interests at her own pace. Just like Hannah's parents, we must recognize the importance of education and encourage our children to pursue their dreams while providing them with the necessary guidance and support to overcome the challenges they may face along the way.

We need to look for ways to foster our children's intrinsic motivation and natural curiosity while avoiding overly critical micromanagement of their every move. Hannah reiterates that her parents were so good not to compare her to other students or to her brother. This helped to strengthen the relationship between Hannah and her parents. No matter the grade she earned, her father's question was always "Did you do your best work?" If yes, she was told she had done a great job, no matter the grade.

We must be sensitive to our children's willingness and openness to apply the principles and strategies discussed within this book. It won't always be easy (speaking from experience!). There are times when my daughter can respond negatively to my encouragement because I'm pressing too hard, expecting her to receive all of my advice with open arms and a fully willing spirit. I've learned that, sometimes, it's better that I lead through modeling and encouragement. Hannah shares that her parents modeled an example of hard work, dedication, and overcoming difficulty. They, too, had faced the challenges of learning English when they became refugees, and they had to find new jobs, churches, and community networks in every new place they lived. Even when they got down at times, they always kept going and dedicated themselves to doing the best they could. Witnessing their hardworking behavior drove her to do the same.

Building on the idea of modeling and encouragement, I recall a valuable lesson I learned from a tour guide about parenting. When my wife and I visited Israel, our tour guide, Arie Bar-David, was a Messianic Jew, full of inspiration and wisdom. One of the great insights he shared with our group was about parenting. He encouraged every adult to, when possible, get down on the level of their child by kneeling down when communicating with them. This is a physical act that can remind us to speak their language as we work to communicate in a way that resonates with their level of maturity.

For example, when we, as parents, discipline, we should keep their level of understanding in mind and remember that there are so many ways to get our point across. The best methods usually involve connecting with them through our tone, eyes, body language, and facial expression. Each child has their own language style and a unique way of communicating. It's our job to be mindful of this. If we really want our children to become better learners, we need to look at all the ideas offered in this book from their perspective. We must get to know how our children communicate and, by extension, how they learn so that we can teach them in ways that will truly resonate and connect with them.

In the world we live in today, the pace of change is accelerating at an unprecedented rate, and it shows no signs of slowing down. The skills and knowledge that were essential just a few years ago may no longer be relevant today, and we must constantly adapt and evolve to keep up. As we discussed in Chapter 1, the ability to learn new things is more critical than ever before. We must teach our children to welcome learning as an ongoing process, a journey that never truly ends.

The good news is that with the right mindset and practical steps and strategies discussed in this book, anyone can have productive and fun learning experiences. It starts with intrinsic motivation, a belief in one's ability to control their actions and outcomes, the right learning strategies, a readiness to explore new ideas, and even preparation in advance to learn new information. It means being open-minded and curious, asking questions, and seeking out new information and experiences.

By adopting this approach to learning, we can unlock our young learners' full potential, both personally and professionally. We can help them develop the skills and knowledge they need to thrive in a constantly evolving world, and we can stay ahead of the curve in an increasingly competitive global marketplace.

So as we close this book and our journey together, let us remember the importance of learning. Let us continue to challenge ourselves and help our children push beyond their boundaries and never stop growing and evolving, for it is only by embracing the power of learning that they can truly achieve their full potential and positively impact the world around them.

# APPENDIX: REFERENCE LIST

Disclaimer: The provided list contains external links to sources and references. These links have not been activated by the publisher, and therefore, we cannot guarantee their accuracy, relevance, timeliness, or completeness beyond the date of publication. The content on these sites is subject to change over time. Though our intention in providing these external links is to offer additional references and potential sources of information, we highly encourage readers to exercise discretion and independent judgment when accessing these links, as the nature and content of the sites may change over time. We are not liable for any errors, omissions, or damages resulting from the use of or reliance on the information found on these external sites. By accessing these links, you acknowledge and accept all associated risks.

## Introduction and Prologue

[1] Thomas Edison, New World Encyclopedia

[2] 1850-1877: Education: Overview, Encyclopedia.com

[3] Thomas Edison, Biography.com

[4] Oprah Winfrey, Biography.com

[5] Oprah opens up to Hoda Kotb about how her childhood trauma informed her life's work, Today.com

[6] The Man Who Saved Oprah Winfrey, Washingtonpost.com

[7] 37 Quotes From Thomas Edison That Will Inspire Success, Inc.com

[8] Boekaerts, Monique. "Self-regulated learning at the junction of cognition and motivation." *European Psychologist* 1, no. 2 (1996): 100.

[9] A Brief Biography of Thomas Edison, nps.gov

# Part I

## Introduction

[1] Abraham Lincoln's 'angel mother' and the second 'mama' who outlived him, Washingtonpost.com

[2] The Two Mothers Who Molded Lincoln, History.com

[3] Yau, Priscilla S., Yongwon Cho, Jacob Shane, Joseph Kay, and Jutta Heckhausen. "Parenting and adolescents' academic achievement: the mediating role of goal engagement and disengagement." *Journal of Child and Family Studies* 31, no. 4 (2022): 897-909.
The impact parents have on academic performance was detailed in this 2022 study by Priscilla Yau and colleagues from the University of California. 220 high school students participated to identify the various kinds of parental support children receive and how it can both positively and, in some cases, negatively influence adolescent academic achievement. The study collected the opinions of participating adolescents via a survey. It found that supportive characteristics such as being highly responsive and setting up clear rules were some of the most effective in facilitating a child's learning. The study also identified other positive parenting characteristics including warmth (i.e., expressing love toward the child), involvement (i.e., spending time with the child), and autonomy-support (i.e., guiding the child toward independence) to all be linked to academic success. The high ranking of each of these characteristics was positively associated with an increase in the student's GPA scores.

Not to be overlooked, the research also found that there are certain negative parenting characteristics that can lead to academic difficulties. Guilt induction (i.e., causing the child to feel guilty) and devaluation (i.e., invalidating the child's thoughts and expressions) can negatively impact academic performance. An example of devaluation would be when the child feels that their mother or father always finishes their sentences whenever they talk. Guilt induction can be felt when mothers or fathers blame the child for other family members' problems. Both of these negative parenting characteristics can be categorized under the umbrella of parental psychological control, which refers to a parent's attempts to manipulate and control their children's thoughts and behavior. Some parents will use these control tactics to keep children emotionally dependent on them.

[4] Aguirre-Dávila, Eduardo, Miguel Morales-Castillo, and Manuel Moreno-Vásquez. "Parenting, autonomy and academic achievement in the adolescence." *Journal of Family Studies* (2021): 1-14. 229 mothers and their adolescents were surveyed—mothers were mailed a questionnaire to complete. Students whose mothers returned the questionnaire received their survey during school hours, where their survey could be completed under the supervision of teachers and research assistants. The goal of the surveys was to evaluate parenting styles (from the perspective of both mothers and their children). The parenting styles under consideration included the expression of affection, communication, involvement, and rule-setting—and the provision of multidimensional autonomy including social (i.e., when the adolescent takes initiative in social contexts as an expression of their individual identity), cognitive (i.e., when adolescents have ownership in planning, organizing, and guiding decision-making), and motivational autonomy (i.e., when the child is intrinsically driven to carry out an action). The goal was to see how these styles of parenting impact a child's grades and academic achievement in math, language, and the natural and social sciences. Many of these parenting strategies, particularly the opportunity for a child to show autonomy with different aspects of their personality, as well as the communication, affection, and involvement of parents, were shown to positively impact students' grades and academic achievement, as measured by GPA scores. Notably, these strategies were associated with improved academic performance in language learning and math—two of the most foundationally important subjects for children to master.

# Chapter 1: Modeling

[1] Mother Teresa, Biography.com

[2] Kong, Siu-Cheung, and Yi-Qing Wang. "The influence of parental support and perceived usefulness on students' learning motivation and flow experience in visual programming: Investigation from a parent perspective." *British Journal of Educational Technology* 52, no. 4 (2021): 1749-1770. Parents were asked to complete an observation survey after evaluating their children's (aged 6–12) learning during a two-day coding fair. In total, 1,196 parents completed the survey. The results of this study revealed that parents' perceived usefulness of the tasks learned during the fair and parental support offered, as a result, could effectively foster students' learning efficiency and motivation. It can also lead to a student's flow experience while learning. This research also showed that a parent's perception of how useful and relevant a subject, task, or educational program is (i.e., our perceived usefulness) can be passed on to our children through simple conversations and modeling.

[3] Captain 'Sully' and Passengers Reunite for 'Miracle on the Hudson' Anniversary: 'We're Like Extended Family'

4 Mother Teresa, The humble sophisticate

# Chapter 2: Elucidation

In three different research studies listed below, the value and need for Elucidation can be seen. In these studies, parental involvement was studied in three different ways—home-based and school-based involvement and academic socialization. All three of these studies sought to determine which of these forms of parental involvement was most helpful in predicting a child's GPA and academic attainment (the highest level of schooling they would achieve).

[1] Day, Elizabeth, and Aryn M. Dotterer. "Parental involvement and adolescent academic outcomes: Exploring differences in beneficial strategies across racial/ethnic groups." *Journal of Youth and Adolescence* 47, no. 6 (2018): 1332-1349. This study utilized data from the Education Longitudinal Study 2002–2013 (56% female, N = 4429),

which followed 10th graders through high school and ten years post–high school, to examine the links between parental involvement strategies and academic outcomes (grade point average and educational attainment). The first study used a longitudinal design since it not only included a large sample of 4,500 students but also tracked their development over the course of 10 years. Participants included white, African American, and Hispanic/Latino adolescents from low-SES families. This study used recursive partitioning, a novel analytic strategy used for exploring higher-order interactions and nonlinear associations among factors (e.g., parental educational involvement strategies) to predict an outcome (e.g., grade point average or educational attainment) through stepwise partitioning. The results showed that the combination of greater academic socialization and school-based involvement was beneficial for all adolescents' grade point averages, whereas the combination of home-based involvement with academic socialization and school-based involvement yielded mixed results. Greater academic socialization and home-based involvement appeared beneficial for educational attainment among African American and Hispanic/Latino adolescents but not white adolescents. More home-based involvement and less academic socialization were associated with less educational attainment for white adolescents. Overall, the findings showed different combinations of parental educational involvement strategies were beneficial for adolescents across racial/ethnic groups, which may have implications for practice and policy. It is interesting to note that the reports from parents in this study highlighted their feeling that academic socialization had a minimal impact. In other words, the parents didn't think that how they talked to their kids about school made that big of a difference. However, reports from their children showed different results. According to the adolescents, academic socialization was perceived to have a stronger, more significant effect on their academic achievement.

[2] Benner, Aprile D., Alaina E. Boyle, and Sydney Sadler. "Parental involvement and adolescents' educational success: The roles of prior achievement and socioeconomic status." *Journal of Youth and Adolescence* 45, no. 6 (2016): 1053-1064. This study investigated the associations between four aspects of parents' educational involvement (i.e., home- and school-based involvement, educational expectations, academic advice) and young people's proximal (i.e., grades) and distal academic outcomes (i.e., educational attainment). Attention was also placed on whether these relations varied as a function of family

socioeconomic status or adolescents' prior achievement. The data were drawn from 15,240 10th grade students (50% females; 57% White, 13% African American, 1% Latino, 9% Asian American, and 6% other race/ethnicity) participating in the Education Longitudinal Study of 2002. The study observed significant links between both school-based involvement and parental educational expectations and adolescents' cumulative high school grades and educational attainment. Moderation analyses revealed that school-based involvement seemed to be particularly beneficial for more disadvantaged youth (i.e., those from low-SES families, those with poorer prior achievement), whereas parents' academic socialization seemed to better promote the academic success of more advantaged youth (i.e., those from high-SES families, those with higher prior achievement).

[3] Duan, Wenjie, Yuan Guan, and He Bu. "The effect of parental involvement and socioeconomic status on junior school students' academic achievement and school behavior in China." *Frontiers in Psychology* 9 (2018): 952. This survey was conducted on 19,487 Chinese junior school students to elucidate the moderating role of socioeconomic status (SES) in the relationship between parental involvement (i.e., home-based involvement and academic socialization) and junior school students' performance in school (i.e., academic achievement and school behavior). The data includes 10,042 males and 9,445 females (mean age = 14.52, SD = 1.24). It was taken from the 2013–2014 Chinese Educational Panel Survey (CEPS) that was administered by the National Survey Research Center at Renmin University of China. It found that home-based involvement had no significant impact on academic achievement. However, the two other types of involvement—academic socialization and school-based involvement—were significant predictors of achievement, with academic socialization being the strongest.

[4] Singapore Math, https://www.singaporemath.com/

## Chapter 3: Feedback

[1] Raising a Moral Child, https://www.nytimes.com/2014/04/12/opinion/sunday/raising-a-moral-child.html

[2] *Mindset: The New Psychology of Success* by Carol S. Dweck, https://www.amazon.com/Mindset-Psychology-Carol-S-Dweck/dp/1400062756/ref=tmm_hrd_swatch_0

[3] Wisniewski, Benedikt, Klaus Zierer, and John Hattie. "The power of feedback revisited: A meta-analysis of educational feedback research." *Frontiers in Psychology 10* (2020): 3087. A 2020 analysis of over 435 research studies explored the role of feedback in education. Each of the studies dealt with the role of feedback in different categories of educational performance—academic (or cognitive, including student achievement, retention, cognitive test performance), motivational (including intrinsic motivation, locus of control, self-efficacy, and persistence), behavioral (or self-regulation, and how students behave in classrooms), and physical (or the development of motor skills). In total, there were 994 samples reviewed and over 61,000 participants. For this analysis, feedback was defined as information provided by an agent regarding aspects of one's performance for understanding. The results showed that providing meaningful feedback had a relatively strong effect on academic performance. With physical performance, the connection to meaningful feedback was very strong, as was the tie to behavioral/self-regulation performance (though behavioral performance came in third of the four). For motivational performance, meaningful feedback did not have as much of an effect (it was a weak to moderate effect). Overall, feedback was shown to strongly influence cognitive abilities. This study also reiterated the idea that not all feedback is the same. Simple forms of reinforcement and punishment, for instance, have low effects on development, while high-information feedback is more effective. With high-information feedback, the timing is important, as is the reason why feedback is being given. The appropriateness of the timing relates to where the students are in their learning process, moving from focusing on the task, the strategies underlying the task, and the self-regulation of the process. When the child is learning something and feedback is given not just about the task itself but how the task is being handled (what strategies they use), the child will learn how to perform the task better the next time they do it.

[4] What is self-talk? https://www.healthdirect.gov.au/self-talk

# Part II

## Introduction

[1] Flying Over Adversity: Aspiring to Be a Pilot, flyingmag.com

[2] Jessica's History, jessicacox.com

[3] Remembering the incredible Inez Cox, rightfootedmovie.com

[4] Being Overlooked, flyingmag.com

## Chapter 4: Motivation

[1] Giannis Antetokounmpo: From poverty in Greece to NBA's most lucrative player - Olympics.com

[2] The Humble Superstar: New Giannis Antetokounmpo Biography Explores Champion's Family Life, Legacy - Wisconsinlife.org

[3] Giannis Antetokounmpo Is the Pride of a Greece That Shunned Him - NYTimes.com

[4] Zaccone, Maria Cristina, and Matteo Pedrini. "The effects of intrinsic and extrinsic motivation on students learning effectiveness. Exploring the moderating role of gender." *International Journal of Educational Management* (2019). In a 2019 study, researchers Zaccone and Pedrini tested 1,491 students from three different countries—Burundi, Morocco, and India—who participated in a digital competencies course. The work aimed to not rely on a composite GPA score to measure the student's learning performance but instead see how performance in a single, specific course would be related to students' motivation. In more detail, the authors measured how well and effectively the students would learn in the course based on two different scales.

The first scale was a four-item questionnaire aimed at measuring the informatics skills of participants, including items such as "I'm comfortable working with informatics as I am in working by hand" and "I can learn how to use new informatics tools." A total score of learning was created using the standardized mean score of these items. Then, the authors set up a measure of growth in informatic skills by considering it as the difference between students' learning score at T1 (i.e., after the course) and students' learning score at T0 (prior to the course). A similar procedure was applied to the measurement of growth in the usage of the computer. A nine-item scale was used to assess the increase of computer usage by the participants.

Further, the students' motivation for learning was measured by means of the four-item scale. Specifically, this motivation scale measured the degree of pleasure and satisfaction that the students experienced while learning and participating in the course. Just as in the work by Steinmayr and Spinath above, the author used hierarchical linear regression analysis to explore the effect of motivation on learning effectiveness (i.e., learning effectiveness was a dependent variable). Additionally, and interestingly, the authors also examined whether the relationship between the level of motivation and learning effectiveness was further modulated by gender or the country where students studied.

As a result, the authors found a positive association between the two types of skill improvements (growth in informatics skills and growth in computer usage) and the level of intrinsic (i.e., internal, see below) motivation. In other words, increased levels of such motivation were also correspondingly associated with improved learning and course grades. The authors concluded that the motivation behind students' course participation played a crucial role in their course performance. Specifically, the students who signed up to an educational program for the pleasure of doing it, i.e., had a high internal motivation to participate in the course, were also among those who were the most effective throughout the course. Importantly, the authors found no effect of gender and country of learning on the association between motivation and academic achievements, which implies that this effect is equally present in both male and female students across different countries/cultures. Taken together, this large-scale study demonstrated that motivation can have a substantial positive impact on learning effectiveness because it provides a potentially lasting (for the duration of the course) personal commitment.

The Zaccone and Pedrini study also provides helpful insight about extrinsic motivation, as it also measured the degree to which a student's decision to enroll in the course was motivated by the existence of tangible incentives and external rewards—extrinsic motivations such as getting an increase in salary, reduced fear of making mistakes, or better performance at work—and how this motivation impacted their performance.

As a result of their study, the authors reported that extrinsic motivation either had no effect on course performance or even had a negative association. In other words, students who signed up for the course driven by extrinsic motivation saw a relatively poorer outcome. Without strong intrinsic motivation, the students were not able to keep up with the course demands and were potentially distracted by other tasks and responsibilities that they valued more that were outside of the course.

[5] Neuville, Sandrine, Mariane Frenay, and Etienne Bourgeois. "Task value, self-efficacy and goal orientations: Impact on self-regulated learning, choice and performance among university students." *Psychologica Belgica* 47, no. 1 (2007).

[6] Al-Harthy, Ibrahim S., and Said S. Aldhafri. "The relationship among task-value, self-efficacy and academic achievement in Omani students at Sultan Qaboos University." *International Review of Social Sciences and Humanities* 7, no. 2 (2014): 15-22. This work tested whether task value can predict students' self-efficacy and whether the task value can be related to students' academic achievements. To assess the levels of task value and self-efficacy, a large and randomly selected group of students enrolled in different courses at Sultan Qaboos University (N = 284) filled out task value and self-efficacy questionnaires. Furthermore, grade point average (GPA) in these participants served as an objective measure of academic performance. As a result, the findings revealed a positive relationship between the magnitude of the task value and self-efficacy. This means that the strength of self-efficacy was associated with higher task value. Importantly, both of these variables were also positive predictors of students' GPAs. In other words, those students who valued the learning process were also demonstrating higher

academic performance as measured via the GPA. Note that the female students showed higher task value and less self-efficacy compared with male students. The authors concluded that university instructors need to pay attention to the value students attach to their courses.

[7] Metallidou, Panayiota, and Anastasia Vlachou. "Children's self-regulated learning profile in language and mathematics: The role of task value beliefs." *Psychology in the Schools* 47, no. 8 (2010): 776-788. This study investigated the relationship between teachers' evaluation of fifth and sixth graders (N = 263 pupils from Central Greece) and students' task value. The task value was measured by means of the subscale of task value beliefs from the Motivational Self-Regulated Learning Questionnaire (MSLQ). The results of a task-value analysis demonstrated that students with high task-value beliefs in math were described as more cognitively, metacognitively, and motivationally competent learners as compared to students with lower task-value beliefs. These results also confirm previous findings that students' higher task values are closely linked to their corresponding levels of motivation, metacognition, and strategic action.

[8] Lee, Daeyeoul, Sunnie Lee Watson, and William R. Watson. "The relationships between self-efficacy, task value, and self-regulated learning strategies in massive open online courses." *International Review of Research in Open and Distributed Learning* 21, no. 1 (2020): 23-39. Lee and colleagues examined the relationships between task value and self-regulated learning strategies and academic performance in massive open online course (MOOC) learners. For this purpose, the authors worked with a total of 184 participants who enrolled in two MOOCs and who completed multiple surveys. By running a correlational analysis, the authors could show a positive linear relationship between task value and the use of self-regulated learning strategies. In more detail, the analyses revealed that task value was a significant predictor of the use of self-regulated learning strategies. Specifically, learners who had high task value showed statistically significant higher average self-regulated learning scores than those who had low task value. Therefore, these findings demonstrated that task value is an important factor that influences not academic performance per se but the self-regulated learning. Importantly, task values are as important for online learning as they are for the in-class option.

[9] José Rizal, New World Encyclopedia

[10] "Yes, Dr. Jose Rizal was a real ophthalmologist" by Ma. Dominga B. Padilla, MD, FPAO, paojournal.com

[11] Taylor, G., Jungert, T., Mageau, G. A., Schattke, K., Dedic, H., Rosenfield, S., and Koestner, R. (2014). "A self-determination theory approach to predicting school achievement over time: The unique role of intrinsic motivation." *Contemporary Educational Psychology* 39(4), 342-358. This study considered the relationship of specific types of motivation in relation to overall academic achievement. Their work examined which types of motivation that were most beneficial for academic achievement, over time, in different school contexts and cultures. The authors examined the combined findings of 18 previous studies and found that intrinsic motivation had a moderately strong, positive relationship to school achievement. Intrinsic motivation had a significantly stronger positive relationship to school achievement for high school and college students than for elementary school students. On the other hand, and in contrast, extrinsic motivation resulted in a negative relationship with academic school performance, or GPA.

[12] Howard, Joshua L., Julien Bureau, Frédéric Guay, Jane XY Chong, and Richard M. Ryan. "Student motivation and associated outcomes: A meta-analysis from self-determination theory." *Perspectives on Psychological Science* 16, no. 6 (2021): 1300-1323. In this work, the authors conducted a meta-analysis that tested the role of motivation in an impressive sample of 344 studies, which had a total of 223,209 participants! In this study, motivation was examined in relation to students' overall feeling of well-being and level of goal orientation. The findings demonstrated that intrinsic motivation was related to students' academic success and overall feeling of well-being. In line with previous studies reported above, external motivation, such as the desire to obtain rewards, was associated with decreased well-being. External motivation was also negatively related to the academic performance of students. The authors could conclude that intrinsic motivation is one of the key factors for successful learning and general academic performance in school.

[13] Wilken, Eric Conrad. "The effects of extrinsic motivation on high school attendance." PhD diss., Lindenwood University, 2016. This study found extrinsic motivation to be helpful in encouraging school attendance.

[14] Shim, Jae Eun, Juhee Kim, Yoonna Lee, Kristen Harrison, Kelly Bost, Brent McBride, Sharon Donovan, et al. "Fruit and vegetable intakes of preschool children are associated with feeding practices facilitating internalization of extrinsic motivation." *Journal of Nutrition Education and Behavior* 48, no. 5 (2016): 311-317. This study found extrinsic motivation to be helpful in encouraging children to eat vegetables.

[15] Amorose, Anthony J., Dawn Anderson-Butcher, Tarkington J. Newman, Mickey Fraina, and Aidyn Iachini. "High school athletes' self-determined motivation: The independent and interactive effects of coach, father, and mother autonomy support." *Psychology of Sport and Exercise* 26 (2016): 1-8. This study found extrinsic motivation to be helpful in motivating athletic performance.

[16] Vallerand, Robert J., and Gaétan F. Losier. "An integrative analysis of intrinsic and extrinsic motivation in sport." *Journal of Applied Sport Psychology* 11, no. 1 (1999): 142-169. This study found extrinsic motivation to be helpful in motivating athletic performance.

[17] Azzahro, Rana, Ana Maghfiroh, and Niken Reti Indriastuti. "Maintaining Students' Extrinsic Motivation in Online Learning: Teachers' Problem." In International Conference of Education, Social, and Humanities (1ST INCESH). Web of Science, 2021. This study found extrinsic motivation to be helpful with some aspects of online learning.

[18] Barajas, Nancy H. "The Influence of Extrinsic Motivational Factors on Upper Elementary Students in Reading." PhD diss., 2020. This research found extrinsic motivation to be efficient when learning specific tasks. The analysis explored the role of several common extrinsic motivation strategies—recognition, competition, compliance, and grades—on upper elementary students whose reading abilities were at least two grade levels below what they should be. It was found that at least one (if not all) of those forms of motivation positively influenced and encouraged the students' reading abilities.

## Chapter 5: Beliefs

[1] Perry Jr., William G. *Forms of Intellectual and Ethical Development in the College Years: A Scheme*. Jossey-Bass Higher and Adult Education Series. Jossey-Bass Publishers, 350 Sansome St., San Francisco, CA 94104, 1999.

[2] Kizilgunes, Berna, Ceren Tekkaya, and Semra Sungur. "Modeling the relations among students' epistemological beliefs, motivation, learning approach, and achievement." *Journal of Educational Research* 102, no. 4 (2009): 243-256.

[3] Does Job Hopping Help Or Hurt Your Career? - Robert Half Talent Solutions

[4] Job hopping is the Gen Z way - By Cate Chapman, editor at LinkedIn News

[5] Workers Are Changing Jobs, Raking In Big Raises—and Keeping Inflation High - *Wall Street Journal*

[6] Gen Z Characteristics Employers Need to Understand - Robert Half Talent Solutions

[7] Trautwein, Ulrich, and Oliver Lüdtke. "Epistemological beliefs, school achievement, and college major: A large-scale longitudinal study on the impact of certainty beliefs." *Contemporary Educational Psychology* 32, no. 3 (2007): 348-366. This study surveyed 2,854 students in Germany and found that the epistemic belief of certainty of knowledge is associated with lower grades.

[8] Listverse - https://listverse.com/2019/05/14/10-quotes-from-experts-who-were-proved-wrong/

[9] Darryl F. Zanuck Quotes. BrainyQuote.com, BrainyMedia Inc, 2022. https://www.brainyquote.com/quotes/darryl_f_zanuck_401896, accessed October 18, 2022.

[10] 1922, *The Truth About Henry Ford* by Sarah T. Bushnell, Chapter 4: "The First Car and the First Race," Quote Page 55 to 57, The Reilly & Lee Company, Chicago, Illinois. (Google Books Full View) https://books.google.com/books?id=YXuMzVQLOAAC&q=fad#v=snippet&q=fad&f=false

[11] Cano, Francisco. "Epistemological beliefs and approaches to learning: Their change through secondary school and their influence on academic performance." *British Journal of Educational Psychology* 75, no. 2 (2005): 203-221. This research was performed with a group of 1,600 students.

[12] Muwonge, C. M., Schiefele, U., Ssenyonga, J., and Kibedi, H. (2019). „Modeling the relationship between motivational beliefs, cognitive learning strategies, and academic performance of teacher education students." *South African Journal of Psychology* 49(1), 122-135. This study examined a large sample of 1,081 students by asking them to fill out a questionnaire that, among other things, measured the level of perceived academic control. The control questions could be "If I try hard enough, then I will understand the study material" or "If I study in appropriate ways, then I will be able to learn the material in this program."

[13] Bill & Melinda Gates Foundation - Foundation Fact Sheet - https://www.gatesfoundation.org/about/foundation-fact-sheet

[14] Bill & Melinda Gates Foundation - Our Story - https://www.gatesfoundation.org/about/our-story

[15] Best advice: Gates on Gates - *Fortune*

[16] Maguire, Eleanor A., David G. Gadian, Ingrid S. Johnsrude, Catriona D. Good, John Ashburner, Richard SJ Frackowiak, and Christopher D. Frith. "Navigation-related structural change in the hippocampi of taxi drivers." *Proceedings of the National Academy of Sciences* 97, no. 8 (2000): 4398-4403.

## Chapter 6: Optimization

[1] Making Process Improvements Stick - Harvard Business Review

[2] The Ultimate Guide to Process Optimization - Wrike

[3] Wittman, J. "The Forgetting Curve." California State University, Stanislaus (2018). Hermann Ebbinghaus (1850-1909) was a German psychologist who founded the experimental psychology of memory. In recognition of his work in psychology, the "forgetting curve"—the loss of learned information—is sometimes referred to as the "Ebbinghaus Forgetting Curve."

[4] van der Schuur, W. A., Baumgartner, S. E., Sumter, S. R., and Valkenburg, P. M. (2015). "The consequences of media multitasking for youth: A review." *Computers in Human Behavior* 53, 204-215.

[5] Judd, Terry. "Making sense of multitasking: Key behaviors." *Computers & Education* 63 (2013): 358-367. A custom monitoring system was used to capture and analyze 3,372 computer session logs of students undertaking self-directed study within an open-access computer laboratory. Each session was broken down into a sequence of tasks within a series of time segments. Segments and sessions were then analyzed and classified as conforming to one of three core behaviors— little or no task switching (focused), task switching without multitasking (sequential), and multitasking. Multitasking was much more common than focused or sequential behaviors. Multitasking was present in more than 70%, was most frequent in over 50%, and occurred exclusively in around 35% of all sessions. By comparison, less than 10% of sessions were exclusively focused and only 7% were exclusively sequential. Once initiated, focused and multitasking behaviors appear to be quite stable. Students were much more likely to continue with them than to switch to an alternate behavior. Sequential behavior is far less stable and appears to represent a transitional state between multitasking and focused behaviors.

[6] Kokoç, Mehmet. "The mediating role of attention control in the link between multitasking with social media and academic performances among adolescents." *Scandinavian Journal of Psychology* 62, no. 4 (2021): 493-501. This study examined the mediating role of attention control as a component of self-regulation in the link between social

media multitasking and academic performances in a sample of adolescents who were recruited from high school students (N=637). A correlational research design was used in the study.

[7] van der Schuur, Winneke A., Susanne E. Baumgartner, Sindy R. Sumter, and Patti M. Valkenburg. "Exploring the long-term relationship between academic-media multitasking and adolescents' academic achievement." *New Media & Society* 22, no. 1 (2020): 140-158.

[8] Cooper, Harris, Barbara Nye, Kelly Charlton, James Lindsay, and Scott Greathouse. "The effects of summer vacation on achievement test scores: A narrative and meta-analytic review." *Review of Educational Research* 66, no. 3 (1996): 227-268. A review of 39 studies indicated that achievement test scores decline over summer vacation. The results of the 13 most recent studies were combined using meta-analytic procedures. The meta-analysis indicated that the summer loss equaled about one month on a grade-level equivalent scale or one-tenth of a standard deviation relative to spring test scores. The effect of summer break was more detrimental for math than for reading and most detrimental for math computation and spelling. Also, middle-class students appeared to gain on grade-level equivalent reading recognition tests over the summer while lower-class students lost on them. There were no moderating effects for student gender or race, but the negative effect of summer did increase with increases in students' grade levels. Suggested explanations for the findings include the differential availability of opportunities to practice different academic materials over the summer and differences in the material's susceptibility to memory decay. The income differences also may be related to differences in opportunities to practice and learn.

[9] Alexander, Karl L., Doris R. Entwisle, and Linda Steffel Olson. "Lasting consequences of the summer learning gap." *American Sociological Review* 72, no. 2 (2007): 167-180. This study found that cumulative achievement gains over the first nine years of children's schooling mainly reflected school-year learning, whereas the high SES-low SES achievement gap at ninth grade mainly traces to differential summer learning over the elementary years.

[10] Kuhfeld, Megan. "Surprising new evidence on summer learning loss." *Phi Delta Kappan* 101, no. 1 (2019): 25-29. This research analyzed data from more than 3.4 million students in all 50 states who

took the NWEA MAP Growth reading and mathematics assessments between the 2016-17 and 2017-18 school years.

[11] The secret strength that fuels Stephen Curry and the Golden State Warriors - ESPN.com

[12] Wittman, J. "The Forgetting Curve." California State University, Stanislaus (2018).

[13] The Pomodoro Technique - Francesco Cirillo https://francesco-cirillo.com/products/the-pomodoro-technique. The Pomodoro° Technique is a time management method developed by Francesco Cirillo in the late 1980s. It is a structured method made up of processes, tools, principles, and values to learn how to deal with time and turn it from a vicious predator to an ally to boost productivity. It is based on a series of principles built on self-observation and awareness. Developing these skills makes it possible to change the relationship with time and reach our goals with less effort and anxiety.

[14] Choe, Danbi. "Parents' and adolescents' perceptions of parental support as predictors of adolescents' academic achievement and self-regulated learning." *Children and Youth Services Review* 116 (2020): 105172. This study examined the inconsistencies in parents' and adolescents' reports of parental support and how each report influences on adolescents' academic achievement and self-regulated learning. The analyzed sample consisted of 6,370 adolescents (seventh grade; 51% female) and their parents from the Korean Educational Longitudinal Survey, which was collected in 2015. This study estimated t-test and ANOVA to test inconsistencies of parents' and adolescents' reports of parental support. Path analysis was conducted to confirm the relationship between each perception and adolescents' academic outcomes. Finally, multigroup analysis was conducted on how the model between parental support and academic outcomes changes across the parent-adolescent dyads. This study found that there was the divergence of adolescents' and parents' reports of parental support. Adolescents' report of parental support is more associated with higher adolescent academic outcomes compared to parents' report, but parents' report of academic support is the strongest predictor to adolescents' academic achievement. This study also found some variations among the parent-adolescent dyads in how parents' and adolescents' reports of parental support relate to adolescent outcomes.

[15] Williamson, Vickie M., Deborah Rush Walker, Eric Chuu, Susan Broadway, Blain Mamiya, Cynthia B. Powell, G. Robert Shelton, Rebecca Weber, Alan R. Dabney, and Diana Mason. "Impact of basic arithmetic skills on success in first-semester general chemistry." *Chemistry Education Research and Practice* 21, no. 1 (2020): 51-61. With this study, a large population (N= 1073) was given the MUST at the beginning of the semester. The MUST offers a quick 15-minute assessment of basic mathematics ability without a calculator. Instructors may find it easier than other documented predictors, which may take more time or involve obtaining student records (e.g., math SAT). Results from the MUST support prior findings that mathematics skills correlate with course grades in chemistry. Poor arithmetic automaticity may be an underlying factor in lower performance by many students.

[16] Wang, Qian, Yi Ding, and Qiong Yu. "Working memory load and automaticity in relation to problem-solving in college engineering students." *Journal of Engineering Education* 107, no. 4 (2018): 636-655. The participants for this study were 31 college engineering students enrolled in a fundamental structural analysis course at a university in the northeastern United States. In mathematics contexts, automaticity refers to this quick and effortless recall of basic mathematic factors. The four testing conditions were based on combinations of high or low WML and high or low availability of automaticity: (a) problems with low WML and high automaticity (Condition 1); (b) problems with high WML and high automaticity (Condition 2); (c) problems with low WML and low automaticity (Condition 3); and (d) problems with high WML and low automaticity (Condition 4) for each original structural analysis task.

[17] Roembke, Tanja C., Eliot Hazeltine, Deborah K. Reed, and Bob McMurray. "Automaticity as an independent trait in predicting reading outcomes in middle-school." *Developmental Psychology* 57, no. 3 (2021): 361. Participants (N = 444, after exclusions; n female = 264, n male = 180) were average to struggling middle-school students from an urban area in eastern Iowa that were all native speakers of English and were roughly equally from grades six, seven, and eight (average age: 13 years). Participants completed different masked and unmasked task versions where they read a word and selected a response (e.g., a

pictured referent). Decoding was uniquely predicted by knowledge (unmasked performance), whereas fluency was uniquely predicted by automaticity (masked performance). In the unmasked version, the target appeared until a response was made. In the masked version, the target was covered with the mask after 80 msec. This study sought to examine predictive relationships between automaticity in word level lexical processes and reading outcomes. This was a significant extension of Roembke et al. (2019), with an almost tenfold increase in sample size, a much larger range of items, and a test/retest reliability assessment.

[18] Logan, Gordon D. "Automaticity, resources, and memory: Theoretical controversies and practical implications." *Human Factors* 30, no. 5 (1988): 583-598.

[19] Schneider, Walter, and Richard M. Shiffrin. "Controlled and automatic human information processing: I. Detection, search, and attention." *Psychological Review* 84, no. 1 (1977): 1.

[20] Liu, Qimeng, Xiaofeng Du, Shuxin Zhao, Jian Liu, and Jinfa Cai. "The role of memorization in students' self-reported mathematics learning: a large-scale study of Chinese eighth-grade students." *Asia Pacific Education Review* 20, no. 3 (2019): 361-374. This study examined over 48,000 eighth-grade Chinese students' mathematics performance and use of learning strategies. The mathematics assessment was developed by the CICA-BEQ and is not openly published. Each paper-and-pencil assessment was administered over 90 minutes and comprised 18 items (including 25 subitems), with each participant receiving the same assessment and the same administration instructions.

[21] Warriors' Steph Curry breaks down art of draining half-court shots. https://www.nbcsports.com/bayarea/warriors/warriors-steph-curry-breaks-down-art-draining-half-court-shots

[22] How To Get Into The Flow State by Steven Kotler - https://www.youtube.com/watch?v=XG_hNZ5T4nY

[23] *Flow*, Harper Collins Publishers - https://www.harpercollins.com/products/flow-mihaly-csikszentmihalyi

[24] Claremont Graduate University - https://www.cgu.edu/people/mihaly-csikszentmihalyi/

[25] Sumaya, Isabel C., and Emily Darling. "Procrastination, flow, and academic performance in real time using the experience sampling method." *Journal of Genetic Psychology* 179, no. 3 (2018): 123-131. Questionnaires were given to the participating students to measure their flow and procrastination while completing a research paper, which they were tasked with completing in a set amount of time. In this study, procrastination was measured in the number of days the students did not work on the task. In other words, how long the students waited to start the paper. They were looking to see if there was more procrastination for students who were not in flow versus those who did achieve learning flow. They found no difference between procrastination and flow—the groups who achieved flow and those who didn't waited until two days before the paper was due to start. So, they surmised that procrastination has no correlation or relation to flow. But, the students who achieved flow made a higher grade on the paper. There was a significant difference in the grades the two groups received. It can be surmised from this study that the flow experience leads to better learning outcomes and better grades. This study also highlighted how learning flow is most often achieved when the learner's skills are rightly matched to the task at hand or they feel well equipped and able to handle the project or subject before them.

[26] Wu, Renshuang, Eugene Scott Huebner, Jianhua Zhou, and Lili Tian. "Relations among positivity, positive affect in school, and learning flow in elementary school students: A longitudinal mediation model." *British Journal of Educational Psychology* 91, no. 4 (2021): 1310-1332.

# Part III

## Introduction

[1] The Boy and the Butterfly: The Struggle Makes Us Stronger - https://www.lifeandwhim.com/first-moments-blog/2018/the-struggle-makes-you-stronger

## Chapter 7: Direction Management

[1] A look back at 15 years of mapping the world, Elizabeth Reid, https://blog.google/products/maps/look-back-15-years-mapping-world/

[2] Florence Chadwick, https://biography.yourdictionary.com/florence-chadwick

[3] Schippers, Michaéla C., Dominique Morisano, Edwin A. Locke, Ad WA Scheepers, Gary P. Latham, and Elisabeth M. de Jong. "Writing about personal goals and plans regardless of goal type boosts academic performance." *Contemporary Educational Psychology* 60 (2020): 101823. Using a time-lagged quasi-experimental design, this model was tested with two first-year university goal-setting cohorts and two control cohorts (total n = 2928). The goal-setting cohorts (n = 698 and 711) showed a 22% increase in academic performance versus the control cohorts (n = 810 and 707). This increase depended on (1) the extent of participation in the three-stage goal-setting intervention, (2) the number of words written in the exercise, and (3) the specificity of students' goal-achievement plans (GAP). Contrary to goal-setting theory, which necessitates goal-task specificity, the results revealed that it did not matter whether the students wrote about academic or non-academic goals or a combination of both. Rather, it appeared to be the overall process of writing about their personal goals, the specificity of their strategies for goal attainment, and the extent of their participation in the intervention that led to an increase in their academic performance. This study suggests an important modification to goal-setting theory, namely a potential contagion effect of setting life goals, an academic goal primed in the subconscious, and subsequent academic performance.

[4] Dotson, Ronnie. "Goal setting to increase student academic performance." *Journal of School Administration Research and Development* 1, no. 1 (2016): 45-46. Of the 328 students participating in the study, 69% made adequate growth after goal-setting utilization as compared to only 60% prior to the implementation of goal-setting.

[5] Sides, Jacklyne D., and Joshua A. Cuevas. "Effect of goal setting for motivation, self-efficacy, and performance in Elementary mathematics." *International Journal of Instruction* 13, no. 4 (2020): 1-16. This eight-week study sought to determine the effects of goal-setting on motivation, self-efficacy, and math achievement in elementary students. The quasi-experimental study included 70 students in third and fourth grade math classes. Students in the experimental group were involved in setting an achievement goal for fluency of multiplication facts. The students monitored their progress through a weekly graphing and reflection activity. The results indicated that elementary students involved in setting goals showed an increase in their mathematical performance of multiplication facts. However, based on the results from this study, goal-setting did not have an impact on motivation or self-efficacy. These results support the concept of goal-setting theory in the academic setting, suggesting that it may be beneficial for teachers to include goal-setting in their day-to-day instructional practices, though further research on its effect on affective traits is warranted.

[6] Setting Goals, https://cce.bard.edu/files/Setting-Goals.pdf

[7] "My Goggles Filled Up With Water"- Michael Phelps Swam Blind for Over 175m to Achieve One of His Biggest Career Achievement, https://www.essentiallysports.com/us-sports-news-swimming-news-my-goggles-filled-up-with-water-michael-phelps-swam-blind-for-over-175m-to-achieve-one-of-his-biggest-career-achievement/

[8] A story of the Mystic Neem Karoli Baba and How He inspired Steve Jobs and Zuckerberg, https://metrosaga.com/mystic-neem-karoli-baba/

[9] The Importance of Writing Well & How to Grow as a Writer, https://www.uagc.edu/blog/the-importance-of-writing-well-how-to-grow-as-a-writer

[10] Importance of Goal Setting, https://www.successstartswithin.com/blog/importance-of-goal-setting

[11] The Case Against Setting Goals for Children, https://medium.com/the-ascent/the-case-against-setting-goals-for-children-243a58411542

[12] Pareto Principle (The 80-20 Rule), https://www.simplypsychology.org/pareto-principle.html

## Chapter 8: Time Management

[1] Britton, Bruce K., and Abraham Tesser. "Effects of time-management practices on college grades." *Journal of Educational Psychology* 83, no. 3 (1991): 405.

[2] Valle, Antonio, Bibiana Regueiro, José C. Núñez, Susana Rodríguez, Isabel Piñeiro, and Pedro Rosário. "Academic goals, student homework engagement, and academic achievement in elementary school." *Frontiers in Psychology* 7 (2016): 463.

[3] Valle Arias, Antonio, Isabel Piñeiro Aguín, Susana Rodríguez Martínez, Bibiana Regueiro Fernández, Carlos Freire Rodríguez, and Pedro José Sales Luís de Fonseca Rosário. "Time spent and time management in homework in elementary school students: A person-centered approach." *Psicothema* (2019).

[4] Curcio, Giuseppe, Michele Ferrara, and Luigi De Gennaro. "Sleep loss, learning capacity and academic performance." *Sleep Medicine Reviews* 10, no. 5 (2006): 323-337.

[5] Stefansdottir, Runa, Vaka Rognvaldsdottir, Kong Y. Chen, Erlingur Johannsson, and Robert J. Brychta. "Sleep timing and consistency are associated with the standardised test performance of Icelandic adolescents." *Journal of Sleep Research* 31, no. 1 (2022): e13422.

[6] Seoane, Hernan A., Leandra Moschetto, Francisco Orliacq, Josefina Orliacq, Ezequiel Serrano, María Inés Cazenave, Daniel E. Vigo, and Santiago Perez-Lloret. "Sleep disruption in medicine students and its relationship with impaired academic performance: a systematic review and meta-analysis." *Sleep Medicine Reviews* 53 (2020): 101333.

7 Comparison of rest-break interventions during a mentally demanding task, https://www.ncbi.nlm.nih.gov/pmc/articles/PMC6585675/. This work investigated the role of breaks in vigor and fatigue during learning. The authors showed that a 20-minute unstructured break resulted in increased vigor during learning. On the other hand, a break that was coupled with a physical exercise and a break that was coupled with a relaxation technique (both six to seven minutes), improved rigor *and* reduced later fatigue that was even beyond a simple unstructured break. The exercise break consisted of three minutes of aerobic exercise including running on the spot and a variety of jumping exercises that were alternated every 30 seconds followed by three minutes of a variety of stretching exercises. The relaxation break consisted of a six-minute guided body scan exercise. Individuals were instructed to focus their attention on various body parts and functions such as feet, legs, arms, and breathing and to observe the sensations arising in those regions. In the unstructured rest break, individuals could do what they wanted as long as they remained seated at their desks.

8 "Give me a break!" A systematic review and meta-analysis on the efficacy of micro-breaks for increasing well-being and performance https://journals.plos.org/plosone/article?id=10.1371/journal.pone.0272460. A different meta-analysis work on the topic of what they call micro-breaks during different tasks. The authors combined the effects of 22 different studies (total sample was N = 2335 participants) and found, just as what we usually see, significant but relatively small positive effects on increased rigor and decreased fatigue. They did not find a significant effect on increased performance. But I think there might have been an indirect effect, i.e., breaks improve rigor and reduce fatigue, and then these factors in turn influence performance. The longer the break, the better. Also, breaks work best for highly demanding tasks.

9 Excerpt from *From the Outside: My Journey Through Life and the Game I Love* by Ray Allen

10 The 5 Types of Note-Taking Methods You Need To Learn, https://theglobalscholars.com/the-5-types-of-note-taking-methods-you-need-to-learn/

[11] Shi, Yinghui, Huiyun Yang, Yi Dou, and Yong Zeng. "Effects of mind mapping-based instruction on student cognitive learning outcomes: a meta-analysis." *Asia Pacific Education Review* (2022): 1-15.

[12] Gagic, Zvezdan Z., Sonja J. Skuban, Branka N. Radulovic, Maja M. Stojanovic, and Olivera Gajic. "The Implementation of Mind Maps in Teaching Physics: Educational Efficiency and Students' Involvement." *Journal of Baltic Science Education* 18, no. 1 (2019): 117-131.

[13] Adodo, S. O. "Effect of mind-mapping as a self-regulated learning strategy on students' achievement in basic science and technology." *Mediterranean Journal of Social Sciences* 4, no. 6 (2013): 163-163.

[14] Citation: Sumaya, Isabel C., and Emily Darling. "Procrastination, flow, and academic performance in real time using the experience sampling method." *Journal of Genetic Psychology* 179, no. 3 (2018): 123-131

## Chapter 9: Space Management

[1] Lewinski, Peter. "Effects of classrooms' architecture on academic performance in view of telic versus paratelic motivation: a review." *Frontiers in Psychology* 6 (2015): 746.

[2] Stone, N. (2001). "Designing effective study environments." *Journal of Environmental Psychology* 21, 179–190. Doi: 10.1006/jevp.2000.0193

[3] "Cognitive performance and emotion are indifferent to ambient color" by Christoph von Castell, Daniela Stelzmann, Daniel Oberfeld, Robin Welsch, Heiko Hecht - https://onlinelibrary.wiley.com/doi/abs/10.1002/col.22168

[4] Earthman, G. (2002). "School facility conditions and student academic achievement," in Williams Watch Series: Investigating the Claims of Williams v. State of California, Los Angeles, CA: UCLA's Institute for Democracy, Education, and Access. Available at: http://www.escholarship.org/uc/item/5sw56439 [accessed October 1, 2002].

## Chapter 10: Knowledge Management

[1] Ponce, Héctor R., Richard E. Mayer, and Ester E. Méndez. "Effects of Learner-Generated Highlighting and Instructor-Provided Highlighting on Learning from Text: A Meta-Analysis." *Educational Psychology Review* 34, no. 2 (2022): 989-1024. The present study examines the existing published research about the effectiveness of learner-generated highlighting and instructor-provided highlighting on learning from text. A meta-analysis was conducted of scientifically rigorous experiments comparing the learning outcomes (i.e., performance on memory and/or comprehension tests) of students (i.e., college students and/or K-12 students) who read an academic text with or without being asked to highlight important material (i.e., with or without learner-generated highlighting) or who read an academic text with or without the important material already being highlighted (i.e., with or without instructor-provided highlighting). We found 36 published articles that met these criteria ranging from the years 1938 to 2019, which generated 85 effect sizes. The results showed that learner-generated highlighting improved memory but not comprehension, with average effect sizes of 0.36 and 0.20, respectively; and instructor-provided highlighting improved both memory and comprehension, both with an average effect size of 0.44. Learner-generated highlighting improved learning for college students but not for school students, with average effect sizes of 0.39 and 0.24, respectively; and instructor-provided highlighting improved learning for both college and school students, with average effect sizes of 0.41 and 0.48, respectively.

[2] Karpicke, Jeffrey D., and Janell R. Blunt. "Retrieval practice produces more learning than elaborative studying with concept mapping." *Science* 331, no. 6018 (2011): 772-775. Abstract: "Educators rely heavily on learning activities that encourage elaborative studying, while activities that require students to practice retrieving and reconstructing knowledge are used less frequently. Here, we show that practicing retrieval produces greater gains in meaningful learning than elaborative studying with concept mapping. The advantage of retrieval practice generalized across texts identical to those commonly found in science education. The advantage of retrieval practice was observed with test questions that assessed comprehension and required students to make inferences. The advantage of retrieval practice occurred even when the criterial test involved creating concept maps. Our findings

support the theory that retrieval practice enhances learning by retrieval-specific mechanisms rather than by elaborative study processes. Retrieval practice is an effective tool to promote conceptual learning about science." The learning conditions: "The students first studied a science text under one of four conditions within a single initial learning session. In the study-once condition, students studied the text in a single study period. In the repeated study condition, students studied the text in four consecutive study periods (8). In the elaborative concept mapping condition, students studied the text in an initial study period and then created a concept map of the concepts in the text. The students were instructed about the nature of concept mapping, viewed an example of a concept map, and created their concept maps on paper while viewing the text. This is a typical way concept mapping is used as an elaborative study activity (16–18). Finally, in the retrieval practice condition, students studied the text in an initial study period and then practiced retrieval by recalling as much of the information as they could on a free recall test."

[3] Baddeley, Alan D., and D. J. A. Longman. "The influence of length and frequency of training session on the rate of learning to type." *Ergonomics* 21, no. 8 (1978): 627-635.

[4] Simon, Dominic A., and Robert A. Bjork. "Metacognition in motor learning." *Journal of Experimental Psychology: Learning, Memory, and Cognition* 27, no. 4 (2001): 907.

[5] Schleicher, Andreas. "PISA 2018: Insights and Interpretations." OECD Publishing (2019).

[6] Study Strategies for Before, During, and After Class by Angela Zanardelli Sickler - https://www.facultyfocus.com/articles/teaching-and-learning/study-strategies-class/

[7] Moravec, Marin, Adrienne Williams, Nancy Aguilar-Roca, and Diane K. O'Dowd. "Learn before lecture: A strategy that improves learning outcomes in a large introductory biology class." *CBE—Life Sciences Education* 9, no. 4 (2010): 473-481. Actively engaging students in lecture has been shown to increase learning gains. To create time for active learning without displacing content we used two strategies for introducing material before class in a large introductory

biology course. Four to five slides from 2007/8 were removed from each of three lectures in 2009 and the information introduced in pre-class worksheets or narrated PowerPoint videos. In class, time created by shifting lecture material to learn before lecture (LBL) assignments was used to engage students in application of their new knowledge. Learning was evaluated by comparing student performance in 2009 versus 2007/8 on LBL-related question pairs, matched by level and format. The percentage of students who correctly answered five of six LBL-related exam questions was significantly higher ($p < 0.001$) in 2009 versus 2007/8. The mean increase in performance was 21% across the six LBL-related questions compared with <3% on all non-LBL exam questions. The worksheet and video LBL formats were equally effective based on a cross-over experimental design. These results demonstrate that LBLs combined with interactive exercises can be implemented incrementally and result in significant increases in learning gains in large introductory biology classes.

## Chapter 11: Anxiety Management

[1] 'An anxious nation': Barnes & Noble sees a surge in sales of books about stress by Rachel Siegel - https://www.washingtonpost.com/business/2018/08/02/an-anxious-nation-barnes-noble-sees-surge-sales-books-about-stress/

[2] COVID-19 pandemic triggers 25% increase in prevalence of anxiety and depression worldwide - https://www.who.int/news/item/02-03-2022-covid-19-pandemic-triggers-25-increase-in-prevalence-of-anxiety-and-depression-worldwide

[3] The Best Books About Anxiety of 2022 - https://psychcentral.com/reviews/best-books-about-anxiety

[4] Spielberger, C. D. (1978). "The State-Trait Anxiety Inventory: Its theoretical and empirical foundations." In C. D. Spielberger and I. G.

Sarason (Eds.), *Stress and Anxiety* (Vol. 5, pp. 3-20). Washington, DC: Hemisphere Publishing Corporation.

[5] Plante, I., Lecours, V., Lapointe, R., Chaffee, K. E., and Fréchette-Simard, C. (2022). "Relations between prior school performance and later test anxiety during the transition to secondary school." *British Journal of Educational Psychology* 92(3), 1068-1085.

[6] Bischofsberger, L., Burger, P. H., Hammer, A., Paulsen, F., Scholz, M., and Hammer, C. M. (2021). "Prevalence and characteristics of test anxiety in first year anatomy students." *Annals of Anatomy-Anatomischer Anzeiger* 236, 151719.

[7] Weems, C.F., Scott, B.G., Graham, R.A., et al. "Fitting Anxious Emotion-Focused Intervention into the Ecology of Schools: Results from a Test Anxiety Program Evaluation." *Prevention Science* 16, 200–210 (2015). https://doi.org/10.1007/s11121-014-0491-1

[8] Yeo, L.S., Goh, V.G., and Liem, G.A.D. "School-Based Intervention for Test Anxiety." *Child Youth Care Forum* 45, 1–17 (2016). https://doi.org/10.1007/s10566-015-9314-1

[9] von der Embse, Nathaniel, Dane Jester, Devlina Roy, and James Post. "Test anxiety effects, predictors, and correlates: A 30-year meta-analytic review." *Journal of Affective Disorders* 227 (2018): 483-493.

[10] Owens, M., Stevenson, J., Hadwin, J. A., and Norgate, R. (2014). "When does anxiety help or hinder cognitive test performance? The role of working memory capacity." *British Journal of Psychology* 105(1), 92-101.

[11] Cizek, G. J., and Burg, S. S. (2006). *Addressing Test Anxiety in a High-Stakes Environment: Strategies for Classroom and Schools.* Corwin Press.

[12] Plante, I., Lecours, V., Lapointe, R., Chaffee, K. E., and Fréchette-Simard, C. (2022). "Relations between prior school performance and later test anxiety during the transition to secondary school." *British Journal of Educational Psychology* 92(3), 1068-1085.

[13] Hart, Ray, Michael Casserly, Renata Uzzell, Moses Palacios, Amanda Corcoran, and Liz Spurgeon. "Student Testing in America's Great City Schools: An Inventory and Preliminary Analysis." Council of the Great City Schools (2015).

[14] Huntley, Christopher D., Bridget Young, James Temple, Melissa Longworth, Catrin Tudur Smith, Vikram Jha, and Peter L. Fisher. "The efficacy of interventions for test-anxious university students: A meta-analysis of randomized controlled trials." *Journal of Anxiety Disorders* 63 (2019): 36-50.

## Chapter 12: Help Management

[1] Lim, Chee, Habibah Ab Jalil, Aini Ma'rof, and Wan Saad. "Peer learning, self-regulated learning and academic achievement in blended learning courses: A structural equation modeling approach." *International Journal of Emerging Technologies in Learning (IJET)* 15, no. 3 (2020): 110-125.

[2] *Greenlights* by Matthew McConaughey https://greenlights.com/

[3] Vygotsky, L. S., and Cole, M. (1978). *Mind in Society: Development of Higher Psychological Processes.* Harvard University Press.

[4] Sakaiya, S., Shiraito, Y., Kato, J., Ide, H., Okada, K., Takano, K., and Kansaku, K. (2013). "Neural correlate of human reciprocity in social interactions." *Frontiers in Neuroscience* 7:239. doi: 10.3389/fnins.2013.00239

[5] Schilbach, L., Timmermans, B., Reddy, V., Costall, A., Bente, G., Schlict, T., et al. (2013). "Toward a second-person neuroscience." *Behavioral and Brain Sciences* 36, 393–462. doi: 10.1017/S0140525X12000660

[6] Guionnet, S., Nadel, J., Bertasi, E., Sperduti, M., Delaveau, P., and Fossati, P. (2012). "Reciprocal imitation: toward a neural basis of social interaction." *Cerebral Cortex* 22, 971–978. doi: 10.1093/cercor/bhr177

[7] Schilbach, L., Wohlschlaeger, A., Kraemer, N., Newen, A., Shah, N., Fink, G., et al. (2006). "Being with virtual others: neural correlates of social interaction." *Neuropsychologia* 44, 718–730. doi: 10.1016/j.neuropsychologia.2005.07.017

[8] Martín-Arbós, Sergi, Elena Castarlenas, and Jorge-Manuel Duenas. "Help-seeking in an academic context: A systematic review." *Sustainability* 13, no. 8 (2021): 4460.

[9] Schenke, Katerina, Arena C. Lam, AnneMarie M. Conley, and Stuart A. Karabenick. "Adolescents' help seeking in mathematics classrooms: Relations between achievement and perceived classroom environmental influences over one school year." *Contemporary Educational Psychology* 41 (2015): 133-146.

## Chapter 13: Effort Management

[1] Life Lessons from the World's Greatest Athletes by Dr. W.D. Panlilio

[2] Chris Johnson: Talks Near Death Experience, Embracing Culture & Life After NFL - *I Am Athlete.* https://www.youtube.com/watch?v=1V2AuKJaah8

[3] Chris Johnson's Speed Workout by Josh Staph, https://www.stack.com/a/chris-johnsons-nine-speed-building-exercises/

[4] Inzlicht, M., Shenhav, A., and Olivola, C. Y. (2018). „The effort paradox: Effort is both costly and valued." *Trends in Cognitive Sciences* 22(4), 337-349.

[5] Resilience definition: https://www.merriam-webster.com/dictionary/resilience

[6] American Psychological Association. "What you need to know about willpower: The psychological science of self-control." Washington: APA (www.apa.org/helpcenter/willpower. pdf) (2012).

[7] The mindset that brings unlimited willpower by David Robson - https://www.bbc.com/worklife/article/20230103-how-to-strengthen-willpower

[8] Self-control definition: https://www.oed.com/

[9] Zacharia, Janine. "The Bing 'Marshmallow Studies': 50 Years of Continuing Research." (2015).

[10] Mischel, W; Shoda, Y; Rodriguez, M. (26 May 1989). "Delay of gratification in children." *Science* 244 (4907): 933–938.

[11] Ayduk, Ozlem N.; Mendoza-Denton, Rodolfo; Mischel, Walter; Downey, Geraldine; Peake, Philip K.; Rodriguez, Monica L. (2000). "Regulating the interpersonal self: Strategic self-regulation for coping with rejection sensitivity." *Journal of Personality and Social Psychology.*

[12] Schlam, Tanya R.; Wilson, Nicole L.; Shoda, Yuichi; Mischel, Walter; Ayduk, Ozlem (2013). "Preschoolers' delay of gratification predicts their body mass 30 years later." *Journal of Pediatrics.*

[13] Shoda, Yuichi; Mischel, Walter; Peake, Philip K. (1990). "Predicting adolescent cognitive and self-regulatory competencies from pre-school delay of gratification: Identifying diagnostic conditions." *Developmental Psychology.*

[14] Norris, G., and Norris, H. (2021). "Building Resilience Through Sport in Young People With Adverse Childhood Experiences." *Frontiers in Sports and Active Living* 3, 663587.

[15] Ayala, Juan Carlos, and Guadalupe Manzano. "Academic performance of first-year university students: The influence of resilience and engagement." *Higher Education Research & Development* 37, no. 7 (2018): 1321-1335.

[16] Hupfeld, Kelly. "A review of the literature: Resiliency skills and dropout prevention." Scholar Centric (2010).

## Chapter 14: Metacognition Management

[1] Ohtani, K., and Hisasaka, T. (2018). "Beyond intelligence: A meta-analytic review of the relationship among metacognition, intelligence, and academic performance." *Metacognition and Learning* 13(2), 179-212.

[2] de Boer, H., Donker, A. S., Kostons, D. D., and van der Werf, G. P. (2018). "Long-term effects of metacognitive strategy instruction on student academic performance: A meta-analysis." *Educational Research Review* 24, 98-115.

[3] Zhang, J., and Zhang, L. J. (2022). "The effect of feedback on metacognitive strategy use in EFL writing." *Computer Assisted Language Learning*, 1-26.

# AUTHORS

## Dr. Wallace Panlilio II
Ph.D. in Educational Psychology

Dr. Wallace Panlilio II, Ph.D., is an experienced educator and entrepreneur. He holds a Ph.D. in Educational Psychology from the University of the Philippines and has served as a school headmaster for 14 years. He also holds two master's degrees in entrepreneurship and educational leadership and has studied economics and political science at the undergraduate level.

Dr. Wallace is currently the Chief Mentor Officer of Digital Ventures Pte. Ltd., an AI solutions and publishing company. He also played a pivotal role in co-founding several pioneering educational institutions that have provided education to tens of thousands of students over the last decade.

Outside of his professional life, Dr. Wallace is an avid open water swimmer, having competed in various swimming competitions over the past decade. He is also part of a family deeply engaged in various aspects of learning. His wife, Sheryl, works as a school principal with expertise in early childhood education, and his daughter, Selynna, specializes in human resources, blockchain technology, and digital marketing. Dr. Wallace brings a wealth of experience and expertise to the fields of education, entrepreneurship, and parenting.

# Dr. Artyom Zinchenko
Ph.D. in Cognitive and Neuroscience

Artyom Zinchenko, PhD, is an accomplished author and cognitive neuroscientist with extensive experience in the field. He earned his Doctorate in Cognitive Neuroscience from the Max Planck Institute for Cognitive Human and Brain Sciences in Leipzig, where his research focused on emotions and cognitive conflict processing.

Dr. Zinchenko is now a researcher and faculty member at Ludwig-Maximilian University in Munich, where his research interests include cognition-emotion interaction and long-term memory guided attention during visual search. He uses various neurophysiological methods to support his research, such as transcranial magnetic stimulation, electroencephalography, skin-conductance, eye-tracking, and combined EEG-fMRI methodology.

Aside from his research, Dr. Zinchenko is an experienced teacher who has taught courses in EEG methodology, cognitive neuroscience, and data analysis. He is also dedicated to introducing cognitive neuroscience to high school students.

Dr. Zinchenko is a father of two and enjoys helping his children with their studies, which inspires him to continue learning himself. He is currently pursuing new knowledge in areas such as machine learning, statistics, and app design.

# Invitation to Join the Wisest Learners Parenting Community

**Dear Esteemed Reader of "Wisest Learners: Unlock the Secrets to Your Child's Academic Success,"**

We are thrilled to extend a special invitation to you, a valued member of our readership. Your commitment to your child's educational journey inspires us, and we believe you would be a perfect fit for our Wisest Learners Parenting Community.

**What Awaits You in Our Community:**

- Recommended List of Parent Essentials: Explore a curated list of highly recommended parenting resources, including books, movies, podcasts, and more
- Engaging Formats: Explore key parenting strategies through videos, infographics, and checklists.
- Time-Saving Resources: Access concise, impactful tools designed to fit your busy schedule.
- Community Support: Join a network of like-minded parents who share your dedication to nurturing academic success.

**As a Member, You Will:**

- Get early access to new resources and publications.
- Participate in engaging webinars and Q&A sessions with leading educational experts.
- Enjoy a platform to share experiences, challenges, and triumphs with fellow parents.

**How to Join:**

Simply visit https://wisestlearners.com/join-the-community/ and sign up. The process is quick, easy, and opens the door to a wealth of resources.

Your journey as a parent is unique and challenging. Let us support you in making it also rewarding and successful.

Join us today and take the next step in enhancing your child's academic journey!

With warm regards,

The Wisest Learners Team

---

Your participation in our community is not just an addition; it's a milestone in our collective journey towards educational excellence.

# Introducing the Wisest Learners School Accreditation Program

### Empowering Schools to Achieve Educational Excellence

At Wisest Learners, we understand the pivotal role schools play in shaping the future of our children. To elevate this impact, we are proud to introduce the Wisest Learners School Accreditation Program. This program is designed to align schools with the highest standards of educational quality, engaging community stakeholders

— parents, teachers, and students — in a unified effort to foster academic success.

## Program Highlights:

- Comprehensive Training and Coaching: Participating schools will receive expert-led training sessions and continuous coaching to implement best practices in education.
- Support Through Assessments: Regular assessments will be conducted to ensure adherence to the Wisest Learners standards, providing schools with feedback and recommendations for continuous improvement.
- Community Involvement: The program emphasizes the importance of a collaborative approach, engaging parents, teachers, and students in the process of educational enhancement.
- Recognition of Excellence: Accredited schools will be recognized for their commitment to educational quality, receiving a seal of excellence from Wisest Learners.

## BENEFITS FOR ACCREDITED SCHOOLS:

1. Enhanced Educational Outcomes: Through our structured program, schools will witness a measurable improvement in academic performance and student engagement.
2. Community Trust and Prestige: Accreditation signifies a commitment to excellence, boosting the school's reputation among parents and the educational community.
3. Access to a Network of Excellence: Join a community of accredited schools, sharing resources, insights, and best practices.

4. Continuous Support and Development: Benefit from ongoing support and resources from the Wisest Learners team, ensuring sustained growth and development.

**Join the Movement:**

- Schools interested in joining the Wisest Learners School Accreditation Program can apply through our website https://wisestlearners.com/join-the-community/.
- The application process involves an initial assessment, followed by a detailed roadmap for accreditation.

Together, let's create an educational environment where every student thrives. Your school's journey towards excellence starts with the Wisest Learners School Accreditation Program.

Join us in this transformative journey!

Warm regards,

The Wisest Learners Team

---

Through collective effort and a commitment to quality, we can create an educational landscape that nurtures the leaders of tomorrow.

DR. WALLACE PANLILIO II & DR. ARTYOM ZINCHENKO